SOUTH-EAST ASIA
phrasebook

David Bradley

Jason Roberts

Joe Cummings

Anita Ramly, Paul Woods &
Kristina Sarwao Rini

John U Wolff

Nguyen Xuan Thu

South-East Asia phrasebook
1st edition – March 1997

Published by
Lonely Planet Publications Pty Ltd ABN 36 005 607 983
90 Maribyrnong St, Footscray, Victoria 3011, Australia

Lonely Planet Offices
Australia Locked Bag 1, Footscray, Victoria 3011
USA 150 Linden St, Oakland CA 94607
UK 10a Spring Place, London NW5 3BH
France 1 rue du Dahomey, 75011 Paris

Cover photograph
Central Market, Kota Bahn, Malaysia
Photograph by Richard l'Anson

ISBN 0 86442 435 3

text © Lonely Planet Publications 1997
cover photograph © Richard l'Anson

Printed by Colorcraft Ltd, Hong Kong

Contents

Acknowledgements

The Burmese chapter was based on an original manuscript by David Bradley, and developed at Lonely Planet with the assistance of Vicky Bowman and San San Hnin Tun. David is a lecturer in linguistics and Burmese at La Trobe University in Melbourne. The Khmer chapter was written by Jason Roberts who is a translator, based in Phnom Penh. Anita Ramly, a native speaker currently living in Kuala Lumpur, wrote the Malay. The Indonesian was based on an original manuscript by Margit Meinhold, updated by Paul Woods and Kristiana Sarwao Rini, with assistance from Tina Gultom. Many thanks to Zaniah Marshallsay for assistance with the final manuscript. The Lao and Thai chapters were written by Joe Cummings, author of Lonely Planet's Thai and Lao phrasebooks and guides to Laos and Thailand. Thanks to Peeti for his assistance with the Thai and to Ratry Chanty for his assistance with the Lao. John U. Wolff wrote the Tagalog chapter. John is Professor of Linguistics and Asian Studies at Cornell University in New York. Vietnamese was written by Nguyen Xuan Thu, author of Lonely Planet's *Vietnamese phrasebook*, with thanks to Giung Van Phan for his help.

This book was edited by Lou Callan and proofread by Sally Steward. Penelope Richardson was responsible for design and illustrations, and David Kemp designed the cover.

From the Publisher

Abbreviations have been used in some chapters. You'll find a list of these after the Introduction in the relevant chapters. Unless otherwise indicated, synonyms in the other language are separated by a slash.

A Note on Tones

Sometimes the pitch at which a word or syllable is pronounced can determine its meaning. These changes in pitch are called tones. The four tonal languages in this book are Burmese, Lao, Thai and Vietnamese. The particular tones relevant to each language are discussed in each chapter. For people from non-tonal backgrounds, it can be hard at first to learn tones. It's less daunting, however, when you realise that they exist in English too. We mainly use tones in English for emphasis or emotion. Think about the different stresses, and hence meaning, between 'He's thought less' and 'He's thoughtless'. Think also about the difference between 'He left, didn't he?' and 'He left, didn't he!'. You can see how different the meanings are when different tones are used. The first rule in learning and using tones in a tonal language is to avoid overlaying your native intonation patterns. The best way to learn about tones is to listen to native speakers. Take a little time to practice the tones and you'll soon have them mastered.

BURMESE

Burmese

Burmese is in the Tibeto-Burman language family. As the national language, it has over 40 million speakers, more than 30 million of whom use it as their first language. Thus it has more speakers than any other Tibeto-Burman language, including Tibetan.

Burmese has some minor dialect differences; the standard dialect is that of Mandalay and Yangon, which is spoken throughout the central area of Myanmar, and taught in schools everywhere. Rakhine (Arakanese) in the west and Tavoyan in the south are slightly different, while Intha (spoken by the people of Inle Lake), Yaw, Danu and Taungyo are more divergent. There are many other languages spoken in Myanmar, some of them in the same language family and others quite unrelated. Nevertheless Burmese is spoken by nearly everyone in the country; and widespread literacy has been achieved through schools and adult literacy programmes.

Since 1989, the government prefers the literary form 'Myanmar' to refer to the country, its language and its people as a whole. The former English name 'Burma' is derived from the spoken form. The English form of many other places and groups was also changed at the same time. In this phrasebook, we use Myanmar to refer to the country, and Burmese for the language (as it is more commonly referred to outside the country). For placenames, the current name is used and then the former name appears in parentheses; for example, Yangon (Rangoon); Rakhine (Arakan). The spelling used in this chapter is the revised spelling introduced in 1980, as formulated by the Myanmar (Burma) Language Commission.

Abbreviations Used in This Chapter

f   said by/to females
m   said by/to males

Pronunciation

In this chapter, Burmese pronunciation follows that used in the textbooks by Okell, the most up-to-date Burmese course available.

Vowels

Burmese vowel sounds occur in open, nasalised and stopped forms. Nasalisation of vowels is like that in French; speakers of English or other languages can approximate this by putting a weak 'n' at the end of such a syllable. In this chapter the nasalisation is indicated by *n* after the vowel, as in *ein* ,'house'.

non-nasalised

i	like 'e' in 'be'
e	like 'a' in 'bay'
eh	like first 'e' in 'elephant'
a	like 'a' in 'father'
aw	as the British pronounce 'law'
o	like 'o' in 'go' or the French 'au'
u	like 'oo' in 'too'

nasalised   stopped

nasalised	stopped	
in	*iq*	like 'sin'
ein	*eiq*	like 'lane'
	eq	as in 'bet'
an	*aq*	like 'man'

oun	ouq	like 'bone'
un	uq	like 'foot'
ain	aiq	as in the English 'might'
aun	auq	as in 'brown'

Consonants

Consonants only occur at the beginning of a syllable; there are no consonants that occur after the vowel.

b, d, j, g, m, n, ng,	as in English; the **w** sound can occur
s, sh, h, z, w, l, y	on its own, or in combination with other consonants
th	as in 'thin'
dh	as in 'the' or 'their'
ny	similar to the consonants at the beginning of the British 'new'
hm, hn, hny, hng, hl	made with a puff of air just before the nasal or **l** sound
p', t', s', c', k'	aspirated
p, t, c, k	unaspirated

Aspirated Consonants

The aspirated sounds are made with a puff of air; this is the way the letters 'p', 't', 'k' are pronounced in English at the beginning of a word. When these sounds are unaspirated they sound like the 'p', 't', 'k' after an 's', as in 'spin', 'stir' and 'skin'.

The unaspirated **c** and aspirated **c'** are similar to the 'ch' in 'church'. Remember that **sh** as in 'ship', **s** as in 'sip', and the aspirated **s'** are three different sounds. Another difficulty is in saying the **ng** at the beginning of a syllable; try saying 'hang on', then leave off the 'ha' to get an idea of the sound.

Like most languages, Burmese changes when spoken rapidly. One change, even in slow speech, is the aspirated and unaspirated sounds **p', p; t', t; s', s; c', c** and **k', k** within a word becoming the voiced sounds **b, d, z, j** and **g**, and the **th** sound becoming the voiced sound **dh**. This happens automatically to the consonant at the beginning of the second, third or later syllable in a word, unless the syllable before it is a stopped syllable. For example:

yauq-cà	'man'	the **c** does not become **j** because of the stopped syllable
băzaq	'mouth'	the original **s** becomes **z**

Tones

Burmese tones are largely a matter of relative stress between adjoining syllables. There are three tones, plus two other possibilities.

Creaky High Tone

This is made with the voice tense, producing a high-pitched and relatively short, creaky sound, such as occurs with the English words 'heart' and 'squeak'. It is indicated by an acute accent above the vowel, for example *ká*, 'dance'.

Plain High Tone

The pitch of the voice starts quite high, then falls for a fairly long time, similar to the pronunciation of words like 'squeal', 'car' and 'way'. It is indicated by a grave accent above the vowel, for example *kà* which, conveniently, is also the Burmese word for 'car'.

Low Tone

The voice is relaxed, stays at a low pitch for a fairly long time, and does not rise or fall in pitch. It is indicated by no accent above the vowel, for example *ka,* 'shield'.

Stopped Syllable

This is a very short and high-pitched syllable, on a high pitch, cut off at the end by a sharp catch in the voice (a glottal stop); this is like the sound in the middle of the exclamation, 'oh-oh', or the Cockney pronunciation of 't' in a word like 'bottle'. It is indicated in this book by a 'q' after the vowel, for example *kaq,* 'join'. However, the 'q' is not pronounced.

Reduced (Weak) Syllable

This is a shortened syllable, usually the first of a two-syllable word, which is said without stress, like the first syllable of 'again' in English. Only the vowel 'a', sometimes preceded by a consonant, occurs in a reduced syllable; this is indicated by a ˘ above the vowel. For example *ălouq,* 'work'. Any syllable but the last in a word can be reduced.

Transliteration

In Burmese writing, *c, c', j* are written using the letters for *k, k', g* plus *y* or *r*, so anglicised forms of Burmese often represent them as *ky, gy* and so on. One example of this is the unit of currency, *caq,* which is usually written 'kyat' in the Roman alphabet. Aspirated consonants (*k', s', t'* and *p'*) may be spelt with an 'h' before or after the consonant. A creaky tone may be indicated by a final *t* eg Hpakant (in Kachin State).

Various combinations of letters may be used to represent the same vowel sound: *e* and *eh* are both often transliterated as 'ay'; *ain* may be represented as 'aing', *auq* as 'auk', and so on.

There is no 'r' in Burmese but the sound appears in some foreign words such as *re-di-yo,* 'radio', or *da-reiq-s'an,* 'animal' (Pali). Sometimes it is substituted with a **y**. Similarly there is no 'f' or 'v' in Burmese; loan words containing these consonants often use **p'** and **b** respectively.

In the transliteration system used in this book, transliterated syllables (with the exception of the reduced syllable **ă**) have been separated by hyphens, and breaks between words, or groups of words, by spaces. This is intended to make it easier for the learner. However, native speakers often do not speak with a clear division between words or syllables.

Greetings & Civilities

In formal situations and in cities, the first thing you say when meeting a stranger is *min-găla-ba*, literally 'It's a blessing'. When you already know someone, a greeting can start by asking about their health. This is no more of a genuine request for a medical report than the English 'How are you?', and is usually answered positively.

Greetings

How are you/Are you well?
  k'ămyà (m)/shin (f)   ခင်ဗျား/ရှင် နေကောင်းရဲ့လား။
  ne-kaùn-yéh-là?

(I) am well.
  ne-kaùn-ba-deh   နေကောင်းပါတယ်။

What about you?
  k'ămyà-yàw (m)/shin-   ခင်ဗျားရော/ရှင်ရော
  yàw (f) ne-kaùn-yéh-là?   နေကောင်းရဲ့လား။

Greetings may also be in the form of asking whether you have eaten (the usual answer, even if you're hungry, is yes, unless you are, for example, arriving at someone's house for dinner!); where you are going, or where you have come from. The answers to these questions can be quite vague; the questions are not meant to be intrusive.

Have you eaten?
t'ǎmìn sà-pì-bi-là?   ထမင်းစားပြီးပြီလား။
(I) have eaten.
sà-pì-ba-bi   စားပြီးပါပြီ။
Where are you going?
beh thwà-mǎló-lèh?   ဘယ်သွားမလို့လဲ။

To this, a general, non-specific reply is *di-nà-lè-bèh,* ဒီနားလေးပဲ (literally 'Just around here'). However, you could say:

I'm going back to my hotel.
ho-teh-go pyan-táw-meh   ဟိုတယ်ကို ပြန်တော့မယ်။

Goodbyes
There is no single phrase for 'Goodbye'; rather, one leads up to departure with thanks if someone has helped you. Then you normally say that you were glad to meet them, and say that you are going. You may finally say that you will see them later, as in English. The phrases used also depend on whether you are leaving or being left behind.

Thank you very much!
ǎmyà-jì cè-zù-tin-ba-deh   အများကြီး ကျေးဇူးတင်ပါတယ်။
I'm glad to meet you.
k'ǎmyà (m)/shin (f) -néh   ခင်ဗျား/ရှင်နဲ့
twé-ya-da wùn-tha-ba-deh   တွေ့ ရတာ ဝမ်းသာပါတယ်။

Are you going home?
  pyan-dáw-măla   ပြန်တော့မလား။
Are you leaving now?
  thwà-dáw-măla   သွားတော့မလား။
I'm leaving now.
  thwà-ba-oùn-meh   သွားပါအုံးမယ်။
I'm leaving, OK?
  thwà-meh naw?   သွားမယ်နော်။
I'm going home, OK?
  pyan-meh naw?   ပြန်မယ်နော်။
Please don't go!
  măthwà-ba-néh-oùn!   မသွားပါနဲ့ အုံး။
OK, go (goodbye).
  kaùn-ba-bi   ကောင်းပါပြီ။
See you again/later.
  twé-meh, naw or   တွေ့ မယ်နော်။
  nauq-twé-dhè-da-páw   နောက်တွေ့ သေးတာပေါ့။

Civilities

Thanking & Being Thanked

In Myanmar a smile is often enough. Thanking is reserved for larger favours. If you think something you want is a favour, you could use *cè-zù pyú-pi*, literally 'having thanked you', before the request. This makes it more polite than just *pa/ba* at the end.

Please help.
  cè-zù pyú-pì ku-nyi-pè-ba   ကျေးဇူးပြုပြီ ကူညီပေးပါ။

However, as more people in Myanmar meet foreigners, saying 'Thank you' is becoming more common:

Thanks.
  cè-zù-bèh   ကျေးဇူးပဲ။

Thank you.
   cè-zù tin-ba-deh   ကျေးဇူးတင်ပါတယ်။

The response may be:

It's nothing (You're welcome).
   keiq-sá mǎshí-ba-bù   ကိစ္စမရှိပါဘူး။

Apologies & Sympathy

Unlike in English, expressing sorrow or sympathy frequently with
unknown strangers is not widespread. Don't say 'Sorry' every time
you brush someone in the street or to attract someone's attention.

(I) am sorry.
   wùn-nèh-ba-deh   ဝမ်းနဲပါတယ်။

To express pleasure or congratulate someone you can say:

(I) am glad.
   wùn-tha-ba-deh   ဝမ်းသာပါတယ်။

You can put these phrases after another sentence:

Pleased to meet you.
   twé-yá-da wùn-tha-ba-deh   တွေ့ ရတာ ဝမ်းသာပါတယ်။

One very frequent phrase is:

Don't feel bad about it/Don't
be embarrassed.
   à-mǎna-ba-néh   အားမနာပါနဲ့ ။

People say this when they want to give you something or do something for you, and don't want you to refuse because it's a favour;

but sometimes they will say this even if they hope you will refuse. If someone says this to you and you accept, you should probably thank them. If you want to decline the offer, or be polite, you might reply:

I do feel bad about it.
   à-na-ba-deh   အားနာပါတယ်။

Attracting Someone's Attention

The polite way to attract someone's attention is to say 'you' – *k'ǎmyà*, ခင်ဗျာ, if you are a man and *shin*, ရှင်, if you are a woman. If the person you wish to talk with has an obvious title, you should use that instead: 'teacher', *s'ǎya*, ဆရာ (m), *s'ǎya-má*, ဆရာမ (f); 'military officer (lieutenant)', *siq-bo*, စစ်ဗိုလ်; 'general' *bo-jouq*, ဗိုလ်ချုပ်. You may also tack these words ('you' or any kind of title) onto the end of anything you say, to make a request or statement even more polite.

For monks there is a special honorific vocabulary.

Please come, sir.
   la-ba, k'ǎmyà (m)/shin (f)   လာပါ ခင်ဗျား:/ရှင်။
Good, teacher.
   kaùn-ba-deh, s'ǎya   ကောင်းပါတယ် ဆရာ။
Yes (to a monk; literally
'correct, Buddha')
   hman-ba, p'ǎyà   မှန်ပါ ဘုရား။

Forms of Address

Each Burmese person has a two-syllable name (or sometimes more; infrequently only one). There is no family name, no change of name on marriage, and no abbreviation, except among intimates.

Before this name, one of a variety of titles may be used, like our 'Mr'; but these titles are used according to age, prestige and closeness, not marital status.

	male		female	
to someone older/respected	ù	ဦး	daw	ဒေါ်
to someone the same age	ko	ကို	mámá	မမ
			daw	ဒေါ်
to someone younger/intimate	maun	မောင်	má	မ

Use of a name without one of these titles is also possible among close friends; so a man called Soe Win could be called U Soe Win, Ko Soe Win, Maun(g) Soe Win or just Soe Win, or even Ko Soe; a lady named Khin Than could be called Daw Khin Than or Ma Khin Than; (using just Khin Than, Khin or Than alone would imply quite close friendship).

Pronouns

Instead of a noun, you may use a pronoun; in Burmese there are many different pronouns. The following are the polite forms for use with non-intimates. One unusual feature is that the sex of the speaker determines which pronoun is used for both 'I/we' and 'you'.

	I	you	he/she/it
male speaker	cănaw	k'ămyà	thu
	ကျွန်တော်	ခင်ဗျား	သူ
female speaker	cămá	shin	thu
	ကျွန်မ	ရှင်	သူ

Very often a person's title, occupation or kinship can be used to signify 'you' or 'I'. Examples include:

older man ('uncle')	*ù-lè*	ဦးလေး
older woman ('aunty')	*daw-daw*	ဒေါ်ဒေါ်
man of same age ('big brother')	*ko-ko*	ကိုကို
woman of same age ('big sister')	*má-má*	မမ
professional person (m)	*s'ăya*	ဆရာ
professional person (f)	*s'ăya-má*	ဆရာမ

The term *s'ăya/s'ăya-má* literally means 'teacher' but as it is a term of respect, visitors of all occupations may find that this is the way they are addressed. As noted earlier, pronouns can be left out altogether if the meaning is clear.

(I) want to go	*thwà-jin-deh*

If you want to emphasise that a pronoun is plural, you can add *dó* after it, eg *cămá-dó*, 'we (f)'.

Body Language

As in other Asian countries, you should never touch someone on the head or point your feet at anyone. Women should avoid touching monks or their clothes, or even approaching too close.

Language Difficulties

Do you understand?
  nà-leh-dhǎlà?   နားလည်သလား။

I understand.
  nà-leh-ba-deh   နားလည်ပါတယ်။

(I) don't understand.
  nà-mǎleh-ba-bù   နားမလည်ပါဘူး။

Please say it again.
  pyan-pyàw-ba-oùn   ပြန်ပြောပါအုံး။

I only speak a little.
  nèh-nèh pyàw-daq-ba-deh   နဲနဲပြောတတ်ပါတယ်။

What do you call this in Burmese?
  da bǎma-lo beh-lo   ဒါ ဗမာလို ဘယ်လိုခေါ်သလဲ။
  k'aw-dhǎlèh?

Can you speak ...?	*(k'ǎmyà (m)/shin (f))*	ခင်ဗျား/ရှင် ... လို
	... lo pyàw-daq-thǎlà?	ပြောတတ်သလား။
I speak ...	*... lo pyàw-daq-teh*	... လို ပြောတတ်တယ်။
I can't speak ...	*... lo mǎpyàw-daq-bù*	... လို မပြောတတ်ဘူး။
Burmese	*bǎma-zǎgà*	ဗမာစကား
English	*ìn-gǎleiq-zǎgà*	အင်္ဂလိပ်စကား
French	*pyin-thìq-zǎgà*	ပြင်သစ်စကား
Japanese	*jǎpan-zǎgà*	ဂျပန်စကား

Small Talk
Meeting People
See also Forms of Address, page 17.

What is your name?
  k'ǎmyá (m)/shín (f) na-   ခင်ဗျား/ရှင် နာမည်
  meh beh-lo k'aw-dhǎlèh?   ဘယ်လို ခေါ်သလဲ။

My name is ...
cănáw (m)/cămá (f) ... ló k'aw-ba-deh — ကျွန်တော့်/ကျွန်မ ... လို့ ခေါ်ပါတယ်။

Nationalities

Where do you live?
k'ămyà (m)/shin (f) beh-hma ne-dhălèh? — ခင်ဗျား/ရှင် ဘယ်မှာနေသလဲ။

What is your nationality?
k'ămyà (m)/shin (f) ba-lu-myò lèh? — ခင်ဗျား/ရှင် ဘာလူမျိုးလဲ။

I live in ...	*cănaw (m)/cămá (f) ... pye-hma ne-ba-deh*	ကျွန်တော်/ကျွန်မ ... ပြည်မှာနေပါတယ်။
I am ...	*cănaw (m)/cămá (f) ... lu-myò-ba*	ကျွန်တော်/ကျွန်မ ... လူမျိုးပါ။
China/Chinese	*tăyouq*	တရုတ်
France/French	*pyin-thiq*	ပြင်သစ်
Thailand/Thai	*yò-dăyà*	ယိုးဒယား

For all other nationalities, the words are similar to the English.

Age

How old are you?
k'ămyà (m)/shin (f) ătheq beh-lauq shí-bi-lèh? — ခင်ဗျား/ရှင် အသက် ဘယ်လောက်ရှိပြီလဲ။

I am ... years old.
cănaw (m)/cămá (f) ătheq ... hniq shí-bi — ကျွန်တော်/ကျွန်မ အသက် ... နှစ် ရှိပြီ။

See page 57 for the numbers.

Occupations

What is your occupation?
k'ămyà (m)/shin (f) ba   (ခင်ဗျား/ ရှင်) ဘာအလုပ်လုပ်သလဲ။
ălouq louq-dhălèh?

I am a/ an ...   *cănaw (m)/cămá (f)* ကျွန်တော်/ကျွန်မ ... ပါ။
                        ... ba

artist	*păgyi-s'ăya*	ပန်းချီဆရာ
businessperson	*sì-bwà-yè-dhămà*	စီးပွားရေးသမား
clerk	*săyè*	စာရေး
dentist	*thwà-beq-s'ăya-wun*	သွားဘက်ဆရာဝန်
diplomat	*than-tăman*	သံတမန်
doctor	*s'ăya-wun*	ဆရာဝန်
engineer	*seq-hmú-pyin-nya-s'ăya*	စက်မှုပညာဆရာ
farmer	*leh-dhămà*	လယ်သမား
government worker	*ăhmú-dàn/ăya-shí/ ăsò-yá wun-dàn*	အမှုထမ်း/အရာရှိ/ အစိုးရ ဝန်ထမ်း
journalist	*dhădìn-za-s'ăya*	သတင်းစာဆရာ
lawyer	*shé-ne*	ရှေ့ နေ
nurse	*thu-na-byú*	သူနာပြု
photographer	*daq-poun-s'ăya*	ဓါတ်ပုံဆရာ
soldier	*siq-thà*	စစ်သား
student	*caùn-dhà*	ကျောင်းသား
teacher	*caùn-s'ăya*	ကျောင်းဆရာ
tourist	*k'ăyì-dhe/tò-riq*	ခရီးသည်/တိုးရစ်
waiter	*săbwè-dò*	စားပွဲထိုး
writer	*sa-yè-s'ăya*	စာရေးဆရာ

Some typically Burmese occupations are:

actor	*thăyouq-s'aun*	သရုပ်ဆောင်
agent/broker	*pwèh-sà*	ပွဲစား
driver	*kà-maùn-thămà*	ကားမောင်းသမား
fortune-teller	*be-din-s'ăya*	ဗေဒင်ဆရာ
guide	*làn-hnyun*	လမ်းညွှန်
bazaar seller	*zè-theh*	ဈေးသည်
monk	*p'oùn-gyì*	ဘုန်းကြီး
nat medium (male)	*naq-s'ăya*	နတ်ဆရာ
nat medium (female)	*naq-găday*	နတ်ကတော်
rickshaw driver	*s'aiq-kà-dhămà*	ဆိုက်ကားသမား
sailor	*thìn-bàw-dhà*	သင်္ဘောသား
shop keeper	*s'ain-pain-shin*	ဆိုင်ပိုင်ရှင်
singer	*ăs'o-daw*	အဆိုတော်

I don't have a job.	*ălouq măshí-bù*	အလုပ်မရှိဘူး

Religion

What is your religion?

k'ămyà (m)/shin (f) beh-ba-dha kò-gweh-dhălèh? ခင်ဗျား/ရှင် ဘယ်ဘာသာ
ကိုးကွယ်သလဲ။

I am ...	*cănaw (m)/cămá (f)*	ကျွန်တော်/ကျွန်မ ... ပါ။
	... ba	
Buddhist	*bouq-da ba-dha*	ဗုဒ္ဓ ဘာသာ
Christian	*k'ăriq-yan ba-dha*	ခရစ်ယာန် ဘာသာ
Hindu	*hein-du ba-dha*	ဟိန္ဒူ ဘာသာ
Jewish	*gyù ba-dha*	ဂျူး ဘာသာ
Muslim	*is-lan ba-dha*	အစ္စလမ် ဘာသာ

I am not religious.
p'ăyà-tăyà mă-youn-kyi-bù   ဘုရားတရား မယုံကြည်ဘူး။
I am interested in Buddhism.
bouq-da ba-dha-ko   ဗုဒ္ဓ ဘာသာကို
seiq-win-sà-ba-deh   စိတ်ဝင်စားပါတယ်။

Family

Are you married?
k'ămyà (m)/shin (f)   ခင်ဗျား/ရှင် အိမ်ထောင်ရှိသလား။
ein-daun shí-dhălà?
(I, you, someone) am/is married.
ein-daun shí-ba-deh   အိမ်ထောင်ရှိပါတယ်။
I am not married.
cănaw (m)/cămá (f)   ကျွန်တော်/ကျွန်မ
ein-daun măshí-ba-bù   အိမ်ထောင်မရှိပါဘူး။

Do you have ...?	... *shí-dhălà?*	... ရှိသလား။
I have ...	*cănaw (m)/cămá (f)*	ကျွန်တော်/ကျွန်မ
	... *shí-ba-deh*	... ရှိပါတယ်။
I have no ...	*cănaw (m)/cămá (f)*	ကျွန်တော်/ကျွန်မ
	... *măshí-ba-bù*	... မရှိပါဘူး။

children	*thà-dhămì*	သားသမီး
father	*ăp'e*	အဖေ
mother	*ăme*	အမေ
older brother	*ăko*	အစ်ကို
younger brother	*nyi* (of male)/	ညီ/မောင်
	maun (of female)	
older sister	*ămá*	အစ်မ
younger sister	*hnămá* (of male)/	နှမ/ညီမ
	nyi-má (of female)	

husband/man	*yauq-cà*	ယောက်ျား
wife	*meìn-má*	မိန်းမ
wife (more polite)	*zănì*	ဇနီး

How many brothers and sisters
do you have?
    maun-hnămá beh-hnăyauq   မောင်နှမ ဘယ်နှယောက် ရှိသလဲ။
    shí-dhălèh?

Making Conversation

We're friends.
    dó thăngeh-jìn-dwe-ba   ဒို့ သူငယ်ချင်းတွေပါ။
I'm here on holiday.
    ăleh la-ba-deh   အလည်လာပါတယ်။
We like it here.
    di-hma pyaw-ne-deh   ဒီမှာပျော်နေတယ်။
Do you live near here?
    di-nà-hma ne-dhălà?   ဒီနားမှာနေသလား။

It's very hot, isn't it!
    theiq pu-deh-naw   သိပ်ပူတယ်နော်။
What a cute (baby,
kitten, doll etc)!
    c'iq-săya-lè   ချစ်စရာလေး။
It's lovely.
    hlá-laiq-ta   လှလိုက်တာ။

This is my address.
    da cănáw (m)/cămá (f)   ဒါ ကျွန်တော့်/
    leiq-sa-ba   ကျွန်မ လိပ်စာပါ။
We'll send you one.
    tăk'ú pó-pè-meh   တစ်ခု ပို့ပေးမယ်။

You're right.
  hman-ba-deh   မှန်ပါတယ်။
I don't think so.
  măt'in-bù   မထင်ဘူး။

Useful Phrases
Beautiful (pagodas,
Buddhas)!
  ci-nyo-zăya kaùn-deh   ကြည့်သိုစရာ ကောင်းတယ်။
Really!
  houq-là   ဟုတ်လား
It's wonderful/very good.
  theiq kaùn-laiq-ta   သိပ် ကောင်းလိုက်တာ။
It's amazing.
  án-áw-zăya-bè   အံ့ဩစရာပဲ။
It's strange.
  t'ù-zàn-laiq-ta   ထူးဆန်းလိုက်တာ။
Just a minute.
  k'ăná-lè naw   ခဏလေး နော်။

Getting Around
Finding Your Way

When will the ... leave?	... *beh-ăc'ein t'weq-mălèh?*	... ဘယ်အချိန်ထွက်မလဲ။
plane	*le-yin-byan*	လေယာဉ်ပျံ
train	*mì-yăt'à*	မီးရထား
bus	*baq-săkà*	ဘတ်စကား
riverboat	*thìn-bàw*	သင်္ဘော
jeep	*jiq-kà*	ဂျစ်ကား
taxi	*ăhngà-kà*	အငှါးကား

bicycle	*seq-beìn*	စက်ဘီး
motorcycle	*mo-ta s'ain-keh*	မော်တော်ဆိုင်ကယ်
rickshaw/side-car	*s'aiq-kà*	ဆိုက်ကား

Where is the ...?	*... beh-hma-lèh?*	... ဘယ်မှာလဲ။
airport	*le-zeiq*	လေဆိပ်
railway carriage	*mì-yǎt'à-dwèh*	မီးရထားတွဲ
railway station	*bu-da-youn*	ဘူတာရုံ
bus station	*baq-sǎkà-geiq*	ဘတ်စကားဂိတ်
riverboat jetty	*thìn-bàw-zeiq*	သင်္ဘောဆိပ်

Can I get there by ...?	*... néh thwà-ló yá-mǎlà?*	... နဲ့ သွားလို့ရမလား။
taxi	*ǎhngà-kà*	အငှားကား
bus	*baq-sǎkà*	ဘတ်စကား
bicycle	*seq-beìn*	စက်ဘီး

Directions

Is this the way to ...?
di-làn ... thwà-déh-làn-là?   ဒီလမ်း ... သွားတဲ့လမ်းလား။

What ... is this?	*da ba ... lèh?*	ဒါ ဘာ ... လဲ။
town	*myó*	မြို့
street	*làn*	လမ်း
bus	*baq-sǎkà*	ဘတ်စကား

How do I get to ...?
... ko beh-lo thwà-yá-dhǎlèh?   ... ကို �‌ဘယ်လိုသွားရသလဲ။

Can I walk there?
làn-shauq-yin yá-mǎlà?   လမ်းလျှောက်ရင် ရမလား။

Is it nearby?
di-nà-hma-là?   ဒီနားမှာလား။

Is it far?
wè-dhǎlà?   ဝေးသလား။

left	*beh-beq*	ဘယ်ဘက်
right	*nya-beq*	ညာဘက်
straight (ahead)	*téh-déh*	တည့်တည့်
very far away	*theiq wè-deh*	သိပ်ဝေးတယ်။
not so far away	*theiq mǎwè-bù*	သိပ်မဝေးဘူး။

north	*myauq-p'eq*	မြောက်ဘက်
south	*taun-beq*	တောင်ဘက်
east	*ǎshé-beq*	အရှေ့ဘက်
west	*ǎnauq-p'eq*	အနောက်ဘက်

Buying Tickets

I'd like ...	*cǎnaw (m)/cǎmá (f)*	ကျွန်တော်/ကျွန်မ
	... lo-jin-ba-deh	... လိုချင်ပါတယ်။
one ticket	*leq-hmaq-dǎzaun*	လက်မှတ်တစ်စောင်
two tickets	*leq-hmaq hnǎsaun*	လက်မှတ်နှစ်စောင်
a sleeper (a bed)	*eiq-ya*	အိပ်ရာ
a room (or cabin on a boat)	*ǎk'àn*	အခန်း

How much is it to go to Maymyo?
me-myó thwà-yin   မေမြို့သွားရင် ဘယ်လောက်လဲ။
beh-lauq-lèh?

Bus

Where does this bus go?
di baq-săkà beh-go   ဒီဘတ်စကား ဘယ်ကိုသွားသလဲ။
thwà-dhălèh?

Where should I get off?
beh-hma s'ìn-yá-mălèh?   ဘယ်မှာဆင်းရမလဲ။

Bus No 8 goes there.
baq-săkà nan-baq-shiq   ဘတ်စကား နံပါတ်ရှစ်
ho-beq thwà-deh   ဟိုဘက် သွားတယ်။

Can I sit here?
di-hma t'ain-ló yá-dhălà?   ဒီမှာထိုင်လို့ ရသလား။

Can I put my things here?
cănáw (m)/cămá (f) pyiq-sì ကျွန်တော့်/ ကျွန်မ ပစ္စည်း
di-hma t'à-ló yá-dhălà?   ဒီမှာ ထားလို့ ရသလား။

Train

express train   *ămyan-yăt'à*   အမြန်ရထား
local train   *law-keh-yăt'à*   လော်ကယ်ရထား

How many hours is it by train
to Mandalay?
mì-yăt'à-néh màn-dălè-go မီးရထားနဲ့ မန္တလေးကို
behnă-na-yi-lèh?   ဘယ်နှစ်နာရီလဲ။

Taxi

Most 'taxis' are old jeeps, pick-ups or cars. Increasingly there
are new saloon cars functioning as taxis, particularly in Yangon
(Rangoon). As there are no meters you should bargain for the
price before you get in.

I'd like to sit in the front.
    ăshé-gàn-hma t'ain-jin-deh   အရှေ့ခန်းမှာထိုင်ချင်တယ်။

What time will we reach Bagan
(Pagan)?
    *băgan beh-ăc'ein
    yauq-mălèh?*   ပုဂံ ဘယ်အချိန် ရောက်မလဲ။

Instructions

Please go slowly.
    pyè-pyè thwà-ba   ဖြည်းဖြည်းသွားပါ။

Please wait for me.
    *cănaw(m)/cămá(f)-go
    saún-ne-ba*   ကျွန်တော်/ကျွန်မကိုစောင့်နေပါ။

Stop here.
    di-hma yaq-pa   ဒီမှာ ရပ်ပါ။

Go to the corner of Fifth St.
    ngà-làn-dáun-go thwà-ba   ၆ါးလမ်းထောင့်ကို သွားပါ။

Boat

What time does the boat
leave?
    *thìn-bàw beh-ăc'ein
    t'weq-mălèh?*   သင်္ဘော ဘယ်အချိန်ထွက်မလဲ။

Can I get on board now?
    ăk'ú teq-ló yá-dhălà?   အခု တက်လို့ရသလား။

Accommodation

Finding Accommodation

Is there a ...   *... di-nà-hma*   ... ဒီနားမှာရှိသလား။
near here?   *shí-dhălà?*
    hotel   *ho-teh*   ဟော်တယ်
    guesthouse   *tèh-k'o-gàn*   တည်းခိုခန်း

Checking In

Can foreigners stay here?
　nain-ngan-gyà-thà　နိုင်ငံခြားသား ဒီမှာတည်းလို့ရသလား။
　di-hma tèh-ló yá-dhălà?

May I see the room?
　ăk'àn cí-bayá-ze?　အခန်း ကြည့်ပါရစေ

Is breakfast included in the
price?
　ăk'àn-k'á-dèh-hma　အခန်းခထဲမှာ မနက်စာ ပါသလား။
　măneq-sa pa-dhălà?

Can I pay in kyats?
　caq-néh pè-ló yá-là?　ကျပ်နဲ့ ပေးလို့ရလား။

I will stay for two nights
　hnăyeq t'èh-meh　နှစ်ရက်တည်းမယ်။

How much is ...?　... *beh-lauq-lèh?*　... ဘယ်လောက်လဲ။
　one night　*tăyeq*　တစ်ရက်
　two nights　*hnăyeq*　နှစ်ရက်
　a single room　*tăyauq-k'an*　တစ်ယောက်ခန်း
　a double room　*hnăyauq-k'an*　နှစ်ယောက်ခန်း
　a cheaper room　*zè-po-nèh-déh-ăk'an*　ဈေးပိုနဲတဲ့အခန်း

This room is good.
　di ăk'àn kaùn-deh　ဒီအခန်း ကောင်းတယ်။

(I/We'll) stay here.
　di-hma t'èh-meh　ဒီမှာ တည်းမယ်။

(We'll) stay together.
　ătu-du t'èh-meh　အတူတူ တည်းမယ်။

We'll stay in separate rooms.
　thì-gyà t'èh-meh　သီးခြား တည်းမယ်။

Requests & Complaints

Do you have ...?	... *shí-dhǎlà?*	... ရှိသလား။
an air-conditioned room	*le-è-gàn*	လေအေးခန်း
a better room	*po-kaùn-déh-ǎk'àn*	ပိုကောင်းတဲ့အခန်း
hot water	*ye-nwè*	ရေနွေး
a mosquito net	*c'in-daun*	ခြင်ထောင်
a restaurant	*sà-thauq-s'ain*	စားသောက်ဆိုင်
a telephone	*p'oùn*	ဖုန်း
a toilet	*ein-dha*	အိမ်သာ

Where can I get my clothes washed?
  ǎwuq-beh-hma-shaw-ló   အဝတ် ဘယ်မှာလျှော်လို့ရလဲ။
  yá-dhǎlèh?

Where is the bathroom?
  ye-c'ò-gàn beh-hma-lèh?   ရေချိုးခန်း �‌ဘယ်မှာလဲ။

The room is expensive.
  ǎk'àn zè-jì-deh   အခန်း ဈေးကြီးတယ်။

Will you fix the light?
  daq-mì pyin-mǎlà?   ဓါတ်မီးပြင်မလား။

Can (I/we) leave my bag for three days?
  tiq-ta di-hma thoùn-yeq   သေတ္တာ ဒီမှာ
  t'a-ló yá-dhǎlà?   သုံးရက်ထားလို့ရလား။

Useful Words

clean	*thán-deh*	သန့်တယ်
dirty	*nyiq-paq-deh*	ညစ်ပတ်တယ်
fan (electric)	*pan-ka*	ပန်ကာ

fan (manual)	*yaq-taun*	ယပ်တောင်
key	*tháw*	သော့
noisy	*s'u-nyan-deh*	ဆူညံတယ်
pillow	*gaùn-oùn*	ခေါင်းအုံး

Around Town

Where is the ...?	... *beh-hma-lèh?*	... ဘယ်မှာလဲ။
bank	*ban-daiq*	ဘဏ်တိုက်
market	*zè*	ဈေး
museum	*pyá-daiq*	ပြတိုက်
post office	*sa-daiq*	စာတိုက်

At the Post Office

How much to send ...?	... *pó-yin beh-lauq-lèh?*	... ပို့ရင် ဘယ်လောက်လဲ။
printed matter	*sa-ouq-twe*	စာအုပ်တွေ
airmail letter	*le-jaùn-sa*	လေကြောင်းစာ
registered	*re-siq-sări/sa-yìn*	ရေစစ္စရီ/စာရင်း
express	*ămyan*	အမြန်
surface	*yò-yò*	ရိုးရိုး
a fax	*'fax'*	ဖက်စ်

Please give me ...	... *pè-ba*	... ပေးပါ။
an aerogram	*èh-ya-leq-ta*	အဲယားလက်တာ
a stamp	*dăzeiq-gaùn-tăloùn*	တံဆိပ်ခေါင်းတစ်လုံး
an envelope	*sa-eiq*	စာအိတ်

BURMESE

| a receipt | *pye-za* | ပြေစာ |
| a telephone directory | *teh-li-p'oùn làn-hnyun* | တယ်လီဖုန်းလမ်းညွှန် |

I want to send this letter to America.

di-sa ăme-rì-kà-go pó-jin-deh — ဒီစာ အမေရိကန်ကို ပို့ချင်တယ်။

Telecommunications

I'd like to make a call.

p'oùn-s'eq-c'in-deh — ဖုံးဆက်ချင်တယ်။

Please call this number for me.

di teh-li-p'oùn nan-baq kaw-pè-ba — ဒီတယ်လီဖုံးနံပါတ်ခေါ်ပေးပါ။

Can I send a fax?

fax pó-ló yá-dhălà? — ဖက်စ်ပို့လို့ ရသလား။

If I send a cable (telegram) how much per word?

cè-nàn-yaiq-yin sa-tăloùn beh-lauq-lèh? — ကြေးနန်းရိုက်ရင် စာတစ်လုံး ဘယ်လောက်လဲ။

At the Bank

Official exchange rates are fixed and some things (including most hotel accommodation and travel) must be paid for in hard currency or foreign exchange certificates (FECs). You will be required on arrival to change some foreign currency into FECs (in Burmese 'FEC' or *bǎ-ma daw-la*).

I want to change ...	... *lèh-jin-ba-deh*	... လဲချင်ပါတယ်။
dollars	*daw-la*	ဒေါ်လာ
pounds	*paun*	ပေါင်

foreign currency	*nain-ngan-gyà ngwe*	နိုင်ငံခြားငွေ
money	*paiq-s'an*	ပိုက်ဆံ
travellers' cheques	*k'ǎyì-c'eq-leq-hmaq*	ခရီးချက်လက်မှတ်

Can I cash a cheque?
   c'eq-ko ngwe-lèh-pè-ló   ချက်ကိုငွေလဲပေးလို့ရသလား။
   yá-dhǎlà?

How many kyat to a dollar?
   tǎdawla beh-hnǎcaq-lèh?   တစ်ဒေါ်လာ ဘယ်နှစ်ကျပ်လဲ။

How much will you give me for
100 dollars?
   daw-la tǎya-go beh-lauq   ဒေါ်လာတစ်ရာကို ဘယ်လောက်
   pyan-pè-mǎlèh?   ပြန်ပေးမလဲ။

Please give me smaller change.
   ǎkywe-ǎnouq lèh-pè-ba   အကြွေအနုပ်လဲပေးပါ။

Sightseeing

How much is the entrance fee?
   win-jè beh-lauq-lèh?   ဝင်ကြေး ဘယ်လောက်လဲ။

Is there an English-speaking guide?
   ingǎleiq sǎgà-pyàw-daq-téh   အင်္ဂလိပ်စကားပြောတတ်တဲ့
   làn-hnyun shí-dhǎlà?   လမ်းညွှန် ရှိသလား။

I'd like to buy a map.
   mye-boun-dǎboun   မြေပုံတစ်ပုံဝယ်ချင်ပါတယ်။
   weh-jin-ba-deh

Can I take photographs?
   daq-poun yaiq-ló-yá-dhǎlà?   ဓါတ်ပုံ ရိုက်လို့ရသလား။

When will it open?
   beh-dáw p'wín-mǎlèh?   ဘယ်တော့ဖွင့်မလဲ။

What time will it close?
   beh-dáw peiq-mǎlèh?   ဘယ်တော့ပိတ်မလဲ။

When was it built?
beh-dòun-gá s'auq-thălèh?   ဘယ်တုန်းကဆောက်သလဲ။

bookshop	*sa-ouq-s'ain*	စာအုပ်ဆိုင်
botanical garden	*youq-k'á-be-dá-ú-yin*	ရုက္ခဗေဒဥယျာဉ်
church	*p'ăyà-shí-k'ò-caùn*	ဘုရားရှိခိုးကျောင်း
cinema	*youq-shin-youn*	ရုပ်ရှင်ရုံ
monastery	*p'oùn-jì-caùn*	ဘုန်းကြီးကျောင်း
park	*pàn-jàn*	ပန်းခြံ
university	*teq-kătho*	တက္ကသိုလ်

Paperwork

customs form	*pyiq-sì thwìn-poun-zan*	ပစ္စည်းသွင်းပုံစံ
embassy	*than-yoùn*	သံရုံး
form	*poun-zan*	ပုံစံ
government official	*wun-dàn*	ဝန်ထမ်း
immigration office	*lu-win-hmú cì-jaq-yè-yoùn*	လူဝင်မှု ကြီးကြပ်ရေးရုံး
passport	*paq-săpó*	ပတ်စပို့

In the Country

Weather

What will the weather be like today?
di-né mò-le-wădhá beh-lo-lèh?   ဒီနေ့ မိုးလေဝသ ဘယ်လိုလဲ။
Will it rain tomorrow?
măneq-p'yan mò-ywa-mălà?   မနက်ဖြန် မိုးရွာမလား။

The weather is ...	*mò-le-wădhá* ...	မိုးလေဝသ ...
good	*kaùn-deh*	ကောင်းတယ်။
changeable	*pyaùn-nain-deh*	ပြောင်းနိုင်တယ်။
bad	*s'ò-deh*	ဆိုးတယ်။

wind	*le*	လေ
cloud	*tein*	တိမ်
fog	*hnìn*	နှင်း
rain (verb)	*mò-ywa-deh*	မိုးရွာတယ်
monsoon storm	*mò-theq-le-pyìn*	မိုးသက်လေပြင်း
season	*ya-dhi-ú-dú*	ရာသီဥတု
weather	*mò-le-wădhá*	မိုးလေဝသ

Geographical Terms

beach	*kàn-byin*	ကမ်းပြင်
countryside	*tàw*	တော
field (irrigated)	*leh*	လယ်
hill	*taun/koùn*	တောင်/ကုန်း
island	*cùn*	ကျွန်း
lake	*ain*	အိုင်
lake (small/artificial)	*kan*	ကန်
map	*mye-boun*	မြေပုံ
river	*myiq*	မြစ်
sea	*pin-leh*	ပင်လယ်
town	*myó*	မြို့
track/trail	*làn-jaùn*	လမ်းကြောင်း
village	*ywa*	ရွာ
waterfall	*ye-dăgun*	ရေတံခွန်

Flora

bamboo	*wà*	ဝါး
bark (tree)	*thiq-k'auq*	သစ်ခေါက်
flower	*pàn*	ပန်း
flowering plant	*pàn-bin*	ပန်းပင်
leaf	*yweq*	ရွက်
lotus	*ca*	ကြာ
orchid	*thiq-k'wá-pàn*	သစ်ခွပန်း
pine	*t'ìn-yù-bin*	ထင်းရှူးပင်
rattan	*cein*	ကြိမ်
teak	*cùn-thiq*	ကျွန်းသစ်
tree	*thiq-pin*	သစ်ပင်
wood	*thiq-thà*	သစ်သား

Fauna

bedbug	*jăbò*	ကြမ်းပိုး
bird	*hngeq*	ငှက်
buffalo	*cwèh*	ကျွဲ
cat	*caun*	ကြောင်
chicken	*ceq*	ကြက်
cockroach	*pò-haq*	ပိုးဟပ်
cow	*nwà*	နွား
deer (barking)	*ji*	ချေ
deer (sambhar)	*s'aq*	ဆတ်
dog	*k'wè*	ခွေး
duck	*bèh*	ဘဲ
elephant	*s'in*	ဆင်

fish	*ngà*	ငါး
fly	*yin*	ယင်
horse	*myìn*	မြင်း
insect	*pò-hmwà*	ပိုးမွှား
mosquito	*c'in*	ခြင်
pig	*weq*	ဝက်
rat	*cweq*	ကြွက်
snake	*mwe*	မြွေ
tiger	*cà*	ကျား

Useful Phrases

What ... is that?	*da ba ... lèh?*	ဒါဘာ ... လဲ။
animal	*dăreiq-s'an*	တိရစ္ဆာန်
flower	*pàn-pin*	ပန်းပင်
tree	*thiq-pin*	သစ်ပင်

Is this the way to ...?
  di-làn ... thwà-déh-làn-là? ဒီလမ်း ... သွားတဲ့လမ်းလား။
How far is it to ...?
  ... ko beh-lauq-wè-dhălèh? ... ကို ဘယ်လောက်ဝေးသလဲ။
How many hours will it take?
  beh-hnăna-yi ca-mălèh? ဘယ်နှစ်နာရီကြာမလဲ။
Are there any road signs?
  làn-hnyun-s'aìn-bouq လမ်းညွှန်ဆိုင်းဘုတ်ရှိသလား။
  shí-dhălà?
(I'm/We're) lost.
  làn pyauq-thwà-bi လမ်းပျောက်သွားပြီ။
Is it OK to swim here?
  di-hma ye-kù-ló-yádhălà? ဒီမှာရေးကူးလို့ရသလား။

Food

Most restaurants are privately run. Apart from Burmese food, various Shan dishes are popular. There are also good Chinese restaurants and Indian food stalls in most towns. The food is not as overpoweringly hot as some Thai or Indian food, but chillies are used fairy liberally. Rice is the staple food.

Is there a ... near here?	... di-nà-hma shí-dhǎlà?	... ဒီနားမှာရှိသလား။
Shan noodle stall	shàn-k'auk-swèh-zain	ရှမ်းခေါက်ဆွဲဆိုင်
Chinese restaurant	tǎyouq-s'ain	တရုတ်ဆိုင်
food stall	sà-thauq-s'ain	စားသောက်ဆိုင်
restaurant	sà-daw-s'eq	စားတော်ဆက်

breakfast	mǎneq-sa	မနက်စာ
lunch	né-leh-za	နေ့လည်စာ
dinner	nyá-za	ညစာ
snack/small meal	móun/thǎye-za	မုန့်/သရေစာ
food ('edibles')	sà-ya	စားစရာ

Eating Out

Please bring a ...	... yu-pè-ba	... ယူပေးပါ။
chopsticks	tu	တူ
fork	k'ǎyìn	ခက်ရင်း
spoon	zùn	ဇွန်း
knife	dà	ဓါး
glass	p'an-gweq	ဖန်ခွက်
plate	bǎgan-byà	ပန်းကန်ပြား
bowl	bǎgan-loùn	ပန်းကန်လုံး
cup	k'weq	ခွက်

I can't eat meat.
  ăthà mǎsà-nain-bù   အသား မစားနိုင်ဘူး။

Do you have any drinking water?
  thauq-ye shí-dhǎlà?   သောက်ရေရှိသလား။

What's the best dish to eat today?
  di-né ba-hìn ǎkaùn-zoùn-lèh?   ဒီနေ့ဘာဟင်းအကောင်းဆုံးလဲ။

I didn't order this.
  da mǎhma-bù   ဒါ မမှာဘူး။

Typical Burmese Dishes

clear soup	*hìn-jo*	ဟင်းချို
sizzling rice soup	*s'an-hlaw-hìn-jo*	ဆန်လှော်ဟင်းချို
'12-taste' soup	*s'eh-hnǎmyò-hìn-jo*	ဆယ်နှစ်မျိုးဟင်းချို
mohinga	*móun-hìn-gà*	မုန့်ဟင်းခါး
(rice vermicelli in fish sauce)		
Mandalay moun-ti	*móun-di*	မုန့်တီ
(spaghetti-like noodles with chicken or fish)		
coconut noodles with chicken and egg	*oùn-nó-k'auk-swèh*	အုန်းနို့ခေါက်ဆွဲ
coconut rice	*oùn-t'ǎmìn*	အုန်းထမင်း
fried rice	*t'ǎmìn-gyaw*	ထမင်းကြော်
packet/bamboo section of sticky rice	*kauk-hnyìn-baùn*	ကောက်ညှင်းပေါင်း
beef curry	*ǎmèh-dhà-hìn*	အမဲသားဟင်း
beef in gravy	*ǎmèh-hnaq*	အမဲနှပ်
chicken curry	*ceq-thà-hìn*	ကြက်သားဟင်း
fried chicken	*ceq-thà-jaw*	ကြက်သားကြော်

fried spicy chicken	*ceq-thà-ăsaq-ceq*	ကြက်သားအစပ်ချက်
grilled chicken (satay)	*ceq-thà-gin*	ကြက်သားကင်
pork curry	*weq-thà-hìn*	ဝက်သားဟင်း
pork curry in thick sauce	*weq-thà s'i-byan*	ဝက်သားဆီပြန်
red pork	*weq-tha-ni*	ဝက်သားနီ
sweet chicken	*ceq-thà-ăc'o-jeq*	ကြက်သားအချိုချက်
fish salad	*ngà-dhouq*	ငါးသုပ်
prawn/shrimp curry	*băzun-hìn*	ပုစွန်ဟင်း
steamed fish in banana leaves	*ngà-baùn-douq*	ငါးပေါင်းထုပ်
vegetable curry	*hìn-dhì-hìn-yweq-hìn/ thì-zoun-hìn*	ဟင်းသီးဟင်းရွက်ဟင်း/ သီးစုံဟင်း
sago/tapioca in syrup	*tha-gu-móun*	သာဂူမုန့်
sticky rice cake with jaggery	*móun-zàn*	မုန့်ဆန်း
sticky rice cake (purple)	*kauk-hnyìn-ngăjeiq*	ကောက်ညှင်းချိုပို
sweet fried rice pancakes	*móun-s'i-jaw*	မုန့်ဆီကြော်
toddy palm sugar cake	*t'àn-thì-móun*	ထန်းသီးမုန့်

At the Market
Meat

beef	*ămèh*	အမဲ
chicken	*ceq-thà*	ကြက်သား
pork	*weq-thà*	ဝက်သား

Seafood

catfish	*ngăk'u*	ငါးခူ
eel	*ngăshín*	ငါးရှဉ့်
fish	*ngà*	ငါး
seafood	*pin-leh-za/ ye-thaq-tăwa*	ပင်လယ်စာ/ ရေသတ္တဝါ
shellfish	*k'ăyú*	ခရု
squid	*pyi-jì-ngà*	ပြည်ကြီးငါး
steamed carp	*ngà-thălauq-paùn*	ငါးသလောက်ပေါင်း
steamed fish	*ngà-baùn*	ငါးပေါင်း

Vegetables

banana flower	*hngăpyàw-bù*	ငှက်ပျောဖူး
beans	*pèh-dhì*	ပဲသီး
cabbage	*gaw-bi-douq*	ဂေါ်ဖီထုပ်
carrot	*moun-la-ú-wa*	မုန်လာဥဝါ
cauliflower	*pàn-gaw-p'i*	ပန်းဂေါ်ဖီ
chick peas	*kălăbèh*	ကုလားပဲ
corn (cob)	*pyaùn-bù*	ပြောင်းဖူး
cucumber	*thăk'wà-dhì*	သခွါးသီး
eggplant/aubergine	*k'ăyàn-dhì*	ခရမ်းသီး
mushrooms	*hmo*	မှို
onion	*ceq-thun-ni*	ကြက်သွန်နီ
pumpkin	*p'ăyoun-dhì*	ဖရုံသီး
tomato	*k'ăyàn-jin-dhì*	ခရမ်းချဉ်သီး
vegetables	*hìn-dhì-hìn-yweq*	ဟင်းသီးဟင်းရွက်
white radish	*moun-la-ú-p'yu*	မုန်လာဥဖြူ
zucchini/gourd	*bù-dhì*	ဘူးသီး

Fruit

fruit	*thiq-thì*	သစ်သီး
apple ('flower-fruit')	*pàn-dhì*	ပန်းသီး
avocado ('butter-fruit')	*t'àw-baq-thì*	ထောပတ်သီး
banana	*ngăpyàw-dhì*	ငှက်ပျောသီး
breadfruit	*paun-móun-dhì*	ပေါင်မုန့်သီး
coconut	*oùn-dhì*	အုန်းသီး
custard apple ('influence-fruit')	*àw-za-thì*	ဩဇာသီး
durian	*dù-yìn-dhì*	ဒူးရင်းသီး
lemon	*shauq-thì*	ရှောက်သီး
lime	*than-băya-dhì*	သံပုရာသီး
lychee	*lain-c'ì-dhì*	လိုင်ချီးသီး
mango	*thăyeq-dhì*	သရက်သီး
orange	*lein-maw-dhì*	လိမ္မော်သီး
papaya ('boat-shaped fruit')	*thìn-bàw-dhì*	သင်္ဘောသီး
peach	*meq-mun-dhì*	မက်မွန်သီး
pear	*thiq-taw-dhì*	သစ်တော်သီး
pineapple	*na-naq-thì*	နာနတ်သီး
plum (damson)	*meq-màn-dhì*	မက်မန်းသီး
jujube plum	*zì-dhì*	ဆီးသီး
pomelo	*cwèh-gàw-dhì*	ကျွဲကောသီး
rambutan ('cockscomb fruit')	*ceq-mauq-thì*	ကြက်မောက်သီး
tamarind	*măjì-dhì*	မန်ကျည်းသီး
watermelon	*p'ăyèh-dhì*	ဖရဲသီး

Spices & Condiments

betel quid	*kùn-ya*	ကွမ်းယား
butter	*t'àw-baq*	ထောပတ်
cardamon	*p'a-la-zé*	ဖါလာစေ့
cashews	*thi-ho-zí*	သီဟိုစေ့
chilli sauce	*ngăyouq-yeh*	ငရုတ်ရည်
chilli	*ngăyouq-thì*	ငရုတ်သီး
coriander	*nan-nan-bin*	နံနံပင်
coconut cream	*oùn-nó*	အုန်းနို့
fish sauce	*ngan-pya-yeh*	ငံပြာရည်
galangal (white ginger-like root)	*meiq-thălin*	မိတ်သလင်
garlic	*ceq-thun-byu*	ကြက်သွန်ဖြူ
ghee	*kalà t'àw-baq*	ကုလားထောပတ်
ginger	*gyìn*	ဂျင်း
honey	*pyà-yeh*	ပျားရည်
lemongrass	*zăbălin*	စပါးလင်
lime (for betel)	*t'oùn*	ထုံး
peanuts	*mye-bèh*	မြေပဲ
fried peanuts	*mye-bèh-jaw*	မြေပဲကြော်
raisins	*zăbyiq-thì-jauq*	စပျစ်သီးခြောက်
rose syrup	*hnìn-yeh*	နှင်းရည်
sago/tapioca	*tha-gu*	သာဂူ
salt	*s'à*	ဆား
sesame	*hnàn*	နှမ်း
soy sauce	*pèh-ngan-pya-yeh*	ပဲငံပြာရည်
sugar	*thăjà*	သကြား
tofu/beancurd	*to-hù*	တိုဟူး

| turmeric | *s'ǎnwìn* | ဆနွင်း |
| vinegar | *sha-lǎka-yeh* | ရှာလကာရည် |

Drinks
Cold Drinks

alcohol	*ǎyeq*	အရက်
beer	*bi-ya*	ဘီယာ
coconut juice	*oùn-yeh*	အုန်းရည်
lime juice	*than-bǎya-yeh*	သံပရာရည်
milk	*nwà-nó*	နွားနို့
orange juice	*lein-maw-yeh*	လိမ္မော်ရည်
soft drink	*bí-laq-yeh/p'yaw-yeh*	ဘီလပ်ရည်/ဖျော်ရည်
sugarcane juice	*can-yeh*	ကြံရည်
toddy	*t'àn-yeh*	ထန်းရည်
water	*ye*	ရေ
boiled cold water	*ye-jeq-è*	ရေချက်အေး
hot water	*ye-nwè*	ရေနွေး
cold water	*ye-è*	ရေအေး
bottled water	*thán-ye*	သန့်ရေ
('clean water')		
soda water	*s'o-da*	ဆိုဒါ
wine	*wain*	ဝိုင်

Hot Drinks

Plain green, Chinese (or Shan) tea comes free in all restaurants and teashops. A thermos of it sits on the table of most Myanmar homes. Other drinks (tea, coffee) tend to come pre-mixed in the cup with milk (or condensed milk) and plenty of sugar. If you ask for a black coffee, you may get local coffee (delicious black with a wedge of lime) or instant coffee, known as 'Nes'. Sachets of 'coffee-mix' (coffee, milk powder and sugar) are becoming widespread.

plain green tea	*lăp'eq-yeh-jàn/*	လက်ဖက်ရည်ကြမ်း/
	ye-nwè-jàn	ရေနွေးကြမ်း
coffee	*kaw-fi*	ကော်ဖီ
Indian tea	*leq-p'eq-yeh*	လက်ဖက်ရည်
with milk	*nwà-nó-néh*	နွားနို့နဲ့
with condensed milk	*nó-s'ì-néh*	နို့ဆီနဲ့
with lime	*than-bǎya-dhì-néh*	သံပုရာသီးနဲ့
with sugar	*dhǎjà-néh*	သကြားနဲ့

Shopping

Where is the ..?	*... beh-hma-lèh?*	... ဘယ်မှာလဲ။
market	*zè*	ဈေး
shop	*s'ain*	ဆိုင်
bookshop	*sa-ouq-s'ain*	စာအုပ်ဆိုင်
medicine store	*s'è-zain*	ဆေးဆိုင်
factory	*seq-youn*	စက်ရုံ

Making a Purchase

Do you have ... ?	*... shí-là*	... ရှိလား။
Where can I buy ...?	*... beh-hma weh-yá-mǎlèh?*	... ဘယ်မှာဝယ်ရမလဲ။

How much is ...?	... *beh-lauq-lèh?*	... ဘယ်လောက်လဲ။
one shirt	*èin-ji tǎt'eh*	အင်္ကျီတစ်ထည်
two sewing needles	*aq-hnǎc'aùn*	အပ်နှစ်ချောင်း
four tickets	*leq-hmaq lè-zaun*	လက်မှတ်လေးစောင်
a pair of shoes	*p'ǎnaq tǎyan*	ဖိနပ်တစ်ရန်

If you want to use a number, you should put a counter word after it. Although there are quite a lot of counters used in Burmese, you can get by with just a few. In general *k'ú*, ခု can be used for counting anything but people. See Numbers & Amounts, page 58 for details on how to use counters.

| two snacks | *móun hnǎk'ú* | မုန့် နှစ်ခု |
| three tickets | *leq-hmaq thòun-zoùn* | လက်မှတ်သုံးစောင် |

Bargaining

Shopping means bargaining, except in government shops.

Please reduce the price.
  zè-sháw-ba   ဈေးလျှော့ပါ

It is very expensive.
  zè theiq cì-deh   ဈေးသိပ်ကြီးတယ်။

Do you have a cheaper one?
  da-t'eq zè po-pàw-dé   ဒါထက် ဈေးပိုပေါတဲ့တစ်ခု
  tǎk'ú shí-dhǎlà?   ရှိသလား။

If I buy two, will you reduce
the price?
  hnǎk'ú weh-yin,   နှစ်ခုဝယ်ရင် ဈေးလျှော့ပေးမလား။
  zè-sháw-pè-mǎlà?

I will give you 100 kyat.
  tǎya pè-meh   တစ်ရာပေးမယ်။

I have only 200 kyat.
   ngwe hnǎya-bèh shí-deh   ငွေနှစ်ရာဘဲ ရှိတယ်။

expensive	*zè-cì-deh*	ဈေးကြီးတယ်
cheap	*zè-pàw-deh*	ဈေးပေါတယ်

Souvenirs

betel box	*kun-iq*	ကွမ်းအစ်
Burmese harp	*sàun*	စောင်း
lacquerware	*yùn-deh*	ယွန်းထည်
metal bowl	*p'ǎlà*	ဖလား
small (pagoda) bell	*s'wèh-lèh*	ဆည်းလည်း
small cymbal-like bell	*sì*	စည်း
vase (for offerings to Buddha)	*nyaun-ye-ò*	ညောင်ရေအိုး

Toiletries

comb	*bì*	ဘီး
shampoo	*gaùn-shaw-yeh*	ခေါင်းလျော်ရည်
soap	*s'aq-pya*	ဆပ်ပြာ
toothbrush	*dhǎbuq-tan*	သွားပွတ်တံ
toothpaste	*thwà-taiq-s'è*	သွားတိုက်ဆေး
toilet paper	*ein-dha-thoùn-seq-ku*	အိမ်သာသုံးစက္ကူ

Smoking

cigarette	*sì-gǎreq*	စီကရက်
cheroot	*s'è-bàw-leiq*	ဆေးပေါလိပ်
cheroot (stronger)	*s'è-byìn-leiq*	ဆေးပြင်းလိပ်
matches	*mì-jiq*	မီးခြစ်

BURMESE

No Smoking
s'è-leiq măthauq-yá   ဆေးလိပ်မသောက်ရ

A packet of ...
... tăhtouq   ... တစ်ထုပ်

Excuse me, do you have a
light?
di-hma k'ămyá (m)/shin (f)   ခင်ဗျား/ ရှင် မီးရှိသလား။
mì shí-dhălà?

Please don't smoke.
s'è-leiq măthauq-pa-néh   ဆေးလိပ်မသောက်ပါနဲ့ ။

I'm trying to give up.
s'è-leiq-p'yaq-p'ó   ဆေးလိပ်ဖြတ်ဖို့ ကြိုးစားနေတယ်။
cò-zà-ne-deh

Sizes & Quantities

big	*cì-deh*	ကြီးတယ်
small	*thè-deh*	သေးတယ်
many	*myà-deh*	များတယ်
few	*nèh-deh*	နည်းတယ်
long	*sheh-deh*	ရှည်တယ်
short (length)	*to-deh*	တိုတယ်
high/tall	*myín-deh*	မြင့်တယ်
low/short (height)	*néin-deh*	နိမ့်တယ်
heavy	*lè-deh*	လေးတယ်
light (weight)	*páw-deh*	ပေါ့တယ်

Health

Be aware that the incidence of infectious diseases is high, the standard of public hospitals is very low, and almost no medicines or
other supplies are available from hospitals or government shops.

Where is the ...?	... *beh-hma-lèh?*	... ဘယ်မှာလဲ။
chemist/pharmacy	*s'è-zain*	ဆေးဆိုင်
doctor	*s'ăya-wun*	ဆရာဝန်
dentist	*thwà-s'ăya-wun*	သွားဆရာဝန်
hospital	*s'è-youn*	ဆေးရုံ
private clinic	*ăt'ù-s'è-gàn*	အထူးဆေးခန်း

Please call a doctor.
s'ăya-wun kaw-pè-ba ဆရာဝန် ခေါ်ပေးပါ။

At the Doctor

My ... hurts
cănáw (m)/cămá (f) ... na-deh ကျွန်တော့်/ကျွန်မ ... နာတယ်။

I feel tired.
pin-bàn-ne-bi ပင်ပန်းနေပြီ။

It hurts here.
di-hma na-deh ဒီမှာ နာတယ်။

I have chest pain.
yin-baq áun-ne-deh ရင်ဘတ် အောင့်နေတယ်။

I vomit often.
k'ăná-k'ăná an-deh ခဏခဏ အန်တယ်။

I feel faint.
mù-lèh-deh မူးလဲတယ်။

Is it serious?
theiq ăyè-jì-dhălà? သိပ် အရေးကြီးသလား။

Ailments

AIDS	*ko-k'an-à-cá-s'ìn-déh-yàw-ga*	ကိုယ်ခံအား ကျဆင်းတဲ့ရောဂါ
asthma	*(pàn-na-)yin-caq*	ပန်းနာရင်ကျပ်

cholera	*ka-lá-wùn-yàw-ga*	ကာလဝမ်းရောဂါ
dengue fever	*thwè-lun-touq-kwè*	သွေးလွန်တုပ်ကွေး
diabetes	*s'ì-jo-yàw-ga*	ဆီးချိုရောဂါ
flu	*touq-kwè*	တုပ်ကွေး
hypertension	*thwè-do-yàw-ga*	သွေးထိုးရောဂါ
malaria ('bird fever')	*hngeq-p'yà*	ငှက်ဖျား
rabies	*k'wè-yù-byan-yàw-ga*	ခွေးရူးပြန်ရောဂါ
venereal disease	*ka-lá-dhà yàwga*	ကာလသားရောဂါ
have anaemia	*thwè-à-nèh-deh*	သွေးအားနည်းတယ်
have a cold	*ăe mí-bi*	အအေးမိပြီ
have a cough	*c'àun s'ò-deh*	ချောင်းဆိုးတယ်
have cramps	*cweq teq-teh*	ကြွက်တက်တယ်
have diarrhoea	*wùn-shàw-deh/ wùn-thwà-ne-deh*	ဝမ်းလျှောတယ်/ ဝမ်းသွားနေတယ်
have dysentery	*wùn kaiq-ne-deh*	ဝမ်းကိုက်နေတယ်
have a fever	*p'yà-deh*	ဖျားတယ်
have a headache	*gàun kaiq-ne-deh*	ခေါင်းကိုက်နေတယ်
have pneumonia	*ăs'ouq yaun-ne-deh*	အဆုတ်ရောင်နေတယ်
have a sore throat	*leh-jàun-na-deh*	လည်ချောင်းနာတယ်
have a stomachache	*baiq na-deh*	ဗိုက်နာတယ်
have sunstroke	*ăpu-shaq-teh*	အပူလျှပ်တယ်
have a toothache	*thwà kaiq-teh*	သွားကိုက်တယ်

Specific Needs

I'm allergic to penicillin.

. *cănaw (m)/cămá (f)* ကျွန်တော်/ကျွန်မ
pănăsălin-né mătéh-bù ပင်နီစလင်နဲ့ မတည့်ဘူး။

I'm pregnant.
baiq cì-deh/ko-wun shí-deh   ဗိုက်ကြီးတယ်/ကိုယ်ဝန်ရှိတယ်။

Parts of the Body

back	*càw-gòun*	ကျောကုန်း
chest	*yin-baq*	ရင်ဘတ်
ear	*nǎyweq*	နားရွက်
eye	*myeq-sí*	မျက်စိ
head	*gàun*	ခေါင်း
heart	*hnǎlòun*	နှလုံး
kidney	*cauk-kaq*	ကျောက်ကပ်
leg/foot	*c'e-dauq*	ခြေထောက်
liver	*ǎthèh*	အသည်း
muscle	*cweq-thà*	ကြွက်သား
nose	*hnǎ'kàun*	နှာခေါင်း
stomach	*ǎsa-ein*	အစာအိမ်
teeth	*thwà*	သွား
throat	*leh-jàun*	လည်ချောင်း

At the Chemist

With the legalisation of border trade with Thailand, China and India, a wide range of Western toiletries and medicines became available in the shops, often at prices lower than those in the West. However, supplies and quality are erratic. If you have specific requirements, you should bring them with you.

How many tablets a day?
tǎné-ko beh-hnǎlòun-lèh?   တစ်နေ့ ကို ဘယ်နှလုံးလဲ။
What medicine is this?
di-s'è ba-s'è-lèh?   ဒီဆေး ဘာဆေးလဲ။

prescription	*s'è-za*	ဆေးစာ
dosage directions	*s'è ăhnyùn*	ဆေးအညွှန်း
aspirin	*eq-săpărin*	အက်စပရင်
bandage (for sprain)	*paq-tì*	ပတ်တီး
insulin	*in-s'u-lin*	အင်ဆူလင်
morphine	*maw-p'èin/ maw-p'ì-yà*	မော်ဖိန်း/ မော်ဖီးယား
pill	*s'è-lòun/s'è-byà*	ဆေးလုံး/ဆေးပြား
sleeping pill	*eiq-s'è*	အိပ်ဆေး
syringe	*s'è-t'ò-aq*	ဆေးထိုးအပ်
vitamin	*à-zè/bi-ta-min*	အားဆေး/ဗီတာမင်

Time & Dates

Telling the Time

What time is it?
beh-ăc'ein shí-bi-lèh? ဘယ်အချိန်ရှိပြီလဲ။

When (in the past)?
beh-dòun-gá-lèh? ဘယ်တုန်းကလဲ။

When (in the future)?
beh-dáw-lèh? ဘယ်တော့လဲ။

At what time?
beh-ăc'ein-hma-lèh? ဘယ်အချိန်မှာလဲ။

The day is divided into four parts:

morning (6 am to midday)	*măneq*	မနက်
midday (noon to 3 pm)	*né-leh*	နေ့လည်
afternoon/evening (3 to 7 pm)	*nyá-ne*	ညနေ
night (7 pm to 6 am)	*nyá*	ည

7 am	*mǎneq k'ú-ħnana-yi*	မနက် ခုနစ်နာရီ
1 pm	*né-leh tǎna-yi*	နေ့ လည် တစ်နာရီ
4.30 pm	*nyá-ne lè-na-yi-gwèh*	ညနေ လေးနာရီခွဲ
10.15 pm	*nyá s'eh-na-yi s'éh-ngà-mǎniq*	ည ဆယ်နာရီဆယ့်ငါးမိနစ်

There are also special words for midday and midnight:

midday	*mùn-déh*	မွန်းတည်
midnight	*thǎgaun*	သန်းခေါင်
hour	*na-yi*	နာရီ
minute	*mǎniq*	မိနစ်

Dates

Giving a date, you start with the year, then the month, day (or phase of moon day for the lunar calendar), and then sometimes the day of the week.

What day (of the week) is it?
    di-né ba-né-lèh?   ဒီနေ့ ဘာနေ့ လဲ။
What is the date?
    di-né beh-hnǎyeq-né-lèh?   ဒီနေ့ ဘယ်နှ ရက်နေ့ လဲ

today	*di-né*	ဒီနေ့
tomorrow	*mǎneq-p'yan*	မနက်ဖြန်
tomorrow morning	*mǎneq-p'yan-mǎneq*	မနက်ဖြန်မနက်
day after tomorrow	*dhǎbeq-k'a*	သဘက်ခါ
next week	*nauq ǎpaq*	နောက် အပတ်
yesterday	*mǎné-gá*	မနေ့ က
yesterday evening	*mǎné-nyá-gá*	မနေ့ညက
last week	*lun-géh-déh-ǎpaq-ká*	လွန်ခဲ့တဲ့ အပတ်က

BURMESE

Days of the Week

Sunday	*tănìn-gănwe-né*	တနင်္ဂနွေနေ့
Monday	*tănìn-la-né*	တနင်္လာနေ့
Tuesday	*in-ga-né*	အင်္ဂါနေ့
Wednesday	*bouq-dăhù-né*	ဗုဒ္ဓဟူးနေ့
Thursday	*ca-dhăbădè-né*	ကြာသပတေးနေ့
Friday	*thauq-ca-né*	သောကြာနေ့
Saturday	*săne-né*	စနေနေ့

Months

The Burmese calendar, still used for some purposes, started with the lunar year corresponding to 638/639 AD. This is known as the Sakkaraj or Thagayit *(dhăgăyiq, သက္ကရာဇ်)* era. For most purposes the Gregorian calendar (solar) is now used instead.

The lunar calendar does not correspond to the Western calendar; the following are approximate equivalents:

	Solar	**Lunar**
January	*zan-năwa-ri*	*pya-dho*
	ဇန်နဝါရီ	ပြာသို
February	*p'e-băwa-ri*	*tăbó-dwéh*
	ဖေဖော်ဝါရီ	တပို့တွဲ
March	*maq*	*tăbàun*
	မတ်	တပေါင်း
April	*e-pyi*	*dăgù*
	ဧပြီ	တန်ခူး
May	*me*	*kăs'oun*
	မေ	ကဆုန်
June	*zun*	*năyoun*
	ဇွန်	နယုန်

July	*zu-lain* ဇူလိုင်	*wa-zo* ဝါဆို
August	*àw-gouq* သြဂုတ်	*wa-gaun* ဝါခေါင်
September	*seq-tinba* စက်တင်ဘာ	*taw-dhălìn* တော်သလင်း
October	*auq-to-ba* အောက်တိုဘာ	*thădìn-juq* သီတင်းကျွတ်
November	*no-win-ba* နိုဝင်ဘာ	*tăzaun-mòun* တန်ဆောင်မုန်း
December	*di-zin-ba* ဒီဇင်ဘာ	*nădaw* နတ်တော်

The lunar year starts with *tăgù*, generally in early to mid April.

Seasons
cool season (October to January)
  s'aùn-ya-dhi   ဆောင်းရာသီ
hot season (February to May)
  nwe-ya-dhi   နွေရာသီ
rainy season (June to September)
  mò-dwìn   မိုးတွင်း

Numbers
Cardinal Numbers

1	၁	*tiq / tă*	တစ်/တ
2	၂	*hniq / hnă*	နှစ်/နှ
3	၃	*thòun*	သုံး
4	၄	*lè*	လေး

5	၅	*ngà*	ငါး
6	၆	*c'auq*	ခြောက်
7	၇	*k'ú-hniq/k'ú-hnă*	ခုနစ်/ခုန
8	၈	*shiq*	ရှစ်
9	၉	*kò*	ကိုး
10	၁၀	*(tă)s'eh*	တစ်ဆယ်
11	၁၁	*s'éh-tiq*	ဆယ့်တစ်
12	၁၂	*s'éh-hniq*	ဆယ့်နှစ်
20	၂၀	*hnăs'eh*	နှစ်ဆယ်
35	၃၅	*thòun-zéh-ngà*	သုံးဆယ့်ငါး
100	၁၀၀	*tăya*	တစ်ရာ
1000	၁၀၀၀	*(tă)t'aun*	တစ်ထောင်
10,000	၁၀၀၀၀	*(tă)thàun*	တစ်သောင်း
100,000	၁၀၀၀၀၀	*(tă)thèin*	တစ်သိန်း
million	၁၀၀၀၀၀၀	*(tă)thàn*	တစ်သန်း

One hundred thousand is often called one *lakh*.

Classifiers (Counters)

Whenever you count things in Burmese, you must put a counter
word (also known as a classifier) after the number. These always
come after the noun being counted. It's like saying 'three *items
of* clothing' or 'three *slices* of cheese'.

  If you are giving a measure (miles, cups, etc) after the noun,
you don't need a counter; groups and round numbers work the
same. And if all this seems too complicated, you may use the
universal counter, *k'ú* (ခု), for any inanimate noun; but not for
monks, people or animals.

• Buddha, temples	*s'u*	ဆု
• Monks, royalty	*pà/bà*	ပါး
• Other high-status humans (also a formal, written form of *yauq*)	*ù*	ဦး
• People	*yauq*	ယောက်
• Animals	*kaun/gaun*	ကောင်
• Plants, rope, thread, hair	*pin/bin*	ပင်
• Round things: fruit, houses, furniture, machines	*lòun*	လုံး
• Flat things	*c'aq/jaq*	ချပ်
• Long things: teeth, fingers, toes, needles, legs, knives	*c'àun/jàun*	ချောင်း
• Clothing (cloth)	*t'eh/deh*	ထည်
• Written things: tickets, letters, newspapers	*saun/zaun*	စောင်
• Tools, instruments (hand)	*leq*	လက်
• Vehicles (large/small)	*sìn* or *sì/zì*	စင်း/စီး
• Books	*ouq*	အုပ်
• Rings-shaped things	*kwìn/gwìn*	ကွင်း
• Leaves (including paper)	*yweq*	ရွက်

Emergencies

Help!	*keh-ba*	ကယ်ပါ။
Watch out!	*dhǎdí t'à-ba*	သတိထားပါ။
Go away!	*thwà-zàn*	သွားဆန်း။
Stop!	*yaq*	ရပ်။
Thief!	*thǎk'ò*	သူခိုး။

Call a doctor!
  s'ǎya-wun-go k'aw-pè-ba!   ဆရာဝန်ကို ခေါ်ပေးပါ။
Call an ambulance!
  lu-na-dìn-gà k'aw-pè-ba!   လူနာတင်ကားခေါ်ပေးပါ။
I am ill.
  ne-mǎkàun-bù   နေမကောင်းဘူး။
I am lost.
  làn pyauq-thwà-bi   လမ်းပျောက်သွားပြီ။
I've been raped.
  mú-dèin cín-k'an-yá-deh   မုဒိမ်းကျင့်ခံရတယ်။
I've been robbed.
  ǎk'ò-k'an-yá-deh   အခိုးခံရတယ်။
My pocket was picked.
  gǎbaiq-hnaiq k'an-yá-deh   ခါးပိုက်နှိုက်ခံရတယ်။
My camera was stolen.
  cǎnáw (m)/cǎmá (f) kin-   ကျွန်တော်/ ကျွန်မ
  mǎra k'ò-k'an-yá-deh   ကင်မရာခိုးခံရတယ်။

I've lost …	*cǎnaw (m)/cǎmá (f) …*	ကျွန်တော်/ ကျွန်မ …
	pyauq-thwà-deh	ပျောက်သွားတယ်။
my bag	*tiq-ta*	သေတ္တာ
my money	*paiq-s'an*	ပိုက်ဆံ

| my passport | *nain-ngan-kù-leq-hmaq* | နိုင်ငံကူးလက်မှတ် |
| my travellers' cheques | *k'ăyì c'eq-leq-hmaq* | ခရီးချက်လက်မှတ် |

Could I use the telephone?
teh-li-p'òun k'ăná   တယ်လီဖုန်း ခဏ
s'eq-ló-yá-dhălà?   ဆက်လို့ရသလား။

I have (medical) insurance.
cănaw(m)/cămá(f) (s'è)   ကျွန်တော်/ကျွန်မ (ဆေး)
a-má-gan shí-ba-deh   အာမခံ ရှိပါတယ်။

INDONESIAN & MALAY

Indonesian & Malay

Indonesian

Indonesian, or Bahasa Indonesia, is the lingua franca of Indonesia. It was adopted as the official language of Indonesia in 1945 and was a symbol of unity and nationalism during the leadership of President Soekarno.

It is derived from Bahasa Melayu as this was once the dominant trade language and the common language of Indonesians who spoke different languages and dialects. In fact, in southern Sumatra Bahasa Melayu is the main language. There are, however, over 300 different languages spoken throughout Indonesia, so you'll find most people use their own local language *(bahasa daerah)* at home, and Bahasa Indonesia to communicate with visitors. Most people you meet in Indonesia (with the exception of those in Irian Jaya) will speak Bahasa Indonesia well.

One of the best aspects of travelling in Indonesia and learning the language is that even your most stumbling attempts to speak Indonesian will be greeted with enthusiasm. Just a few words will be rewarded with the exclamation *'Wah, sudah lancar bahasa Indonesianya'*, which is a compliment on your fluency.

Selamat jalan! – Bon voyage!

Malay

Malay, officially known as Bahasa Melayu, is the country's national language. It is used for official purposes by state and federal governments. While Malay is widely spoken, it is by no means the only language in Malaysia. Due to the multiracial make-up of the country, languages such as Tamil and Mandarin are also spoken. English is Malaysia's second most spoken language and is a compulsory subject in its schools.

Although Malay forms the basis of Bahasa Indonesia, differences lie mainly in word usage. A substantial number of Malay words is derived from English, making it an easy language to learn for English-speaking people. Words such as 'clinic' and 'antibiotic' are incorporated into Malay by a change of spelling – *klinik* and *antibiotik*.

Although standard Malay is spoken in Kuala Lumpur, other Malaysian regions have their own dialects. But standard Malay is understood throughout the country. Remember, even a simple *Terima kasih* ('Thank you') from you will impress the people you meet. *Selamat belajar* – Happy learning!

About This Chapter

In this chapter the Indonesian word or phrase is presented in the second (middle) column, the Malay in the third. Where necessary we have used the abbreviations (I) and (M) to distinguish the Indonesian word or phrase from the Malay. Variants of a word within the same language are separated by a slash.

Pronunciation

Indonesian and Malay are easy languages to pronounce as each letter represents one sound.

Vowels

a   like the 'u' in 'hut'

e   1) as in 'may' or the French *entrée* when stressed;
      2) when unstressed it is hardly pronounced at all, like the
      'e' in 'water' or 'fatter' – *empat* ('four') is pronounced
      'mm-pat'

INDONESIAN / MALAY

i	as the 'i' in 'hit'
o	as in 'raw' but a shorter sound, with lips in more of an 'o' position
u	as the 'u' in 'put'

Diphthongs

There are also three vowel combinations:

ai	sounds like 'i' in 'like'
au	sounds like 'ow' in 'cow'
ua	begins with the sound of 'oo' as in 'too' and ends with the 'ah' sound in 'hut'; as these two sounds are run together, it sounds like there is a 'w' between them.

Consonants

Consonants are pronounced as in English with the exception of the following:

b	1) as 'b' in 'better' at the beginning or middle of a word; 2) as the 'b' in 'rub' (almost a 'p' sound) at the end of a word
c	as 'ch' in 'chair'
g	always pronounced hard, as the 'g' in 'garden'
j	In Malay it is pronounced as the 'j' in 'jam'; In Indonesian it's more of a 'dj' sound
r	pronounced clearly and distinctly and slightly trilled.
h	stressed a little more strongly than in English, as if you were sighing

k   pronounced as the English 'k', but when it's at the end of
        a word you stop short of actually saying it, eg *tidak* is
        pronounced 'tee-da'
ny   as the 'ny' in 'canyon'
ng   as the 'ng' in 'long'
ngg   a combination of 'ng' and a hard 'g' as in 'anger'
kh   as 'ch' in the Scottish *loch*

Stress
Almost all syllables have equal stress but a good rule of thumb is
to put most emphasis on the second-last syllable. The main
exception to this rule is when the second-last syllable has an
unstressed 'e', eg *besar* ('big') is pronounced with the stress on
the last syllable.

Greetings & Civilities
Greetings & Goodbyes
Selamat means 'May your action be blessed' and comes from the
Arabic word, *salam*. Put together with words for 'morning' or
'evening' it means something like 'Have a nice morning/
evening'. All sorts of actions may be blessed, and *selamat* is a
word you will hear quite often.

	INDONESIAN	MALAY
Good morning.	*Selamat pagi.*	*Selamat pagi.*
Hello/Good day.	*Selamat siang.*	*Selamat tengahari.*
Good afternoon.	*Selamat sore.*	*Selamat petang.*
Good evening.	*Selamat malam.*	*Selamat malam.*
Good night. (on retiring)	*Selamat tidur.*	*Selamat malam.*

	INDONESIAN	MALAY
Goodbye.		
(you are leaving)	*Selamat tinggal.*	*Selamat tinggal.*
(you are staying)	*Selamat jalan.*	*Selamat jalan.*
See you later.	*Sampai jumpa lagi.*	*Sampai jumpa lagi.*

Civilities

For many Indonesians and Malaysians it is a sign of polite restraint not to accept an offer when it is first made. Therefore, if you are offering somebody something don't be deterred by their first refusal. Repeat the offer and it will probably be accepted.

When you are visiting somebody in their house you may be served a sweet drink (which is considered better than offering coffee or tea) and sometimes a snack.

Welcome.	*Selamat datang.*	*Selamat datang.*
Enjoy your meal.	*Selamat makan.*	*Selamat makan.*
Enjoy your drink.	*Selamat minum.*	*Selamat minum.*

There are two words for 'Please': *tolong* is used when you are making a request or when you are asking somebody to do something for you; *silakan* is used when you are offering something to somebody.

Please/Help.	*Tolong.*	*Tolong.*
Please shut the door.	*Tolong tutup pintu itu.*	*Tolong tutup pintu itu.*
Please clean my room.	*Tolong bersihkan kamar saya.*	*Tolong bersihkan bilik saya.*
Please come in.	*Silakan masuk.*	*Silakan masuk.*
Please sit down.	*Silakan duduk.*	*Silakan duduk.*

You will find that 'Thank you' is used less frequently than in English.

	INDONESIAN	MALAY
Thank you.	*Terima kasih.*	*Terima kasih.*
You're welcome.	*Kembali/*	*Kembali/*
	Sama-sama. (slang)	*Sama-sama.* (slang)
Excuse me.	*Permisi/Ma'afkan*	*Permisi/Ma'afkan*
	saya.	*saya.*
Pardon/What did you say?	*Ma'af?*	*Ma'af?*
I'm sorry, …	*Ma'af, …*	*Ma'af, …*

Forms of Address

In Indonesia you will hear various forms of address. The most usual are *ibu* and *bapak* which literally mean 'mother' and 'father'. They are also used in situations which require a greater degree of formality, as in the passport office, for instance.

In Malaysia *encik* and *puan* are used. These are the Malay equivalents of 'Mr' and 'Mrs'. It is polite to attach these words to someone's name when you speak to them. The word *cik* is used to address an unmarried woman.

Saudara literally means 'brother' or 'sister' and can be used as a more formal word for 'you' in both Indonesian and Malay. In both languages you'll also often hear the less formal *anda*, but if in doubt about how polite you should be, use *saudara*.

When talking to children you may want to use *dik*, from the word *adik*, meaning younger brother or sister.

Pronouns

I/me/my	*saya*
you/your (sg, inf)	*kamu*
you/your (sg, pol)	*suadara/anda*
he/she/him/her	*dia*
it	*ia*
we/us/our	*kami* (excludes person spoken to)
we/us/our	*kita* (includes person spoken to)
you (pl)	*saudara sekalian* (I)/*kamu sekalian* (M)
they	*mereka*

Body Language

Shaking hands involves only a light, brief touch of the hand, and is suitable for both men and women. Some Muslims don't shake hands with anyone they are not related to, so don't be offended if your offer of a handshake is refused.

It is considered polite to bow from the waist slightly when walking in front of somebody who is seated or when interrupting. Standing with your hands on your hips is considered rude. When sitting, tuck your feet away so they are not pointing towards anyone. Touching people on the head and pointing with your finger is also considered rude.

Language Difficulties

	INDONESIAN	MALAY
Do you speak English?	*Bisa berbicara bahasa Inggris?*	*Bolehkah anda bercakap bahasa Inggeris?*
Do you understand?	*Apakah saudara mengerti?*	*Adakah saudara faham?*

	INDONESIAN	**MALAY**
I understand.	*Saya mengerti.*	*Saya faham.*
I don't understand.	*Saya tidak mengerti.*	*Saya tidak faham.*
How do you say ... in Indonesian/ Malaysian?	*Apa bahasa Indonesianya...?*	*Apa bahasa Malaysianya ...?*
What does this mean?	*Apa artinya ini?*	*Apa maksud ini?*
Please speak slowly!	*Tolong bicara lebih lambat.*	*Tolong berbicara perlahan-lahan.*
Please write that word down for me.	*Tolong tuliskan kata itu untuk saya.*	*Tolong tuliskan perkataan.*

Small Talk
Meeting People

How are you?	*Kenalkan?*	*Apa khabar?*
I'm fine, thanks.	*Khabar baik.*	*Khabar baik.*
What's your name?	*Siapa nama saudara/anda?*	*Siapa nama saudara/anda?*
My name is ...	*Nama saya ...*	*Nama saya ...*

Nationalities

Where are you from?	*Dari mana asal saudara?*	*Dari mana asal saudara?*
I am from ...	*Saya dari ...*	*Saya dari ...*
Australia	*Australia*	*Australia*
Canada	*Kanada*	*Kanada*
England	*Inggris*	*England*
Europe	*Eropa*	*Eropah*

	INDONESIAN	MALAY
Indonesia	*Indonesia*	*Indonesia*
Ireland	*Irlandia*	*Ireland*
Japan	*Jepang*	*Jepun*
Malaysia	*Malaysia*	*Malaysia*
New Zealand	*Selandia Baru*	*New Zealand*
Scotland	*Skotlandia*	*Scotland*
the USA	*Amerika*	*Amerika*

I'm an (Australian).	*Saya orang (Australia).*	*Saya orang (Australia).*

Age

How old are you?	*Berapa umur saudara?*	*Berapa umur saudara?*

I am …	*Umur saya …*	*Umur saya …*
20 years old	*duapuluh ˎ*	*dua puluh tahun*
35 years old	*tigapuluh lima*	*tiga puluh lima tahun*

Occupations

What is your occupation?	*Apa pekerjaan saudara?*	*Apa pekerjaan saudara?*

I am a/an …	*Saya …*	*Saya …*
artist	*seniman*	*seniman*
businessperson	*pengusaha*	*peniaga*
doctor	*dokter*	*doktor*
factory worker	*pekerja pabrik*	*pekerja kilang*
farmer	*petani*	*petani*
journalist	*wartawan*	*wartawan*
lawyer	*ahli hukum*	*peguam*

	INDONESIAN	MALAY
mechanic	*montir*	*mekanik*
musician	*pemain musik*	*pemain musik*
nurse	*perawat*	*jururawat*
public servant	*pegawai negeri*	*pegawai am*
sailor	*pelaut*	*pelaut*
scientist	*ahli sains*	*ahli sains*
secretary	*sekretaris*	*setiausaha*
student (school)	*pelajar*	*pelajar*
student (university)	*mahasiswa*	*mahasiswa*
teacher	*guru*	*guru*
unemployed	*menganggur*	*menganggur*
writer	*penulis*	*penulis*

INDONESIAN / MALAY

Religion

Most Indonesians and Malaysians are Muslim, some are Christian, a few are Hindu and Buddhist. Some people you meet may feel uncomfortable if you do not profess a religion, often equating atheism with communism. Therefore, you will maintain better relations by claiming to have a religion.

What is your religion?	*Apa agama saudara?*	*Apa agama saudara?*
My religion is …	*Agama saya …*	*Agama saya …*
Buddhism	*Budha*	*Budha*
Catholicism	*Katolik*	*Katolik*
Christianity	*Kristen*	*Kristian*
Hindu	*Hindu*	*Hindu*
Judaism	*Yahudi*	*Yahudi*
Islam	*Islam*	*Islam*

Family

Questions about you and your life will be asked quite frequently, in particular, *Sudah nikah?* (I) or *Sudah kahwin?* (M) ('Are you already married?'). Unless you are indeed married, the appropriate answer is *Belum!* ('Not yet!'). *Tidak* ('No') is grammatically fine to use, but most people won't understand why you should not be married or not thinking about it.

	INDONESIAN	MALAY
Are you married?	*Sudah nikah?*	*Sudah kahwin?*
I'm not married yet.	*Saya belum nikah.*	*Saya belum kahwin.*
I am married.	*Saya sudah nikah.*	*Saya sudah kahwin.*
Do you have any children?	*Punya anak?*	*Punya anak?*
I don't have any children.	*Saya tidak punya anak.*	*Saya tidak punya anak.*
I don't have any children yet.	*Saya belum punya anak.*	*Saya belum punya anak.*
This is my ...	*Ini ... saya.*	*Ini ... saya.*
mother	*ibu*	*emak*
father	*bapak*	*ayah*
older sister	*kakak*	*kakak*
older brother	*abang*	*abang*
younger sister	*adik perempuan*	*adik perempuan*
younger brother	*adik laki-laki*	*adik laki-laki*
child	*anak*	*anak*
son	*anak laki-laki*	*anak laki-laki*
daughter	*anak perempuan*	*anak perempuan*

	INDONESIAN	MALAY
husband	*suami*	*suami*
wife	*istri*	*isteri*
friend	*teman*	*kawan/sahabat*
boyfriend	*pacar*	*teman lelaki*
girlfriend	*teman*	*teman wanita*
partner	*pasangan*	*pasangan*

Interests

What is your hobby?	*Apa hobi anda?*	*Apa hobi anda?*
I like …	*Saya suka …*	*Saya suka …*
I don't like …	*Saya tidak suka …*	*Saya tidak suka …*
discos	*disko*	*disko*
film	*filem*	*filem*
going shopping	*berbelanja*	*berbelanja*
music	*musik*	*musik*
playing games	*bermain game*	*bermain game*
playing sport	*berolahraga*	*berolahraga*
reading books	*membaca buku*	*membaca buku*
travelling/going out	*berjalan-jalan*	*berjalan-jalan*
watching TV	*nonton televisi*	*tonton televisyen*

Making Conversation

Where are you going?	*Mau kemana?*	*Mau kemana?*
What is this called?	*Apa ini?*	*Apa ini?*
I/We love it here.	*Saya/Kami suka disini.*	*Saya/Kami suka di sini.*

	INDONESIAN	**MALAY**
Do you live here?	*Tinggal di sini?*	*Tinggal di sini?*
What do you think?	*Apa pendapat anda?*	*Apa pendapat anda?*
Can I take a photo (of you)?	*Boleh saya potret?*	*Boleh saya ambil gambar anda?*
Can I take a photo (of that)?	*Boleh saya potret itu?*	*Boleh saya ambil gambar?*
Beautiful, isn't it?	*Cantik, kan?*	*Cantik, kan?*
That's strange!	*Anehnya!*	*Anehnya!*
That's OK/alright.	*Betul/Baik.*	*Betul/Baik.*

Useful Phrases

I'm ready.	*Saya siap.*	*Saya siap.*
Slow down!	*Pelan-pelan!*	*Perlahan-lahan!*
Look!	*Lihat!*	*Lihat!*
Listen!	*Dengarlah!*	*Dengarlah!*
Hurry up!	*Cepat-cepat!*	*Cepat-cepat!*
Go away!	*Pergi!*	*Pergi!*
Watch out!	*Awas!*	*Awas!*
It is possible.	*Mungkin.*	*Mungkin.*
It is not possible.	*Tidak mungkin.*	*Tidak mungkin.*
I forgot.	*Saya lupa.*	*Saya lupa.*
It is important.	*Penting.*	*Penting.*
It is not important.	*Tidak penting.*	*Tidak pentingo.*
It doesn't matter.	*Tidak apa-apa.*	*Tidak mengapa.*

Getting Around

Transport in Indonesia includes the ubiquitous Balinese *bemo* – a pick-up truck with two rows of seats down each side. Bemos usually run standard routes and depart when full, but can also be chartered like a taxi. They are sometimes known as *angkots,* from *angkutan* (transport) and *kota* (city). A step up from the bemo is the small minibus known either as an *oplet, mikrolet* or *kolt* – since they are often Mitsubishi Colts. Then there's the *becak*, or bicycle-rickshaw which is found in most major cities. The *bajaj* is a three-wheeled vehicle which is powered by a noisy, two-stroke engine, and is only found in Jakarta. In quieter towns, you may find *andongs* and *dokars* which are horse-drawn carts.

When travelling in Malaysia you can choose between buses, taxis and trains. In cities, taxis and buses are the most common forms of transport. Taxis are more concentrated in the city centre so if you are staying in a suburban area, a bus or minibus may be a better choice. They are cheap, more frequent and offer many different routes. Long-distance taxis are available for those who don't like travelling by bus.

Finding Your Way

	INDONESIAN	MALAY
Where is the …?	*Dimana …?*	*Di mana …?*
airport	*lapangan terbang*	*lapangan terbang*
city bus station	*terminal bis kota*	*terminal bas kota*
city bus stop	*halte bis kota*	*perhentian bas kota*
inter-city bus station	*terminal bis antar kota*	*terminal bas antara-kota*
ticket counter	*kaunter tikit*	*kaunter tikit*
train station	*stasiun kereta api*	*stesen keretapi*
What time does the … leave?	*Jam berapa … berangkat?*	*Pukul berapakah … berangkat?*
city bus	*bis kota*	*bas kota*
inter-city bus	*bis antar kota*	*bas antara-kota*

	INDONESIAN	MALAY
train	*kereta api*	*keretapi*
plane	*pesawat udara*	*pesawat terbang*

Directions

How can I get to ...?	*Bagaimana saya pergi ke ...?*	*Bagaimana saya pergi ke ...?*
Is it far?	*Jauh?*	*Jauh?*
Is it near?	*Dekat?*	*Dekat?*
Is it near here?	*Dekat dari sini?*	*Dekat dari sini?*
Go straight ahead!	*Jalan terus!*	*Jalan terus!*
What ... is this?	*Ini ... apa?*	*Ini ... apa?*
street	*jalan*	*jalan*
city	*kota*	*kota*
village	*desa*	*desa/kampung*
Turn left ...	*Belok kiri ...*	*Belok kiri ...*
Turn right ...	*Belok kanan ...*	*Belok kanan ...*
at the T-junction	*di pertigaan*	*di pertigaan*
at the traffic lights	*di lampu lalu lintas*	*di lampu lalu lintas*
in front of	*didepan*	*di hadapan*
next to	*disamping*	*di samping/ di sebelah*
behind	*dibelakang*	*di belakang*
opposite	*berhadapan dengan*	*berhadapan dengan*
north	*utara*	*utara*
south	*selatan*	*selatan*
east	*timur*	*timur*
west	*barat*	*barat*

	INDONESIAN	**MALAY**
Buying Tickets		
How much is a … from Jakarta to Medan?	*Berapa harganya satu … dari Jakarta ke Medan?*	*Berapa harganya satu … dari Jakarta ke Medan?*
one-way ticket	*tiket satu jalan*	*tiket satu jalan*
return ticket	*tiket pulang pergi*	*tiket balik pergi*
Two tickets to …	*Dua karcis ke …*	*Dua tiket ke …*
I'd like to buy a return ticket.	*Saya mau beli satu tiket pulang pergi.*	*Saya mau beli satu tiket balik pergi.*
Where can I buy a night bus ticket?	*Dimana saya bisa beli tiket bis?*	*Di manakah boleh saya beli tiket bas malam?*
I'd like to book a seat for Monday.	*Saya mau pesan satu kursi untuk hari Senin.*	*Saya mahu tempah satu kerusi untuk hari Isnin.*
ticket	*karcis*	*tiket*
ticket window	*loket*	*kaunter*
1st class	*kelas satu*	*kelas satu*
economy class	*kelas ekonomi*	*kelas ekonomi*

Air		
Is there a flight to Medan on Monday?	*Apakah ada pesawat ke Medan pada hari Senin?*	*Apakah ada pesawat ke Medan pada hari Isnin?*
What time is the flight to Medan on Monday?	*Jam berapa pesawat berangkat ke Medan pada hari Senin?*	*Pukul berapa pesawat berangkat ke Medan pada hari Isnin?*

	INDONESIAN	MALAY
What time do I have to be at the airport?	*Jam berapa saya harus ada di lapangan udara?*	*Pukul berapa saya harus ada di la pangan terbang?*

Bus

	INDONESIAN	MALAY
What time is the … bus?	*Jam berapa bis yang …?*	*Pukul berapa bas yang …?*
next	*berikutnya*	*berikutnya*
last	*terakhir*	*terakhir*

Where is the nearest bus station?	*Dimana setasiun bis yang terdekat?*	*Dimana stesan bas yang terdekat?*
Does this bus go to …?	*Apakah bis ini pergi ke …?*	*Adakah bas ini pergi ke …?*
Is there a night bus to …?	*Apakah ada bis malam yang ke …?*	*Adakah bas malam ke …?*
What time does the bus arrive at …?	*Jam berapa bisnya sampai di …?*	*Pukul berapakah bas akan tiba di …?*
Could you let me know when we arrive at …?	*Tolong beritahu saya kalau sudah sampai di …*	*Tolong beritahu saya kalau sudah sampai di …*
I want to get off!	*Saya mau turun!*	*Saya mau turun!*

Train

What station is this?	*Ini stasiun apa?*	*Stesen apa ini?*
What is the next station?	*Apa stasiun yang berikutnya?*	*Apakah stesen yang berikutnya?*
Which platform does the train leave from?	*Dari platform berapa keretapi berangkat?*	*Dari peron berapa berangkat?*

	INDONESIAN	MALAY
Where do I need to change trains?	*Dimana saya harus ganti kereta?*	*Di mana saya harus ganti keretapi?*
Does this train stop at ...?	*Adakah keretapi ini berhenti di ...?*	*Adakah keretapi ini berhenti di ...?*
Is this seat free?	*Kursi ini kosong?*	*Adakah kerusi ini kosong?*
This seat is taken.	*Sudah ada orangnya.*	*Sudah ada orangnya.*
Would you mind if I open the window?	*Boleh saya buka jendela?*	*Boleh saya buka tingkap?*

Taxi

Please take me to ...?	*Tolong antar saya ke ...?*	*Tolong hantar saya ke ...?*
this address	*alamat ini*	*alamat ini*
the airport	*lapangan terbang*	*lapangan terbang*
How much does it cost to go to ...?	*Berapa ongkosnya ke ...?*	*Berapa harganya untuk pergi ke ...?*
Does that include the luggage?	*Itu termasuk ongkos bagasi?*	*Adakah itu termasuk harga beg?*
That's too much!	*Terlalu mahal!*	*Terlalu mahal!*

Instructions

Here is fine, thank you.	*Berhenti disini.*	*Berhenti disini.*
The next street, please.	*Jalan berikutnya.*	*Jalan berikutnya.*
Continue!	*Terus!*	*Terus!*
Careful!	*Hati-hati!*	*Hati-hati!*
Stop!	*Berhenti/Stop!*	*Berhenti/Stop!*

	INDONESIAN	MALAY
Please slow down.	*Pelan-pelan saja.*	*Perlahan-lahan.*
Please hurry.	*Tolong cepat sedikit.*	*Tolong cepat sedikit.*
Please wait here.	*Tunggu disini.*	*Tolong tunggu di sini.*
I'll be right back.	*Saya akan segera kembali.*	*Saya akan segera kembali.*

Useful Words & Phrases

The train is …	*Keretapinya …*	*Keretapinya …*
delayed (intentional)	*ditunda*	*ditunda*
delayed (unexpected)	*tertunda*	*tertunda*
cancelled	*dibatalkan*	*dibatalkan*
on time	*tepat*	*tepat*

Where can I rent a car?	*Dimana saya bisa sewa mobil?*	*Di manakah saya boleh menyewa kereta?*
Where can I hire a bicycle?	*Dimana saya bisa sewa sepeda?*	*Di mana tempat sewa basikal?*
How much is it daily/weekly?	*Berapa ongkos sewanya per hari/minggu?*	*Berapa harga sewanya setiap hari/setiap minggu?*
Does that include insurance?	*Apa itu termasuk asuransi?*	*Adakah itu termasuk insuran?*

How long does the trip take?	*Berapa lama perjalanannya?*	*Berapa lama perjalanannya?*
I want to get off at …	*Saya mau turun di …*	*Saya mau turun di …*
Where are we now?	*Dimana kita sekarang?*	*Dimana kita sekarang?*

	INDONESIAN	**MALAY**
airport	*lapangan udara*	*lapangan terbang*
corner	*sudut*	*pojok*
economy class	*kelas ekonomi*	*kelas ekonomi*
full	*penuh*	*penuh*
intersection	*persimpangan*	*persimpangan*
reservation office	*kantor pemesanan*	*pejabat tempahan*
street	*jalan*	*jalan*
timetable	*daftar waktu*	*jadual*

Accommodation
Finding Accommodation

Where is a …?	*Dimana ada …?*	*Di mana ada …?*
hotel	*hotel*	*hotel*
cheap hotel	*hotel yang murah*	*hotel yang murah*
nice hotel	*hotel yang bagus*	*hotel yang bagus*

Checking In

Is there a room available?	*Ada kamar yang kosong?*	*Ada bilik kosong?*
I'd like a room …	*Saya perlu satu kamar …*	*Saya perlu bilik …*
for one person	*untuk se orang*	*untuk se orang*
for two people	*untuk dua orang*	*untuk dua orang*
with a bathroom	*dengan kamar mandi*	*dengan bilik mandi*
with a fan	*dengan kipas angin*	*dengan kipas angin*
with a TV	*dengan TV*	*dengan TV*
with a window	*dengan jendela*	*dengan tingkap*

INDONESIAN / MALAY

	INDONESIAN	MALAY
I'm going to stay for …	Saya mau menginap untuk …	Saya mau menginap untuk …
one day	satu hari	satu hari
one week	satu minggu	satu minggu
What is the daily rate?	Berapa tarip hariannya?	Berapa kadar hariannya?
Does the price include breakfast?	Apa harganya termasuk sarapan?	Apa harganya termasuk makan pagi?
Is there a discount for students?	Ada diskaun untuk pelajar?	Ada diskaun untuk pelajar?
Can I see the room?	Boleh saya lihat kamarnya?	Boleh saya lihat biliknya?
I don't like this room.	Saya tidak suka kamar ini.	Saya tidak suka bilik ini.
Do you have a better room?	Ada kamar yang lebih bagus?	Ada bilik yang lebih bagus?
I'll take this room.	Saya mau kamar ini.	Saya mahu bilik ini.

Requests & Complaints

Can I use the telephone?	Boleh pakai telpon?	Boleh saya guna talipon?
Please change my sheets.	Tolong ganti sepreinya.	Tolong ganti cadar saya.
My room needs to be cleaned.	Tolong bersihkan kamar saya.	Tolong bersihkan bilik saya.
The window is broken.	Jendelanya rusak.	Tingkap ini rosak.

	INDONESIAN	MALAY
I can't open the door/window.	Saya tidak bisa buka pintunya/ jendelanya.	Saya tidak boleh buka pintuini/ tingkap ini.
The toilet is broken.	WCnya rusak.	Tandas ini rosak.
Where can I wash my clothes?	Dimana saya bisa mencuci baju saya?	Di mana saya boleh mencuci baju?
When will they be ready?	Kapan bisa diambil?	Bilakah boleh siap?
The room smells.	Kamarnya bau.	Bilik ini berbau.
It's too dark.	Terlalu gelap disini.	Terlalu gelap disini.
It's too noisy.	Terlalu ribut disini.	Terlalu bising di sini.
Please spray my room.	Tolong semprot kamar saya.	Tolong sembur bilik saya.
There are mosquitoes in it.	Ada nyamuk.	Ada nyamuk.

Checking Out

Please prepare my/our bill.	Tolong siapkan rekening saya/kami.	Tolong sediakan bil saya/kami.
Please call me a taxi.	Tolong panggilkan taksi.	Tolong panggilkan teksi.
Can I pay by …?	Bisa bayar dengan …?	Boleh saya bayar dengan …?
credit card	kartu kredit	kad kredit
travellers' cheque	cek wisata	cek pengembaraan

INDONESIAN / MALAY

INDONESIA / MALAY

	INDONESIAN	MALAY
Can I leave my things here until …?	*Bisa titip barang-barang saya sampai …?*	*Boleh saya tinggalkan barang-barang saya sehingga …?*
this afternoon	*nanti siang*	*tengahari ini*
this evening	*nanti sore*	*petang ini*
tonight	*nanti malam*	*malam ini*

Useful Words

address	*alamat*	*alamat*
air-con	*AC*	*alat penyejuk/ pendingin udara*
clean	*bersih*	*bersih*
dirty	*kotor*	*kotor*
key/lock	*kunci*	*kunci*
noisy	*ribut*	*bising*
pillow	*bantal*	*bantal*
quiet	*sepi*	*senyap*
soap	*sabun mandi*	*sabun mandi*
soap (detergent)	*sabun cuci*	*sabun cuci*
towel	*handuk*	*tuala*
water	*air*	*air*

Around Town

Where is a …?	*Dimana ada …?*	*Di mana ada …?*
bank	*bank*	*bank*
embassy	*kedutaan besar*	*kedutaan besar*
hospital	*rumah sakit*	*hospital*
hotel	*hotel*	*hotel*
police station	*kantor polisi*	*stesen polis*
post office	*kantor pos*	*pejabat pos*

	INDONESIAN	MALAY
public telephone	*telepon umum*	*telepon umum*
public toilet	*WC umum*	*tandas awam*
town square	*alun-alun*	*medan perbandaran*

At the Post Office

	INDONESIAN	MALAY
I want to send a …	*Saya mau kirim …*	*Saya mau kirim …*
letter	*surat*	*surat*
parcel	*paket*	*bungkusan*
telegram	*kawat*	*telegram*
Please send it by …	*Tolong kirim dengan ...*	*Tolong kirim dengan ...*
airmail	*pos udara*	*pos udara*
surface mail	*pos biasa*	*pos biasa*
express (overseas)	*ekspres (luar negeri)*	*ekspres (luar negeri)*
express (domestic)	*kilat (dalam negeri)*	*kilat (dalam negeri)*
How much does it cost to send this to …?	*Berapa ongkos kirim ini ke …?*	*Berapa harga kiriman ini ke …?*
aerogram	*aerogram*	*aerogram*
envelope	*amplop*	*sampul surat*
mailbox	*kotak pos*	*peti surat*
postcards	*kartu pos*	*pos kad*
receiver (letter)	*penerima*	*penerima*
sender (letter)	*pengirim*	*pengirim*
stamps	*perangko*	*setem*

INDONESIA / MALAY

	INDONESIAN	MALAY
Telephone		
I want to call …	*Saya mau menelpon …*	*Saya mahu menelefon …*
The number is …	*Nomernya …*	*Nombornya …*
How much is a three-minute call?	*Berapa ongkos telpon untuk tiga menit?*	*Berapa harganya untuk panggilan tiga minit?*
I want to make a long-distance call to Australia.	*Saya mau menelpon ke Australia.*	*Saya mahu membuat panggilan jauh ke Australia.*
I want to make a reverse-charges/collect call.	*Saya mau menelpon yang panggilan reverse charge.*	*Saya mahu membuat panggilan telefon dibayar oleh si penerima.*
May I speak to …?	*Boleh bicara dengan …?*	*Boleh saya bercakap dengan …?*
At the Bank		
I want to change …	*Saya mau menukar …*	*Saya mau menukar …*
(Australian) $	*dolar (Australi)*	*dolar (Australia)*
a cheque	*cek*	*cek*
a travellers' cheque	*cek turis*	*cek pengembaraan*
Where can I cash a travellers' cheque?	*Dimana saya bisa menguangkan cek perjalanan turis?*	*Di mana boleh saya tunaikan cek pengembaraan?*
What is the exchange rate?	*Berapa kursnya?*	*Berapa kadar pertukarannya?*

	INDONESIAN	MALAY
Can I transfer money here from my bank?	*Bisakah menransfer uang dari?*	*Bolehkah saya memindahkan wang dari bank saya ke sini?*
bankdraft	*surat wesel*	*draf bank*
cash	*uang kontan*	*wang tunai*
bill/note	*uang kertas*	*wang kertas*
coins	*uang logam*	*matawang*
money	*uang*	*duit*

Sightseeing

Where is the tourist office?	*Dimana ada kantor wisata?*	*Di mana pejabat pelancung?*
Are there any tourist attractions near here?	*Ada tempat pariwisata dekat sini?*	*Ada tempat tarikan pelancung dekat sini?*
I'm looking for the …	*Saya mencari …*	*Saya mencari …*
What time does it open/close?	*Jam berapa buka/tutup?*	*Pukul berapa buka/tutup?*
How much does it cost to get in?	*Berapa bayaran masuk?*	*Berapa bayaran masuk?*
What is that building?	*Itu gedung apa?*	*Bangunan apa itu?*
Do you have a local map?	*Saudara punya peta lokal?*	*Saudara ada peta tempatan?*
May I take photographs?	*Boleh saya ambil foto?*	*Boleh saya ambil foto gambar?*

INDONESIAN / MALAY

	INDONESIAN	**MALAY**
May I take your photograph?	*Boleh saya foto saudara?*	*Boleh saya ambil foto gambar saudara?*
castle	*benteng*	*istana*
church	*gereja*	*gereja*
cinema	*bioskop*	*panggung wayang*
concert	*konser*	*konsert*
market	*pasar*	*pasar*
mosque	*mesjid*	*masjid*
museum	*musium*	*musium*
puppet theatre	*tempat wayang kulit*	*panggung wayang kulit*
temple	*candi*	*candi*
theatre	*gedung sandiwara*	*gedung sandiwara*
nightclub	*kelab malam*	*kelab malam*
village	*desa*	*desa/kampung*
zoo	*kebun binatang*	*zoo/kebun binatang*

Paperwork

name	*nama*	*nama*
address	*alamat*	*alamat*
date of birth	*tanggal lahir*	*tarikh lahir*
place of birth	*tempat lahir*	*tempat lahir*
age	*umur*	*umur*
sex	*jenis kelamin*	*jenis kelamin/jantina*
nationality	*kebangsaan*	*bangsa*
religion	*agama*	*agama*
profession	*pekerjaan*	*pekerjaan*
reason for travel	*maksud kunjungan*	*maksud perjalanan*

	INDONESIAN	MALAY
marital status	*status perkawinan*	*status perkahwinan*
single	*belum kawin*	*bujang*
married	*kawin*	*kahwin*
divorced	*cerai*	*cerai*
widow	*janda*	*janda*
widower	*duda*	*duda*
identification	*surat keterangan*	*surat pengenalan*
passport number	*nomor paspor*	*nombor paspot*
visa	*visa*	*visa*
birth certificate	*surat keterangan lahir*	*surat beranak*
driving licence	*SIM (Surat Ijin Mengemudi)*	*lesen memandu*
customs	*bea cukai*	*kastam*
immigration	*imigrasi*	*imigresen*
purpose of visit	*maksud kunjungan*	*maksud perjalanan*
holiday	*liburan*	*cuti*
business	*pekerjaan*	*perniagaan*
visiting relatives	*kunjungan keluarga*	*melawat keluarga*

In the Country
Weather

What's the weather like?	*Bagaimana cuacanya?*	*Bagaimana cuacanya?*
Today it is …	*Hari ini …*	*Hari ini …*
cloudy	*mendung*	*mendung*
cold	*dingin*	*sejuk*
flooding	*banjir*	*banjir*

INDONESIAN / MALAY

	INDONESIAN	MALAY
hot	*panas*	*panas*
humid	*lembab*	*lembab*
raining heavily	*hujan lebat*	*hujan lebat*
raining lightly	*gerimis*	*hujan renyai*
warm	*hangat*	*hangat*
wet	*basah*	*basah*
windy	*berangin*	*berangin*
dry season	*musim kemarau*	*musim kemarau*
fog	*kabut*	*kabut*
rain	*hujan*	*hujan*
rainy season	*musim hujan*	*musim hujan*
storm	*badai*	*taufan/ribut*
sun	*matahari*	*matahari*

(literally 'eye of the day')

Geographical Terms

beach	*pantai*	*pantai*
cave	*gua*	*goa/gua*
forest	*hutan*	*hutan*
hill	*bukit*	*bukit*
hot spring	*mata air panas*	*mata air panas*
island	*pulau*	*pulau*
lake	*danau*	*tasik*
mountain	*gunung*	*gunung*
river	*sungai*	*sungai*
sea	*laut*	*laut*
valley	*lembah*	*lembah*
waterfall	*air terjun*	*air terjun*

	INDONESIAN	MALAY
Flora & Agriculture		
agriculture	*pertanian*	*pertanian*
cloves	*cengkeh*	*cengkeh*
coconut palm	*pohon kelapa*	*pohon kelapa/pokok kelapa*
corn	*jagung*	*jagung*
firewood	*kayu bakar*	*kayu bakar*
flower	*bunga*	*bunga*
fruit tree	*pohon buah*	*pohon buah/pokok buah*
harvest (v)	*panenpemungutan*	*penuaian*
irrigation	*pengairan*	*pengairan*
leaf	*daun*	*daun*
planting	*menanam*	*menanam*
rice field	*sawah*	*sawah*
rice terrace	*petak sawah*	*petak sawah*
sugar cane	*tebu*	*tebu*
tobacco	*tembakau*	*tembakau*
Fauna		
ant	*semut*	*semut*
bird	*burung*	*burung*
buffalo	*kerbau*	*kerbau*
butterfly	*kupu-kupu*	*kupu-kupu*
cat	*kucing*	*kucing*
chicken	*ayam*	*ayam*
cockroach	*kecoa/lipas*	*kecoa/lipas*
cow	*sapi*	*lembu*
crocodile	*buaya*	*buaya*
dog	*anjing*	*anjing*
fish	*ikan*	*ikan*

	INDONESIAN	MALAY
fly	*lalat*	*lalat*
horse	*kuda*	*kuda*
monkey	*monyet*	*monyet*
mosquito	*nyamuk*	*nyamuk*
pig	*babi*	*babi*
sheep	*domba*	*biri-biri*
snake	*ular*	*ular*
spider	*laba-laba*	*labah-labah*
tiger	*harimau*	*harimau*

Camping

camping	*berkemah*	*berkemah*
campsite	*tempat kemah*	*tempat perkhemahan*
mat	*tikar*	*tikar*
penknife	*pisau lipat*	*pisau lipat*
rope	*tali*	*tali*
tent	*tenda*	*khemah*
torch (flashlight)	*senter*	*lampu suluh*

Useful Words & Phrases

Is it safe to swim here?	*Aman berenang disini?*	*Selamat berenang di sini?*
Where is the nearest village?	*Dimana desa yang paling dekat?*	*Di mana kampung yang paling dekat?*
Is it safe to climb this mountain?	*Aman mendaki gunung ini?*	*Selamat mendaki gunung ini?*
Do I need a guide?	*Apakah saya perlu pemandu wisata?*	*Adakah saya perlukan pemandu pelancung?*

	INDONESIAN	**MALAY**
compass	*kompas*	*kompas*
diving	*menyelam*	*menyelam*
fishing	*memancing*	*memancing*
hunting	*berburuh*	*memburu*
mountain climbing	*mendaki gunung*	*mendaki gunung*
surfing	*bermain selancar*	*bermain selancar*
swimming	*berenang*	*berenang*

Food

In Indonesia and Malaysia the best places to try local food are the *warung* in Indonesia or the *gerai* in Malaysia. These food stalls are found along the streets. Night markets *(pasar malam)* are also good places for cheap food.

Where is a ...?	*Dimana ada ...?*	*Di mana ada ...?*
food stall	*warung*	*gerai*
night market	*pasar malam*	*pasar malam*
restaurant	*rumah makan*	*restoran*
cheap restaurant	*rumah makan murah*	*restoran murah*

breakfast	*makan pagi/sarapan*	*sarapan/makan pagi*
lunch	*makan siang*	*makan tengahari*
dinner	*makan malam*	*makan malam*

Eating Out

Is there a table for (five) available?	*Ada meja untuk (lima) orang?*	*Ada meja untuk (lima) orang?*
Please bring ... the menu	*Boleh minta ... daftar makanan*	*Boleh bawa ... daftar makanan, menu*

	INDONESIAN	MALAY
a glass of water	*segelas air putih*	*segelas air putih*
the bill	*bon*	*bil*
I can't eat …	*Saya tidak boleh makan …*	*Saya tidak boleh makan …*
milk and cheese	*susu dan keju*	*susu dan keju*
eggs	*telur*	*telur*
meat	*daging*	*daging*
prawns	*udang*	*udang*
This isn't cooked properly.	*Ini belum matang.*	*Ini belum cukup masak.*
Not too spicy please.	*Jangan terlalu pedas, ya.*	*Jangan terlalu pedas, ya.*
This is delicious.	*Makanan ini enak.*	*Makanan ini enak.*
May we have our bill please?	*Tolong kasi bonnya.*	*Tolong beri bil kami.*

If you are a vegetarian you can say *tanpa daging* ('without meat') or *sayur saja* ('vegetables only').

Typical Indonesian Dishes

Bubur Ayam
　　Indonesian porridge with chicken, usually sweetened and made from rice, black sticky rice or mung beans

Cap Cai
　　mixed, fried vegetables; sometimes served with meat

Gado-gado
　　steamed beansprouts and mixed vegetables with a spicy peanut sauce

Mie Kuah
noodle soup
Martabak
savoury Indonesian pancake stuffed with meat, egg and
vegetables; there is also a sweet version
Nasi Campur
steamed rice with a bit of everything
Nasi Goreng
fried rice with vegetables and sometimes meat
Sate
small pieces of various types of meat on a skewer served
with a spicy peanut sauce
Sop Ayam
chicken soup

Typical Malaysian Dishes

Assam Laksa
noodles served with a sour, fish-based gravy, garnished
with pineapple, cucumber, chillies, onions and mint leaves.
The best place to try this noodle dish is in Penang; it is also
known as *Penang Assam Laksa*.
Curry Laksa
noodles in curry gravy and garnished with beancurd, fish
balls, chicken, seafood and bean sprouts
Hainanese Chicken Rice
the rice is cooked with chicken stock and served with
steamed chicken and a bowl of soup; with roasted chicken
it is known as Malay Chicken Rice
Murtabak
minced and curried beef or chicken wrapped in flaky pastry,
served with pinkish pickled onions

Nasi Ayam
   steamed chicken-flavoured rice served with either steamed
   or roasted chicken, chicken broth, chilli-ginger sauce and
   soy sauce

Nasi Campur
   steamed rice served with your choice of curry, fried fish or
   meat and vegetables

Nasi Lemak
   steamed coconut rice served with fried anchovies, sambal
   and peanuts. Chicken/beef rendang can be added upon
   request.

Satay
   marinated meat on skewers served with peanut sauce

Rojak
   a Malaysian salad similar to the Indonesian *gado-gado*;
   beanshoots, pineapple, cucumber, mangoes, and fried bean
   curd with peanut sauce

Roti Canai
   flaky bread served with a curry of your choice

Yong Tau Foo
   vegetables and beancurd are stuffed with fish meat and
   served with a spicy, chilli/soy sauce; tasty with noodles

At the Market

The market is a dynamic focal point of life. In the market the most
intriguing array of local produce will be laid out for sale.

| How much is this? | *Berapa harganya ini?* | *Berapa harganya ini?* |
| How much is a kg of …? | *Berapa sekilo …?* | *Berapa sekilo …?* |

	INDONESIAN	MALAY
A kg of …, please.	*Minta … sekilo.*	*Minta sekilo …*
I don't want that one.	*Jangan yang itu.*	*Saya tidak mahu yang itu.*
Please give me another one.	*Tolong kasi saya yang lainnya.*	*Tolong beri saya yang lain.*

Meat — *Daging* — *Daging*

beef	*daging sapi*	*daging lembu*
brains	*otak*	*otak*
chicken	*ayam*	*ayam*
duck	*daging bebek*	*daging itik*
heart	*jantung*	*jantung*
lamb	*domba*	*kambing*
liver	*hati*	*hati*
mutton/goat	*kambing*	*kambing*

Seafood — *Ikan* — *Ikan*

crab	*kepiting*	*ketam*
freshwater fish	*ikan tambak*	*ikan air tawar*
lobster	*udang karang*	*udang kara/galah*
mussels	*kerang*	*kupang*
oysters	*tiram*	*tiram*
prawns/shrimp	*udang*	*udang*
saltwater fish	*ikan laut*	*ikan laut*
squid	*cumi-cumi*	*sotong*

Vegetables — *Sayur* — *Sayur*

beans	*buncis*	*kacang buncis*
cabbage	*kol*	*kobis*
carrot	*lobak merah*	*lobak merah*

	INDONESIAN	MALAY
cauliflower	*bunga kol*	*bunga kobis*
corn	*jagung*	*jagung*
cucumber	*ketimun*	*timun*
eggplant	*terong*	*terong*
mushrooms	*jamur*	*cendawan*
onion	*bawang bombay*	*bawang merah*
potato	*kentang*	*kentang*
pumpkin	*labu merah*	*labu*
tomato	*tomat*	*tomato*

Fruit	*Buah*	*Buah*
apples	*apel*	*epal*
banana	*pisang*	*pisang*
cempedak	*cempedak*	*cempedak*
coconut	*kelapa*	*kelapa*
durian	*durian*	*durian*
jackfruit	*nangka*	*nangka*
lemon	*jeruk nipis*	*limau*
mango	*mangga*	*mangga*
mangosteen	*manggis*	*manggis*
orange	*jeruk manis*	*oren*
pawpaw	*papaya*	*papaya, betik*
peanuts	*kacang*	*kacang*
pineapple	*nanas*	*nanas*
starfruit	*belimbing*	*belimbing*
strawberry	*arbei*	*strawberi*

Spices & Condiments		
chilli	*cabe*	*cili/lada*
cinnamon	*kayu manis*	*kayu manis*

	INDONESIAN	MALAY
cloves	*cengkeh*	*cengkeh*
curry	*kari*	*kari*
garlic	*bawang putih*	*bawang putih*
ginger	*jahe*	*halic*
oil	*minyak*	*minyak*
pepper	*lada*	*lada*
salt	*garam*	*garam*
soy sauce	*kecap asin*	*kicap masin*
sweet soy sauce	*kecap manis*	*kicap manis*
sugar	*gula*	*gula*
turmeric	*kunyit*	*kunyit*
vinegar	*cuka*	*cuka*

Drinks

beer	*bir*	*bir*
coffee	*kopi*	*kopi*
chocolate	*coklat*	*coklat*
citrus juice	*es jeruk*	*jus limau*
coconut milk	*es kelapa*	*air kelapa*
cordial	*sirup*	*sirap*
ginger tea	*teh jahe*	*teh halia*
milk	*susu*	*susu*
rice wine	*brem*	*tuak*
tea	*teh*	*teh*
with/without milk	*dengan/tanpa susu*	*dengan/tanpa susu*
with/without sugar	*dengan/tanpa gula*	*dengan/tanpa gula*
water	*air putih*	*air putih*
boiled water	*air matang*	*air masak*

	INDONESIAN	MALAY
Useful Words		
ashtray	*asbak*	*tempat abu rokok*
bitter	*pahit*	*pahit*
cold	*dingin*	*dingin/sejuk*
eat	*makan*	*makan*
fresh	*segar*	*segar*
fry (v)	*goreng*	*goreng*
hot	*panas*	*panas*
salty	*asin*	*masin*
sour	*asam*	*masam*
sweet	*manis*	*manis*
toothpick	*tusuk gigi*	*cungkil gigi*
unripe/uncooked	*mentah*	*mentah*

Shopping

	INDONESIAN	MALAY
Where is the ...?	*Dimana ada ...?*	*Di mana ada ...?*
barber	*tukang cukur rambut*	*tukang cukur rambut*
bookshop	*toko buku*	*kedai buku*
chemist	*apotik*	*farmasi*
grocery	*toko makanan*	*kedai makanan*
market	*pasar*	*pasar*
night market	*pasar malam*	*pasar malam*
shopping centre	*pusat pertokoan*	*pusat membeli-belah*
tailor	*penjahit*	*tukang jahit*

Bargaining

In Malaysia and Indonesia bargaining is customary in the market or for services like taxis and pedicabs, but not in shops and restaurants, or wherever prices are marked. This is known as fixed price or *harga pas*. It is quite common for tourists to be charged more than the local people, as they are often considered to be wealthy. If you want to know the common price *(harga biasa)*, ask an independent bystander.

	INDONESIAN	**MALAY**
I want to buy …	*Saya mau beli …*	*Saya mau beli …*
How much is it?	*Berapa harganya ini?*	*Berapa harganya ini?*
That's too much.	*Terlalu mahal.*	*Terlalu mahal.*
I don't have much money.	*Saya tidak ada banyak uang.*	*Saya tidak punya banyak wang.*
Can you lower the price?	*Boleh kurang?*	*Boleh kurang?*
I'll give you …	*Saya bayar …*	*Saya bayar …*
No more than …	*Tidak lebih dari …*	*Tidak lebih dari …*

Souvenirs

gold	*emas*	*emas*
handicraft	*kerajinan tangan*	*kraftangan*
handmade batik	*batik tulis*	*batik tulis*
jewellery	*perhiasan*	*barang kemas*
masks	*topeng*	*topeng*
paintings	*lukisan*	*lukisan*
pottery	*keramik*	*tembikar*
printed batik	*batik cap*	*batik cap*
puppets	*wayang kulit*	*boneka*
silver	*perak*	*perak*
souvenir	*kenang-kenangan*	*cenderamata*
statue	*patung*	*patung*

	INDONESIAN	MALAY
stone carving	*ukiran batu*	*ukiran batu*
woodcarving	*ukiran kayu*	*ukiran kayu*

Toiletries

baby's bottle	*botol bayi*	*botol bayi*
baby powder	*bedak bayi*	*bedak bayi*
condoms	*kondom*	*kondom*
contraceptive	*kontrasepsi*	*pencegah hamil*
laxative	*obat cuci perut*	*julap*
moisturiser	*krim pelembab*	*krim pelembab*
mosquito repellent	*obat nyamuk*	*ubat nyamuk*
razor blade	*silet*	*pisau cukur*
sanitary napkins	*duk/softex/tuala wanita*	*duk/softex/tuala wanita*
shampoo	*sampo*	*syampu*
shaver	*pisau cukur*	*pisau cukur*
shaving cream	*krim cukur*	*krim cukur*
sunblock cream	*krim pengangkal terbakar sinar matahari*	*krim pencegah matahari*
tampons	*tampon*	*tampon*
tissues	*tisu*	*tisu*
toilet paper	*kertas kamar kecil*	*kertas tandas*
toothbrush	*sikat gigi*	*berus gigi*
toothpaste	*pasta gigi*	*ubat gigi*

Photography

I'd like a film for this camera.	*Minta filem untuk kamera ini.*	*Saya mahu filem untuk kamera ini.*
How much is it for processing?	*Berapa ongkos cuci cetak?*	*Berapa harga cuci cetak?*

	INDONESIAN	MALAY
When will it be ready?	*Kapan selesainya?*	*Bila boleh siap?*
Do you repair cameras here?	*Bisa memperbaiki kamera disini?*	*Boleh perbaiki kamera di sini?*
B&W (film)	*(filem) hitam*	*(filem) hitam putih*
camera	*kamera*	*kamera*
colour (film)	*(filem) berwarna*	*(filem) berwarna*
develop	*mencuci*	*mencuci*
film	*filem*	*filem*
photograph	*foto*	*foto*

Smoking

A packet of cigarettes, please.	*Minta rokok satu bungkus.*	*Minta rokok satu bungkus.*
Do you have a light?	*Boleh minta api?*	*Boleh minta api?*
cigarettes	*rokok*	*rokok*
matches	*korek api*	*mancis*
pipe	*pipa rokok*	*paip*
tobacco	*tembakau*	*tembakau*

Sizes & Comparisons

big	*besar*	*besar*
bigger	*lebih besar*	*lebih besar*
biggest	*paling besar*	*paling besar*
too big	*terlalu besar*	*kebesaran*
very big	*sangat besar*	*sangat besar*
small	*kecil*	*kecil*
smaller	*lebih kecil*	*lebih kecil*

	INDONESIAN	MALAY

Health

Where is a …?	*Dimana ada …?*	*Di mana ada ...?*
chemist/pharmacy	*apotik*	*farmasi*
dentist	*doktergigi*	*doktor gigi*
doctor	*dokter*	*doktor*
hospital	*rumah sakit*	*hospital*
medicine	*obat*	*ubat*

At the Doctor

My ... hurts.	*… saya sakit.*	*… saya sakit.*
I feel nauseous.	*Saya mau muntah.*	*Saya mau muntah.*
I feel dizzy.	*Saya merasa pusing.*	*Saya rasa pening.*

Ailments

allergy	*alergi*	*alergi*
asthma	*asma*	*penyakit lelah*
burns	*luka bakar*	*luka bakar*
cholera	*kolera*	*kolera*
cold	*masuk angin*	*masuk angin*
constipation	*sukar buang air besar*	*sembelit*
diarrhoea	*diarea/mencret/ cirit-birit*	*diarea/cirit-birit*
dysentery	*disentri*	*disentri*
fever	*demam*	*deman*
flu	*selesma*	*selsema*
food poisoning	*keracunan makanan*	*keracunan makanan*
headache	*sakit kepala*	*sakit kepala*
hepatitis	*hepatitis*	*hepatitis*
malaria	*malaria*	*malaria*

	INDONESIAN	**MALAY**
stomachache	*sakit perut*	*sakit perut*
sunburn	*kulit terbakar matahari*	*kulit terbakar matahari*
typhoid	*demam tipus*	*demam kepialu*
venereal disease	*penyakit kelamin*	*penyakit kelamin*

INDONESIAN / MALAY

Useful Words & Phrases

I'm allergic to penicillin/ antibiotics.	*Saya alergi penisilin/antibiotika.*	*Saya alergik kepada penisilin/antibiotik.*
I have low/high blood pressure.	*Saya menderita tekanan darah rendah/tinggi.*	*Saya menderita tekanan darah rendah/tinggi.*
I've been vaccinated.	*Saya sudah divaksinasi.*	*Saya sudah divaksinasi.*
I have my own syringe.	*Saya punya suntikan saya sendiri.*	*Saya punya suntikan saya sendiri.*
Please take us to a hospital.	*Tolong antar kami ke rumah sakit.*	*Tolong hantar kami ke rumah sakit.*
I have medical insurance.	*Saya punya asuransi kesehatan.*	*Saya punya insurans kesihatan.*
I need a receipt for my insurance.	*Saya perlu kwitansi untuk asuransi saya.*	*Saya perlu resit untuk insurans.*

addiction	*kecanduan*	*ketagihan*
contraceptive	*kontrasepsi*	*pencegah hamil*
disease	*penyakit*	*penyakit*
injection	*suntikan*	*suntikan*
poisonous	*beracun*	*beracun*
urine	*air seni*	*kencing*

	INDONESIAN	MALAY
Women's Health		
Could I see a female doctor?	*Ada dokter perempuan disini?*	*Ada doktor perempuan disini?*
Could I see a doctor for females?	*Ada dokter untuk perempuan disini?*	*Ada doktor untuk perempuan disini?*
I'm pregnant.	*Saya hamil.*	*Saya hamil.*
I'm on the pill.	*Saya pakai pil kontrasepsi.*	*Saya pakai pil pencegah hamil.*
I haven't menstruated for … weeks.	*Saya belum mentruasi selama … … minggu.*	*Saya belum datang haid selama … minggu.*

Parts of the Body

arm	*lengan*	*lengan*
back	*punggung*	*punggung*
ear	*telinga*	*telinga*
eye	*mata*	*mata*
face	*wajah*	*muka*
finger	*jari tangan*	*jari tangan*
hands	*tangan*	*tangan*
head	*kepala*	*kepala*
leg/foot	*kaki*	*kaki*
mouth	*mulut*	*mulut*
muscle	*otot*	*otot*
nose	*hidung*	*hidung*
skin	*kulit*	*kulit*
stomach	*perut*	*perut*
tooth	*gigi*	*gigi*

	INDONESIAN	**MALAY**
At the Chemist		
I need medicine for …	*Saya perlu obat untuk …*	*Saya perlu ubat untuk …*
I need a prescription for …	*Saya perlu resep untuk …*	*Saya perlu surat ubat doktor untuk …*
How many times a day?	*Berapa kali sehari?*	*Berapa kali sehari?*
These tablets must be taken three times a day.	*Tablet-tablet ini harus diminum*	*Pil ini harus di ambil tiga kali sehari.*
antibiotics	*antibiotisk*	*antibiotik*
antiseptic	*antiseptik*	*antiseptik*
aspirin	*aspirin*	*aspirin*
bandage	*pembalut*	*kain balut*
penicillin	*penisilin*	*penisilin*
quinine	*kina*	*kuinina*
sleeping pills	*pil tidur*	*pil tidur*
tablet	*tablet*	*pil*
vitamins	*vitamin*	*vitamin*

(side tab) **INDONESIAN / MALAY**

Time & Dates
Telling the Time

Telling the time is fairly straightforward. In Indonesian the word *jam* is used to mean 'hour/o'clock'. In Malaysian the words *pukul* and *jam* are both used but *pukul* is more common.

The words for 'am' and 'pm' are not used. Instead Indonesians say *jam delapan pagi* (literally '8 in the morning') and *jam delapan malam* (literally '8 at night'). The Malaysian equivalents are *pukul lapan pagi* and *pukul lapan malam*.

	INDONESIAN	MALAY
What time is it?	*Jam berapa (sekarang)?*	*Pukul berapa (sekarang)?*
It's three o'clock.	*Jam tiga.*	*Pukul tiga.*

Unlike English, 'five-thirty' is not given in Indonesian as 'half past five' but as 'half to six'. The word for 'half' is *setengah*.

It's five-thirty.   *Jam setengah enam.*

In Malaysian it is expressed as 'half past five', as in English.

It's five-thirty.   *Pukul lima setengah.*

Time is expressed in Indonesian as so many minutes past the hour until it gets past the half hour when it is expressed as the next hour minus so many minutes. The word for 'plus/past' is *lewat* and the word for 'minus/before' is *kurang*.

It's ten past three.	*Jam tiga lewat sepuluh.*
It's quarter past four.	*Jam empat lewat seperempat.*
It's quarter to four.	*Jam empat kurang seperempat.*

In Malaysian the equivalent times are:

It's ten past three.	*Pukul tiga sepuluh minit.*
It's quarter past four.	*Pukul empat suku.*
It's quarter to four.	*Kurang suku pukul empat.*

	INDONESIAN	MALAY
Days of the Week		
Monday	*hari Senin*	*hari Isnin*
Tuesday	*hari Selasa*	*hari Selasa*
Wednesday	*hari Rabu*	*hari Rabu*
Thursday	*hari Kamis*	*hari Khamis*
Friday	*hari Jum'at*	*hari Jumaat*
Saturday	*hari Sabtu*	*hari Sabtu*
Sunday	*hari Minggu*	*hari Minggu/Ahad*
On Monday.	*Pada hari Senin.*	*Pada hari Isnin.*
Months		
January	*Januari*	*Januari*
February	*Februari*	*Februari*
March	*Maret*	*Mac*
April	*April*	*April*
May	*Mei*	*Mei*
June	*Juni*	*Jun*
July	*Juli*	*Julai*
August	*Agustus*	*Ogos*
September	*September*	*September*
October	*Oktober*	*Oktober*
November	*Nopember*	*November*
December	*Desember*	*Disember*
During June.	*Selama bulan Juni.*	*Semasa bulan Jun.*
Seasons		
spring	*musim semi*	*musim bunga*
summer	*musim panas*	*musim panas*
autumn/Fall	*musim gugur*	*musim luruh/gugur*
winter	*musim dingin*	*musim sejuk*

	INDONESIAN	MALAY
Dates		
What date is it today?	*Tanggal berapa hari ini?*	*Tanggal berapa hari ini?*
It's 1 April.	*Tanggal satu April.*	*Tanggal satu April.*
Present		
today	*hari ini*	*hari ini*
tonight	*malam ini*	*malam ini*
this week	*minggu ini*	*minggu ini*
this month	*bulan ini*	*bulan ini*
this year	*tahun ini*	*tahun ini*
now	*sekarang*	*sekarang*
immediately	*sekarang juga*	*sekarang juga*
just now	*baru saja*	*baru saja*
Past		
yesterday	*kemarin*	*kelmarin*
day before yesterday	*kemarin dulu*	*kelmarin dulu*
last night	*tadi malam/kemarin malam*	*malam kelmarin/ semalam*
last week	*minggu lalu*	*minggu lalu*
last month	*bulan lalu*	*bulan lalu*
last year	*tahun lalu*	*tahun lalu*
Future		
tomorrow	*besok*	*esok*
day after tomorrow	*lusa*	*lusa*
next week	*minggu depan*	*minggu depan*
next month	*bulan depan*	*bulan depan*
next year	*tahun depan*	*tahun depan*

Numbers
Cardinal Numbers

	INDONESIAN	MALAY
0	*nol*	*kosong*
1	*satu*	*satu*
2	*dua*	*dua*
3	*tiga*	*tiga*
4	*empat*	*empat*
5	*lima*	*lima*
6	*enam*	*enam*
7	*tujuh*	*tujuh*
8	*delapan*	*lapan*
9	*sembilan*	*sembilan*
10	*sepuluh*	*sepuluh/puluh*
11	*sebelas*	*sebelas/belas*
12	*duabelas*	*dua belas*
13	*tigabelas*	*tiga belas*
14	*empatbelas*	*empat belas*
15	*limabelas*	*lima belas*
16	*enambelas*	*enam belas*
17	*tujuhbelas*	*tujuh belas*
18	*delapanbelas*	*lapan belas*
19	*sembilanbelas*	*sembilan belas*
20	*duapuluh*	*dua puluh*
21	*duapuluh satu*	*dua puluh satu*
22	*duapuluh dua*	*dua puluh dua*
30	*tigapuluh*	*tiga puluh*
40	*empatpuluh*	*empat puluh*
50	*limapuluh*	*lima puluh*
100	*seratus*	*seratus*
200	*duaratus*	*dua ratus*

	INDONESIAN	**MALAY**
1000	*seribu*	*seribu*
2000	*duaribu*	*dua ribu*
1 million	*sejuta*	*sejuta*
2 million	*dua juta*	*dua juta*

Ordinal Numbers

1st	*pertama*	*pertama*
2nd	*kedua*	*kedua*
3rd	*ketiga*	*ketiga*
4th	*keempat*	*keempat*
5th	*kelima*	*kelima*
6th	*keenam*	*keenam*
7th	*ketujuh*	*ketujuh*
8th	*kedelapan*	*kelapan*
9th	*kesembilan*	*kesembilan*
10th	*kesepuluh*	*kesepulah*

the first bus	*bis (yang) pertama*	*bas (yang) pertama*
the third building	*gedung (yang) ketiga*	*bangunan (yang) ketiga*

Emergencies

Help!	*Tolong!*	*Tolong!*
Stop!	*Stop!*	*Berhenti!*
Go away!	*Pergi!*	*Pergi!*
Watch out!	*Awas!*	*Awas!*
Thief!	*Copet!*	*Perompak*
Fire!	*Kebakaran!*	*Api!, Kebakaran!*

INDONESIAN / MALAY

	INDONESIAN	**MALAY**
Could you help me please?	*Boleh minta tolong?*	*Boleh tolong saya?*
There's been an accident!	*Ada kecelakaan!*	*Ada kemalangan!*
Call a doctor!	*Panggil dokter!*	*Panggil doktor!*
Call an ambulance!	*Panggil ambulan!*	*Panggil ambulan!*
I've been robbed!	*Saya dirompak!*	*Saya dirompak!*
I'll get the police!	*Saya akan panggil polisi!*	*Saya akan panggil polis!*
I'm ill.	*Saya sakit.*	*Saya sakit.*
I'm lost.	*Saya kesasar.*	*Saya sesat.*
Where is the police station?	*Dimana ada kantor polisi?*	*Di mana stesen polis?*
Could I please use the telephone?	*Boleh saya pakai telepon?*	*Boleh saya pakai telefon?*
I wish to contact my embassy/consulate.	*Saya mau menghubungi kedutaan besar/konsulat saya.*	*Saya mau menghubungi kedutaan besar/konsulat saya.*
I didn't realize I was doing anything wrong.	*Saya tidak tahu kalau saya salah.*	*Saya tidak sedar yang saya melakukan kesalahan.*
I didn't do it.	*Saya tidak melakukan itu.*	*Saya tidak melakukannya.*

	INDONESIAN	MALAY
I'm sorry/ I apologise.	*Saya menyesal.*	*Saya minta maaf.*
My blood group is (A, B, O, AB) positive/negative.	*Golongan darah saya (A, B, O, AB) positif/negatif.*	*Jenis darah (A, B, O, AB) positif/negatif.*

KHMER

Khmer

The Khmer or Cambodian language is spoken by approximately nine million people in the Kingdom of Cambodia and is understood by many in bordering countries. Written Khmer is based on the ancient Brahmi script of southern India. Arguably one of the oldest languages in South-East Asia, Khmer inscriptions have been dated back to the 7th century A.D. Although separate and distinct from its Thai, Lao, and Burmese neighbours, Khmer shares with them the common roots of Sanskrit and Pali — a heritage of centuries of linguistic and cultural interaction and their shared faith in Theravada Buddhism. More recently, many French words entered the Khmer language during the colonial period, especially medical and technical terms.

Unlike the languages of its bordering countries, Khmer is non-tonal, meaning that there are no special intonations of words which alter their meaning. However, the lack of tones is compensated by the complexity of the Khmer pronounciation.

In this chapter the author has attempted to construct a simple transliteration system, designed for basic communication rather than linguistic perfection. Several Khmer vowels, however, have no English equivalent; thus such words can only be approximated by English spellings. Other words are written as they are pronounced and not necessarily according to the actual vowels used in the words. (Khmer placenames will follow their standard spellings.) As with any language, questions regarding exact pronunciations are best solved by asking a native speaker.

Though English is fast becoming Cambodia's dominant second language, the Khmer still cling to the Francophone pronunciation of the Roman alphabet and most foreign words. This is helpful to remember when spelling Western words and names; thus 'ay—bee—cee' becomes 'ah—bey—sey', and so on. French speakers will definitely have an advantage when addressing the older generation, as most educated Khmers studied French at some point during their schooling. Many household items retain their French names as well, especially those which were introduced to Cambodia by the French, such as *robine*, 'tap/faucet', and *ampuol*, 'light bulb'.

The Khmers sincerely appreciate any effort to learn their language and are very supportive of foreigners who give it even a half-hearted try.

Dialects

Although the Khmer language as spoken in Phnom Penh is generally intelligible nationwide, there are several distinct dialects in other areas of the country. Most notably, the Khmer in Takeo province (south of Phnom Penh) tend to modify or slur hard consonant combinations, especially those with an 'r' in them; thus *bram* ('five') becomes *peam*, *sraa* ('alcohol') becomes *se-aa*, and *baraang* ('French' or 'foreigner') becomes *beang*. In Siem Reap, sharp-eared travellers will notice a very Lao sounding lilt to the local speech. Certain vowels are modified, such as in *poan* ('thousand') which becomes *peuan*, and *kh'sia* ('pipe'), which becomes *kh'seua*.

Pronunciation
Vowels

aa	as in 'father'
i	as in 'kit'
uh	as in 'but'
ii	as in 'feet'

KHMER

ei	a combination of 'uh' and 'ii' above; 'uh-ii'
eu	try pronouncing the sound 'oo' while keeping the lips spread flat rather than rounded
euh	as 'eu' above, but pronounced short and hard
oh	as the 'o' in 'hose' but pronounced short and hard
ow	as in 'glow'
u	as in 'flute' but pronounced short and hard
uu	as in 'zoo'
ua	as the 'ou'in 'tour'
uah	as 'ua' above, but pronounced short and hard
œ	as 'er' in 'her' but more open
aa-œ	a tough one with no English equivalent; like a combination of 'aa' and 'œ'. When placed between consonants it is often pronounced like 'ao'
eua	combination of 'eu' and 'a'
ia	as 'ee-ya', like 'beer' without the 'r'
e	as in 'late'
ai	as in 'side'
ae	as in 'cat'
ay	as 'ai' above but slightly more nasal
ey	as in 'pray'
ao	as in 'cow'
av	another tough one with no English equivalent; like a very nasal 'ao'. The final 'v' is not pronounced.
euv	no English equivalent; like a very nasal 'eu'. The final 'v' is not pronounced.
ooh	as the oo in shoot pronounced short and hard
ohm	as in 'home'
am	as in 'glum'

KHMER

oam	a combination of 'o' and 'am'
a/ah	shorter and harder than 'aa' above
eah	combination of 'e' and 'ah', pronounced short and hard
ih	as the 'ee' in 'teeth', pronounced short and hard
eh	as the 'a' in 'date', pronounced short and hard
awh	as the 'aw' in 'jaw', pronounced short and hard
oah	a combination of 'o' and 'ah', pronounced short and hard
aw	as the 'aw' in 'jaw'

Vowels and diphthongs with an 'h' at the end should be pronounced hard and aspirated (with a puff of air).

In addition to these vowels, the combination of certain vowels and final consonants subtly modifies the vowel sounds, such as in the word *sao-it*, 'to laugh', a combination of the 'aa-œ' vowel and the final consonant 'j', and *poan*, 'thousand', a combination of 'aa' and the final consonant 'n'.

Consonants

Khmer uses some consonant combinations which are rather bizarre to the Westerner ear and equally difficult for the Western tongue, such as 'j-r' in *j'rook*, 'pig', or 'ch-ng' in *ch'ngain*, 'delicious'. For ease of pronunciation such consonants are separated here with an apostrophe.

k	as the 'g' in 'gun'
kh	as the 'k' in 'kill'
ng	as in the final sound of the word 'sing'. Practice by saying 'singing-nging-nging-nging' until you can say 'nging' clearly.
j	as the 'j' in 'jump'

KHMER

ch   as in 'cheese'

ny   as in the final syllable of 'onion' : 'nyun'.

t   a hard, unaspirated 't' sound with no direct equivalent in English. Similar to the 't' in 'stand.'

th   as the 't' in 'two'; never as the 'th' in 'thanks'

p   a hard, unaspirated 'p' sound, as in 'stop'

ph   as the 'p' in 'pond', never as 'ph' in 'phone'

r   as in 'rum' but hard and rolling, with the tongue flapping against the palate. In rapid conversation it is often omitted entirely.

w   as the 'w' in 'woman'; contrary to the common transliteration system, there is no equivalent to the English 'v' sound in Khmer

Greetings & Civilities

Greetings & Goodbyes

Hello.	*johm riab sua/ sua s'dei*	ជំរាបសួរ /សួស្ដី
Welcome.	*sohm swaakohm*	សូមស្វាគមន៍
Goodbye.	*lia suhn hao-y*	លាសិនហើយ
See you later.	*juab kh'nia th'ngay krao-y*	ជួបគ្នាថ្ងៃក្រោយ

Civilities

Please.	*sohm*	សូម
Thank you.	*aw kohn*	អរគុណ
You're welcome.	*awt ei te/sohm anjœ-in*	អត់អីទេ /សូមអញ្ជើញ

Excuse me/I'm sorry.	*sohm toh*	សុំទោស
Yes. (men)	*baat*	បាទ
Yes. (women)	*jaa*	ចាស
No.	*te*	ទេ
Pardon?	*niak niyey tha mait?*	អ្នកនិយាយថាម៉េច?
Enjoy your meal.	*anjœ-in pisaa ao-y baan ch'ngain*	អញ្ជើញពិសាឱ្យបានឆ្ងាញ់

Forms of Address

The Khmer language reflects the social standing of the speaker and subject through various personal pronouns and 'politeness words'. These range from the simple *baat* (for men), and *jaa* (for women), placed at the end of a sentence, meaning 'Yes' or 'I agree', to the very formal and archaic *Reachasahp* or 'Royal language', a separate vocabulary reserved for addressing the King and very high officials. Many of the pronouns are determined on the basis of the subject's age and sex in relation to the speaker. The easiest and most general personal pronoun is *niak*, 'you', which may be used in most situations, with either sex. Women of your age and older can be called *ming* ('aunt') or, for more formal situations, *lowk srei* ('Madam'). Men of your age and older may be called *lowk* ('mister'). *Bawng* is a good informal, neutral pronoun for men or women who are (or appear to be) older than you. For third person, male or female, singular or plural, the respectful form is *koat* and the common form is *ke*.

For women younger than you the terms *b'own* or *niang* may be used. The pronoun *own* may also be used but this is usually reserved for close friends. For men younger than you use the terms *own* or *b'own*.

KHMER

Pronouns

I	kh'nyohm	ខ្ញុំ
you	niak/lowk/bawng	អ្នក /លោក /បង
he/she/they	koat (formal)/ke (common)	គាត់ /គេ
we	yœng	យើង
you (plural)	niak teang awh/awh lowk	អ្នកទាំងអស់ /អស់លោក

Language Difficulties

Do you speak English?
  niak jeh phiasaa awngle te?   អ្នកចេះភាសាអង់គ្លេសទេ?
Does anyone here speak English?
  tii nih mian niak jeh phiasaa   ទីនេះមានអ្នកចេះភាសាអង់គ្លេសទេ?
  awngle te?

Do you understand?
  niak yuhl te/niak s'dap baan te?   អ្នកយល់ទេ /អ្នកស្ដាប់បានទេ?
I understand.
  kh'nyohm yuhl/kh'nyohm   ខ្ញុំយល់/ខ្ញុំស្ដាប់បាន
  s'dap baan
I don't understand.
  kh'nyohm muhn yuhl te/   ខ្ញុំមិនយល់ទេ /ខ្ញុំស្ដាប់មិនបានទេ
  kh'nyohm s'dap muhn baan te

What does this mean?
  nih mian nuh-y tha mait?   នេះមានន័យថាម៉េច?
How do you say ... in Cambodian?
  ... kh'mai tha mait?   ...ខ្មែរថាម៉េច?

Please speak slowly.
  sohm niyay yeut yeut   សូមនិយាយយឺតៗ
Please repeat it.
  sohm niyay m'dawng tiat   សូមនិយាយម្ដងទៀត

KHMER

Write that word down for me.
sohm sawse piak nooh ao-y សូមសរសេរពាក្យនេះឲ្យខ្ញុំ
kh'nyohm

Small Talk
Meeting People
Hi. How are you?
niak sohk sabaay te? អ្នកសុខសប្បាយទេ?
I'm fine.
kh'nyohm sohk sabaay ខ្ញុំសុខសប្បាយ
I'm fine. And you?
kh'nyohm sohk sabaay. ខ្ញុំសុខសប្បាយ ចុះអ្នក?
joh niak?
What is your name?
niak ch'muah ei? អ្នកឈ្មោះអី?
My name is ...
kh'nyohm ch'muah ... ខ្ញុំឈ្មោះ...
I'm staying at ...
kh'nyohm snahk neuv... ខ្ញុំស្នាក់នៅ...

KHMER

Nationalities
Where are you from?
niak mao pii prateh naa? អ្នកមកពីប្រទេសណា?

I am from ...	*kh'nyohm mao pii...*	ខ្ញុំមកពី...
Australia	*prateh Owstraalii*	ប្រទេសអូស្ត្រាលី
Cambodia	*kampujia*	កម្ពុជា
Canada	*prateh Caanaadaa*	ប្រទេសកាណាដា
England	*prateh Awngle*	ប្រទេសអង់គ្លេស
Europe	*ærohp*	អឺរ៉ុប
Ireland	*prateh Iilahn*	ប្រទេសអៃឡង់

Israel	prateh Iisra-ail	ប្រទេសអ៊ីស្រាអែល
Japan	prateh Japohn	ប្រទេសជប៉ុន
New Zealand	prateh Niw Siilahn	ប្រទេស និវស៊ីឡង់
Scotland	prateh skawt	ប្រទេសស្កុត
South Africa	prateh Aafrik d'bohng	ប្រទេសអាប្រិកខាងត្បូង
the USA	prateh Saharawt khaang Amerik	សហរដ្ឋអាមេរិក

Age

How old are you?
niak aayu pohnmaan?   អ្នកអាយុប៉ុន្មាន?

I am ...	kh'nyohm aayu ...	ខ្ញុំអាយុ...
20 years old	m'phei ch'nam	ម្ភៃឆ្នាំ
35 years old	saamsuhp bram ch'nam	សាមសិបប្រាំឆ្នាំ

Occupations

What is your occupation?
niak twœ gaa ei?   អ្នកធ្វើការអី?

I am a/an ...	kh'nyohm jia ...	ខ្ញុំជា...
artist	silapakaw	សិល្បករ
businessperson	niak johmnuin	អ្នកជំនួញ
doctor	kruu paet	គ្រូពេទ្យ
engineer	wisawakaw	វិស្វករ
factory worker	kamakaw rohng jak	កម្មកររោងចក្រ
farmer	kasikaw	កសិករ
journalist	niak kasait	អ្នកកាសែត
lawyer	me thiawii	មេធាវី
mechanic	jiang masuhn	ជាងម៉ាស៊ីន

musician	*niak leng phleng*	អ្នកលេងភ្លេង
office worker	*niak twœ kaa kh'nohng kaariyalai*	អ្នកធ្វើការក្នុងការិយាល័យ
public servant	*rawthakaa*	រដ្ឋការ
scientist	*niak witiasah*	អ្នកវិទ្យាសាស្ត្រ
singer	*niak johmriang*	អ្នកចម្រៀង
student	*nisuht*	និស្សិត
teacher	*kruu bawngrian*	គ្រូបង្រៀន
writer	*niak nipohn*	អ្នកនិពន្ធ

Religion

What is your religion?
  niak kuhn sasanaa awei?   អ្នកកាន់សាសនាអ្វី?

My religion is ...	*kh'nyohm kuhn sasanaa ...*	ខ្ញុំកាន់សាសនា ...
Buddhism	*preah poht*	ព្រះពុទ្ធ
Christianity	*krih*	គ្រិស្ត
Hindu	*hinduu*	ហិណ្ឌូ
Judaism	*yooda*	យូដា
Islam	*islaam*	អ៊ីស្លាម

I am not religious.
  kh'nyohm kh'mian sasanaa te   ខ្ញុំគ្មានសាសនាទេ

Family

Are you married?
  niak riap kaa hao-y reu neuv?   អ្នករៀបការហើយឬទៅ?
I'm not married yet.
  kh'nyohm muhn toan riap kaa te   ខ្ញុំមិនទាន់រៀបការទេ

KHMER

I'm married.
   kh'nyohm riap kaa hao-y   ខ្ញុំរៀបការហើយ
Do you have any children?
   niak mian kown hao-y reu neuv?   អ្នកមានកូនហើយឬនៅ?
I don't have any children.
   kh'nyohm awt mian kown te   ខ្ញុំអត់មានកូនទេ
I don't have any children yet.
   kh'nyohm muhn toan mian kown te   ខ្ញុំមិនទាន់មានកូនទេ

This is my ...	*nih jia ... r'bawh kh'nyohm*	នេះជា ... របស់ខ្ញុំ
mother	*m'daay*	ម្ដាយ
father	*euv pohk*	ឪពុក
older sister	*bawng srei*	បងស្រី
older brother	*bawng brawh*	បងប្រុស
younger sister	*b'own srei*	ប្អូនស្រី
younger brother	*b'own brawh*	ប្អូនប្រុស
child/children	*kown*	កូន
son	*kown brawh*	កូនប្រុស
daughter	*kown srei*	កូនស្រី
husband	*b'dei*	ប្ដី
wife	*prapohn*	ប្រពន្ធ
friend	*muht*	មិត្ត
boyfriend/girlfriend	*sawngsaa*	សង្សារ

Interests

Do you like ...?   *niak johl juht ... te?*   អ្នកចូលចិត្ត...ទេ?
I like ...   *kh'nyohm johl juht ...*   ខ្ញុំចូលចិត្ត...

I don't like ...	kh'nyohm awt johl juht ... te	ខ្ញុំអត់ចូលចិត្ត...ទេ
going shopping	teuv p'saa	ទៅផ្សារ
music	phleng	ភ្លេង
playing games	leng l'baing	លេងល្បែង
playing sports	leng keilaa	លេងកីឡា
reading books	aan siew pheuv	អានសៀវភៅ
travelling/going out	daa-œ leng	ដើរលេង
watching TV	mœl turatuh	មើលទូរទស្សន៍

Making Conversation

Where are you going?
niak teuv naa? អ្នកទៅណា?
(NB: As with many other languages, this is a very common greeting; an exact answer is not necessary)

Where are you from?
niak mao pii prateh naa? អ្នកមកពីប្រទេសណា?

How long have you been in Cambodia?
niak mao dawl srawk kh'mai អ្នកមកដល់ស្រុកខ្មែរប៉ុន្មានថ្ងៃហើយ?
pohnmaan th'ngay hao-y?

I've been in Cambodia
for one week.
kh'nyohm mao srawk ខ្ញុំមកស្រុកខ្មែរមួយអាទិត្យហើយ
kh'mai muy aatuht hao-y

When did you arrive in Cambodia?
niak mao dawl srawk kh'mai អ្នកមកដល់ស្រុកខ្មែរពីអង្កាល់?
pii awngal?

Two weeks ago.
pii aatuht muhn ពីរអាទិត្យមុន

KHMER

How long will you stay (in
Cambodia)?
    neuv srawk kh'mai pohnmaan   នៅស្រុកខ្មែរប៉ុន្មានថ្ងៃទៀត?
    th'ngay tiat?

I'll be staying (another) two
weeks.
    kh'nyohm neuv pii aatuht (tiat)   ខ្ញុំនៅពីរអាទិត្យ (ទៀត)

What is this called?
    nih ke hav thaa mait?   នេះគេហៅថាម៉េច?

Can I take a photo (of you)?
    kh'nyohm aa-it thawt ruup   ខ្ញុំអាចថតរូបអ្នកបានទេ?
    niak baan te?

Can I take a photo (of that)?
    kh'nyohm aa-it thawt ruup   ខ្ញុំអាចថតរូបវាបានទេ?
    wia baan te?

Do you live here?
    niak snahk neuv tii nih reu?   អ្នកស្នាក់នៅទីនេះឬ?

Useful Phrases

It is possible (for you to go).
    niak aa-it teuv baan   អ្នកអាចទៅបាន

It is possible (for you to do).
    niak aa-it twœ baan   អ្នកអាចធ្វើបាន

It is not possible (for you to go).
    niak muhn aa-it teuv baan te   អ្នកមិនអាចទៅបានទេ

I forgot.
    kh'nyohm plet   ខ្ញុំភ្លេច

It is important.
    wia samkhuhn   វាសំខាន់

It's not important/It doesn't matter.
    wia awt samkhuhn te   វាអត់សំខាន់ទេ

KHMER

Getting Around

Getting around in Cambodia is done mostly via cyclo or moto-taxi (called *moto dohp*); real taxis are reserved for long journeys. Most moto dohp drivers speak a bit of English, but cyclo pedallers will definitely test your Khmer abilities.

Finding Your Way

Where is the ...?	... *neuv ai naa?*	នៅឯណា?
bus station	*kuhnlaing laan ch'nual*	កន្លែងឡានឈ្នួល
bus stop	*jamnawt laan ch'nual*	ចំណតឡានឈ្នួល
train station	*s'thaanii roht plæng*	ស្ថានីយរថភ្លើង
airport	*wial yohn hawh*	វាលយន្តហោះ

What time does the ... leave?	... *jein maong pohnmaan?*	...ចេញម៉ោងប៉ុន្មាន?
bus	*laan ch'nual*	ឡានឈ្នួល
train	*roht plæng*	រថភ្លើង
plane	*yohn hawh/k'pal hawh*	យន្តហោះ/កប៉ាល់ហោះ

Directions

How can I get to ...?
phleuv naa teuv ...   ផ្លូវណាទៅ ...?

Is it far?
wia neuv ch'ngaay te?   វានៅឆ្ងាយទេ?

Is it near?
wia neuv juht te?   វានៅជិតទេ?

What ... is this?	... nih ch'muah ei?	... នេះឈ្មោះអ្វី?
street	phleuv	ផ្លូវ
city	krohng	ក្រុង
village	phuum	ភូមិ

Go straight ahead.	teuv trawng	ទៅត្រង់
Turn left ...	bawt ch'weng	បត់ឆ្វេង
Turn right ...	bawt s'dam	បត់ស្ដាំ
at the corner	neuv kait j'rohng	នៅកាច់ជ្រុង
in front of	neuv khaang mohk	នៅខាងមុខ
next to	neuv joab	នៅជាប់
behind	neuv khaang krao-y	នៅខាងក្រោយ
opposite	neuv tohl mohk	នៅទល់មុខ

north	khaang jæng	ខាងជើង
south	khaang d'bowng	ខាងត្បូង
east	khaang kaot	ខាងកើត
west	khaang leit	ខាងលិច

Buying Tickets

ticket window	kuhnlaing tein samboht	កន្លែងទិញសំបុត្រ
ticket	samboht	សំបុត្រ
one-way ticket	samboht jih teuv	សំបុត្រជិះទៅ
return ticket	samboht jih teuv mao	សំបុត្រជិះទៅមក
seat	kav ei/kuhnlaing ahngkuy	កៅអី/កន្លែងអង្គុយ

How much is a ticket to ...?
  'samboht yohn hawh teuv ...   សំបុត្រយន្តហោះទៅ...ថ្លៃប៉ុន្មាន?
  th'lay pohnmaan?

Please give me two tickets.
sohm ao-y samboht pii   សូមឱ្យសំបុត្រពីរ

Bus

bus   *laan ch'nual*   ឡានឈ្នួល

Where is the nearest bus
station?
   kuhnlaing laan ch'nual   កន្លែងឡានឈ្នួលនៅឯណា?
   neuv ai naa?
What time does the ... bus
leave?
   laan ch'nual johng krao-y   ឡានឈ្នួល ...ចេញទៅម៉ោងប៉ុន្មាន?
   jein teuv maong pohnmaan?
Could you let me know when
we arrive at ...?
   sohm brahp kh'nyohm neuv   សូមប្រាប់ខ្ញុំនៅពេលយើងដល់...
   pehl yæng dawl ...
I want to get off (here)!
   kh'nyohm jawng joh (tii nih)!   ខ្ញុំចង់ចុះ (ទីនេះ)!

Train

train   *roht plæng*   រថភ្លើង

Is this seat free?
   kuhnlaing nih damne te?   កន្លែងនេះទំនេរទេ?
This seat is taken.
   kuhnlaing nih awt damne te   កន្លែងនេះអត់ទំនេរទេ
What station is this?
   nih jia s'thaanii naa?   នេះជាស្ថានីយណា?
What is the next station?
   bawntoap pii nih keu   បន្ទាប់ពីនេះគឺស្ថានីយអ្វី?
   s'thaanii ei?

Taxi

taxi	*tahk sii*	តាក់ស៊ី

Please take me to ...	*sohm juun*	សូមជូនខ្ញុំទៅ ...
	kh'nyohm teuv ...	
this address	*aadreh/*	អាសយដ្ឋាននេះ
	aasayathaan nih	
the airport	*wial yohn hawh*	វាលយន្តហោះ

How much is it to ...?
teuv ... th'lay pohnmaan? ទៅ...ថ្លៃប៉ុន្មាន?
That's too much!
th'lay pek! ថ្លៃពេក!

Instructions

Here is fine, thank you.
chohp neuv tii nih kaw baan ឈប់នៅទីនេះក៏បាន
The next street, please.
teuv phleuv muy tiat ទៅផ្លូវមួយទៀត
Continue!
teuv mohk tiat! ទៅមុខទៀត!

Please slow down.
sohm bawntaw-y l'beuan សូមបន្ថយល្បឿន
Please hurry.
sohm prawnyap bawnteht សូមប្រញាប់បន្តិច

Please wait here.
sohm rohng jam neuv tii nih សូមរង់ចាំនៅទីនេះ
I'll be right back.
kh'nyohm mao wein eileuv hao-y ខ្ញុំមកវិញឥឡូវហើយ

Useful Words & Phrases

The (train) is ...   *roht plæng...*   រថភ្លើង...
  delayed   *mao yeut*   មកយឺត
  cancelled   *treuv ph'aak*   ត្រូវផ្អាក

How long does the trip to ... take?
  twæ damnaa-æ teuv ... awh   ធ្វើដំណើរទៅ...អស់ប៉ុន្មានម៉ោង?
  pohnmaan maong?
I want to get off at ...
  kh'nyohm jawng joh neuv ...   ខ្ញុំចង់ចុះនៅ...
I am lost.
  kh'nyohm wohngweng phleuv   ខ្ញុំវង្វេងផ្លូវ
Where can I hire a bicycle?
  ke mian gawng jual neuv   តើមានកង់ជួលនៅឯណា?
  ai naa?
Where are we now?
  eileuv yæng neuv kuhnlaing   ឥឡូវយើងនៅកន្លែងណា?
  naa?
Where is the restroom?
  bantohp tuhk neuv ai naa?   បន្ទប់ទឹកនៅឯណា?

Accommodation
Finding Accommodation

Where is a ...?   *... neuv ai naa?*   ...នៅឯណា?
  hotel   *sahnthaakia/ohtail*   សណ្ឋាគារ/អូតែល
  cheap hotel   *sahnthaakia/*   សណ្ឋាគារ/អូតែលថោក
    ohtail thaok

I've already found a hotel.
  kh'nyohm mian ohtail hao-y   ខ្ញុំមានអូតែលហើយ
I'm staying at ...
  kh'nyohm snahk neuv ...   ខ្ញុំស្នាក់នៅ...

What is the address?
 aasayathaan nih neuv ai naa?   អាសយដ្ឋាននេះនៅឯណា?
Could you write down the
address, please?
 sohm sawse aasayathaan   សូមសរសេរអាសយដ្ឋានឱ្យខ្ញុំ
 ao-y kh'nyohm

Checking In

Do you have a room?
 niak mian bantohp tohmne te?   អ្នកមានបន្ទប់ទំនេរទេ?

I'd like a room ...	*kh'nyohm sohm*	ខ្ញុំសុំបន្ទប់...
	bantohp ...	
for one person	*samruhp muy niak*	សំរាប់មួយនាក់
for two people	*samruhp pii niak*	សំរាប់ពីរនាក់
with a bathroom	*dail mian bantohp tuhk*	ដែលមានបន្ទប់ទឹក
with a fan	*dail mian dawnghahl*	ដែលមានកង្ហារ
with a window	*dail mian bawng-uit*	ដែលមានបង្អួច

I'm going to stay for ...	*kh'nyohm nuhng snahk tii nih ...*	ខ្ញុំនឹងស្នាក់ទីនេះ...
one day	*muy th'ngay*	មួយថ្ងៃ
one week	*muy aatuht*	មួយអាទិត្យ

How much does it cost per day?
 damlay muy th'ngay pohnmaan?   តំលៃមួយថ្ងៃប៉ុន្មាន?
Does the price include breakfast?
 damlay bantohp khuht teang   តំលៃបន្ទប់គិតទាំងអស់ពេលព្រឹកឬ?
 m'hohp pel pruhk reu?
Can I see the room?
 kh'nyohm sohm mæl bantohp   ខ្ញុំសុំមើលបន្ទប់បានទេ?
 baan te?

I don't like this room.
  kh'nyohm muhn johl juht
  bantohp nih te
ខ្ញុំមិនចូលចិត្តបន្ទប់នេះទេ

Do you have a better room?
  niak mian bantohp l'aw
  jiang nih te?
អ្នកមានបន្ទប់ល្អជាងនេះទេ?

I'll take this room.
  kh'nyohm yohk bantohp nih
ខ្ញុំយកបន្ទប់នេះ

I'm not sure how long I'm
staying.
  kh'nyohm muhn duhng thaa
  kh'nyohm nuhng snahk
  pohnmaan th'ngay te
ខ្ញុំមិនដឹងថាខ្ញុំនឹងស្នាក់ប៉ុន្មានថ្ងៃទេ

Requests & Complaints

My room needs to be cleaned.
  bantohp kh'nyohm treuv
  kaa sam-aat
បន្ទប់ខ្ញុំត្រូវការសំអាត

I can't open the door/window.
  kh'nyohm baok t'wia/
  bawng-uit muhn baan
ខ្ញុំបើកទ្វារ/បង្អួចមិនបាន

I've locked myself out.
  kh'nyohm plet sao
  kh'nohng bantohp
ខ្ញុំភ្លេចសោរក្នុងបន្ទប់

The toilet is broken.
  bawng-kohn khow-it hao-y
បង្គន់ខូចហើយ

Can you get it fixed?
  niak aa-it juah jul wia
  baan te?
អ្នកអាចជួសជុលវាបានទេ?

The room smells.
  bantohp mian kluhn muhn l'aw បន្ទប់មានក្លិនមិនល្អ

It's too noisy.
  bantohp th'lawng pek   បន្ទប់ផ្ដុំពេក

Where can I wash my clothes?
  kh'nyohm aa-it baok khao av   ខ្ញុំអាចបោកខោអាវនៅកន្លែងណា?
  neuv kuhnlaing naa?

Please wash these clothes for me.
  sohm baok khao av nih   សូមបោកខោអាវនេះឱ្យខ្ញុំ
  ao-y kh'nyohm

When will they be ready?
  hao-y angkal?   ហើយអង្កាល់?

Can I use the telephone?
  kh'nyohm aa-it braa-æ   ខ្ញុំអាចប្រើទូរស័ព្ទបានទេ?
  turasahp baan te?

Checking Out

I'm leaving this hotel.
  kh'nyohm jaak jein pii   ខ្ញុំចាកចេញពីអូតែលនេះហើយ
  ohtail nih hao-y

Please prepare my/our bill.
  sohm kuht luy   សូមគិតលុយ

Call me a taxi please.
  sohm juay hav taksii mao   សូមជួយហៅតាក់ស៊ីមក

Can I pay by ...?   *kh'nyohm aa-it*   ខ្ញុំអាចប្រើ...បានទេ?
                     braa-æ ... baan te?

  credit card   *kaad kredit*   កាតក្រេឌីត
  travellers' cheque *saik*   សែក

NB credit cards are rarely accepted in Cambodia, and traveller's cheques must usually be cashed before using.

Can I leave my things here until ...?

kh'nyohm aa-it ph'nyaa-æ		ខ្ញុំអាចផ្ញើរវ៉ាន់របស់
eiwuhn r'bawh kh'nyohm		ខ្ញុំនៅទីនេះដល់...បានទេ?
neuv tii nih dawl ... baan te?		

| this afternoon | l'ngiak nih | ល្ងាចនេះ |
| this evening | yohp nih | យប់នេះ |

Useful Words

air-con	masuhn trawjeahk	ម៉ាស៊ីនត្រជាក់
clean	s'aat	ស្អាត
dirty	krawkhwuhk/kuhkrik	ក្រខ្វក់
electricity	phlæng/phlæng ahkisahnii	ភ្លើង /ភ្លើងអគ្គិសនី
garden	suan ch'baa	សួនច្បារ
key/lock	kown sao/sao	កូនសោរ /សោរ
lift	johndaa-æ yown	ជណ្ដើរយន្ត
noisy	th'lawng/uu-aw	ថ្លង់ /អ៊ូអរ
pillow	kh'nao-y	ខ្នើយ
quiet	s'nguht	ស្ងាត
rent (v)	jual	ជួល
sheet	kamraal puuk	កំរាលពូក
soap	sabuu	សាប៊ូ
soap (detergent)	sabuu masaav	សាប៊ូម្សៅ
towel	kuhnsaing	កន្សែង
water	tuhk	ទឹក

Around Town

Where is a ...?	... neuv ai naa?	...នៅឯណា?
bank	th'niakia	ធនាគារ
consulate	kohng sul	កុងស៊ុល
embassy	s'thaantuut	ស្ថានទូត
hotel	sahnthaakia/ohtail	សណ្ឋាគារ/អូតែល
police station	poh polih/s'thaanii nohkohbaal	ប៉ុស្ត៍ប៉ូលីស / ស្ថានីយនគរបាល
post office	praisuhnii	ប្រៃសណីយ
public telephone	turasahp saathiaranah	ទូរស័ព្ទសាធារណៈ
public toilet	bawngkohn saathiaranah	បង្គន់សាធារណៈ

At the Post Office

I want to buy ...	kh'nyohm jawng tein ...	ខ្ញុំចង់ទិញ...
postcards	kaad postal	កាតប៉ុស្តាល់
stamps	taim	តែមប្រិ៍

I want to send a ...	kh'nyohm jawng ph'nyaa-æ ...	ខ្ញុំចង់ផ្ញើ...
letter	samboht	សំបុត្រ
parcel	kuhnjawp	កញ្ចប់
telegram	turalek/telegraam	ទូរលេខ/តេលេក្រាម
fax	faek/turasaa	ហ្វាក់/ទូរសារ

Please send it by ...	sohm ph'nyaa-æ wia ...	សូមផ្ញើវា...
airmail	taam yohn hawh	តាមយន្តហោះ
surface mail	taam k'pal tuhk	តាមកប៉ាល់ទឹក

envelope	*sraom samboht*	ស្រោមសំបុត្រ
mailbox	*pra-awp praisuhnii*	ប្រអប់ប្រៃសណីយ
postage	*damlay taim*	តំលៃតែមប្រើ

Telephone

I want to call ...
    *kh'nyohm jawng turasahp
    teuv ...*
    ខ្ញុំចង់ទូរស័ព្ទទៅ...

The number is ...
    lek turasahp keu ...
    លេខទូរស័ព្ទគឺ...

I want to speak for three minutes.
    *kh'nyohm jawng niyay tai
    bei niatii*
    ខ្ញុំចង់និយាយតែបីនាទី

How much does a three-minute
call cost?
    *turasahp teuv bei niatii treuv
    awh pohnmaan?*
    ទូរស័ព្ទទៅបីនាទីត្រូវអស់ប៉ុន្មាន?

I've been cut off.
    turasahp dait kh'sai
    ទូរស័ព្ទដាចាច់ខ្សែ

The line is busy.
    turasahp kampohng joab r'wuhl
    ទូរស័ព្ទកំពុងជាប់រវល់

May I speak to ...?
    sohm juab jia muy ...
    សុំជួបជាមួយ...

Wrong number.
    hav j'ralawm lek
    ហៅច្រឡំលេខ

Hello, is ... there?
    hello, ... neuv te?
    ហេឡូ ...នៅទេ?

Yes, he/she is here.
    baat, koat neuv
    បាទ គាត់នៅ

One moment, (please).
    sohm jam muy plaet
    សូមចាំមួយភ្លែត

KHMER

At the Bank

I want to change ...   *kh'nyohm jawng dow...*   ខ្ញុំចង់ដូរ...
   US $ *dolaa amerik*   ដុល្លាអាមេរិក
   Australian $ *dolaa owstraalii*   ដុល្លាអូស្រ្តាលី
   money   *luy*   លុយ
   a travellers' cheque   *saik*   សែក

Where can I cash a travellers'
cheque?
   kh'nyohm aa-it dow saik   ខ្ញុំអាចដូរសែកនៅឯណា?
   neuv ai naa?

What is the exchange rate for
US dollars?
   muy dolaa dow baan   មួយដុល្លាដូរបានប៉ុន្មាន?
   pohnmaan?

What time do banks open?
   th'niakia baok maong   ធនាគារបើកម៉ោងប៉ុន្មាន?
   pohnmaan?

Can I transfer money here
from my bank?
   kh'nyohm aa-it p'te luy pii   ខ្ញុំអាចផ្ទេរលុយពី
   th'niakia kh'nyohm mao nih   ធនាគារខ្ញុំមកនេះបានទេ?
   baan te?

How long will it take to
arrive?
   wia treuv sii r'yeah pel   វាត្រូវស៊ីរយៈពេលប៉ុន្មានទើបមកដល់?
   pohnmaan tæp mao dawl?

Has any money arrived for me?
   mian luy mao dawl samrahb   មានលុយមកដល់សំរាប់ខ្ញុំទេ?
   kh'nyohm te?

Sightseeing

Where is the Ministry of Tourism?
krawsuang tesajaw neuv ai naa?   ក្រសួងទេសចរណ៍នៅឯណា?

How far is the ...?
... ch'ngaay pohnmaan?   ... ឆ្ងាយប៉ុន្មាន?

I am going to the ...
kh'nyohm teuv ...   ខ្ញុំទៅ ...

I am looking for the ...
kh'nyohm rohk ...   ខ្ញុំរក ...

What time does it open?
wia baok maong pohnmaan?   វាបើកម៉ោងប៉ុន្មាន?

What time does it close?
wia buht maong pohnmaan?   វាបិទម៉ោងប៉ុន្មាន?

Do you have a local map?
niak mian phain tii samruhp   អ្នកមានផែនទីសំរាប់តំបន់នេះទេ?
tambawn nih te?

May I take photographs?
kh'nyohm aa-it thawt ruup   ខ្ញុំអាចថតរូបបានទេ?
baan te?

May I take your photograph?
kh'nyohm aa-it thawt ruup   ខ្ញុំអាចថតរូបអ្នកបានទេ?
niak baan te?

I'll send you a copy.
kh'nyohm nuhng ph'nyaa-æ   ខ្ញុំនឹងផ្ញើមួយសន្លឹកឱ្យអ្នក
muy suhnluhk ao-y niak

Please take a photo of me.
sohm ao-y niak thawt ruup   សូមឱ្យអ្នកថតរូបខ្ញុំ
kh'nyohm

bookshop	*hahng luak siew pheuv*	ហាងលក់សៀវភៅ
cinema	*rowng kohn*	រោងកុន

market	*p'saa*	ផ្សារ
museum	*saarahmohntii*	សារមន្ទី
park	*suan*	សួន
restaurant	*resturaan/ phowjuhniiyathaan*	ភោជនីយដ្ឋាន
temple	*wawt*	វត្ត
theatre	*rowng l'khaon*	រោងល្ខោន

Paperwork

Ministry of Tourism	*krawsuang tesajaw*	ក្រសួងទេសចរណ៍
Ministry of Foreign Affairs	*krawsuang kaa bawrateh*	ក្រសួងការបរទេស
Ministry of the Interior	*krawsuang mahaa p'tey*	ក្រសួងមហាផ្ទៃ
name	*ch'muah*	ឈ្មោះ
address	*aadreh/aasayathaan*	អាសយដ្ឋាន
date of birth	*th'ngay khai kamnaot*	ថ្ងៃខែកំណើត
place of birth	*tii kuhnlaing kamnaot*	ទីកន្លែងកំណើត
age	*aayu*	អាយុ
sex	*phet*	ភេទ
nationality	*suhnjiat*	សញ្ជាតិ
race	*johnjiat*	ជនជាតិ
religion	*sasanaa*	សាសនា
profession	*wijia jiiweah*	វិជ្ជាជីវៈ
reason for travel	*mulahet twæ damnaa-æ*	មូលហេតុធ្វើដំណើរ

marital status	*s'thaanaphiap kruasaa*	ស្ថានភាពគ្រួសារ
single	*neuv liw*	នៅលីវ
married	*riap kaa hao-y*	រៀបការហើយ
divorced	*leng kh'nia*	លែងគ្នា
widow	*me mai*	មេម៉ាយ
widower	*puah mai*	ពោះម៉ាយ
identification	*buhn samkoal kh'luan*	បណ្ណសំគាល់ខ្លួន
	attahsuhnyianabuhn	អត្តសញ្ញាណបណ្ណ
passport number	*lek likhuht ch'lawng dain*	លេខលិខិតឆ្លងដែន
visa	*wisaa/tithaakaa*	វីសា/ទិដ្ឋាការ
birth certificate	*buhn kamnaot*	បណ្ណកំណើត
driving licence	*buhn baok baw*	បណ្ណបើកបរ
customs	*koy*	គយ
immigration	*aandao praweh*	អន្តោប្រវេសន៍
purpose of visit	*kowl bamnawng mao*	គោលបំណងមក
	dawl srawk kh'mai	ដល់ស្រុកខ្មែរ
holiday	*daa-æ leng*	ដើរលេង
business	*aajiiwakam*	អាជីវកម្ម
visiting relatives	*juab sait nyiat*	ជួបសាច់ញាតិ

In the Country
Weather
What's the weather like?
   thiataakah mait teuv?   ធាតុអាកាសម៉េចទៅ?

It's ...	wia ...	វា...
cloudy	mian pohpohk j'raa-œn	មានពពកច្រើន
cold	trawjeak	ត្រជាក់
flooding	leit tuhk	លិចទឹក
hot	k'dav	ក្តៅ
humid	s'oh	សួះ
raining heavily	mian phliang khluhng	មានភ្លៀងខ្លាំង
raining lightly	mian phliang teht/ r'lam	មានភ្លៀងតិច/ លើម
windy	mian k'shawl khluhng	មានខ្យល់ខ្លាំង

cloud	pohpohk	ពពក
dry season	khai bruhng	ខែប្រាំង
earth	dei	ដី
fog	ahp	អ័ព្រ
moon	khai	ខែ
rain	phliang	ភ្លៀង
rainy season	khai phliang	ខែភ្លៀង
storm	pyuh	ព្យុះ
sun	preah aatuht	ព្រះអាទិត្យ

Geographical Terms

beach	ch'ne samoht	ឆ្នេរសមុទ្រ
bridge	spian	ស្ពាន
cave	ruung ph'nohm	រូងភ្នំ
forest	prey	ព្រៃ

hill	*tual*	ទួល
island	*kawh*	កោះ
lake	*buhng*	បឹង
mountain	*ph'nohm*	ភ្នំ
plain	*wial*	វាល
river	*tohnle*	ទន្លេ
sea	*samoht*	សមុទ្រ
valley	*j'rolohng*	ជ្រលង
waterfall	*tuhk chuu*	ទឹកជ្រោះ

Flora & Agriculture

agriculture	*kasikam*	កសិកម្ម
coconut palm	*daa-œm downg*	ដើមដូង
corn	*powt*	ពោត
firewood	*oh*	ឧស
flower	*ph'kaa*	ផ្កា
harvest (verb)	*j'rowt kaht*	ច្រូតកាត់
irrigation	*kaa bawnghow tuhk*	ការបង្ហូរទឹក
leaf	*sluhk chœ*	ស្លឹកឈើ
planting (vegetables)	*kaa dam doh*	ការដាំដុះ
planting (rice)	*stuung*	ស្ទូង
rice field	*wial srai*	វាលស្រែ
sugar cane	*ampeuv*	អំពៅ
tobacco	*th'nam juak*	ថ្នាំជក់

Fauna

| ant | *srawmao-it* | ស្រមោច |
| bird | *jaap/sat slaap* | ចាប/ សត្វស្លាប |

cat	*ch'maa*	ឆ្មា
chicken	*moan*	មាន់
cow	*kow*	គោ
crocodile	*krawpœ*	ក្រពើ
dog	*ch'gay*	ឆ្កែ
fish	*trei*	ត្រី
fly	*ruy*	រុយ
horse	*seh*	សេះ
leech	*ch'læng*	ឈ្លើង
monkey	*swaa*	ស្វា
mosquito	*muh*	មូស
pig	*j'ruuk*	ជ្រូក
snake	*puah*	ពស់
spider	*ping piang*	ពីងពាង

KHMER

Camping

camping	*kaa bawh johmrohm*	ការបោះជំរំ
camping ground	*kuhnlaing bawh johmrohm*	កន្លែងបោះជំរំ
stove	*jœng kraan*	ជើងក្រាន
tent	*tawng*	តង់

Useful Words & Phrases

Is it safe to swim here?
   hail tukk neuv tii nih mian sohwatthaphiap reu te?　　ហែលទឹកនៅទីនេះមានសុវត្ថិភាពឬទេ?

Where is the nearest village?
   mian phum neuv juht nih te?　　មានភូមិនៅជិតនេះទេ?

Do I need a guide?
kh'nyohm treuv kaa niak   ខ្ញុំត្រូវការអ្នកនាំផ្លូវទេ?
noam phleuv te?
Is this path safe to walk on?
phleuv nih mian sohwatthaphiap   ផ្លូវនេះមានសុវត្ថិភាពដែរឬទេ?
dai reu te?
Are there any landmines in this area?
neuv m'dohm nih mian miin   នៅម្ដុំនេះមានមីនឬទេ?
reu te?

backpack	*krawbowp spiay*	ក្របូបស្ពាយ
compass	*trei wisai*	ត្រីវិស័យ
diving	*kaa muit tuhk*	ការមុជទឹក
fishing	*kaa stuit trei*	ការស្ទូចត្រី
hunting	*kaa prian*	ការព្រាន
map	*phain tii*	ផែនទី
mountain climbing	*kaa laong ph'nohm*	ការឡើងភ្នំ
penknife	*kambuht tow-it*	កាំបិតតូច
rope	*kh'sai*	ខ្សែ
swimming	*kaa hail tuhk*	ការហែលទឹក
torch (flashlight)	*puhl*	ពិល

KHMER

Food

Where is a ...?	*... neuv ai naa?*	...នៅឯណា?
cheap restaurant	*haang baay/*	ហាងបាយថោក
	resturaan thaok	
restaurant	*resturaan/*	ភោជនីយដ្ឋាន
	phowjuhniiyathaan	

| food stall | kuhnlaing luak m'howp | កន្លែងលក់ម្ហូប |
| market | p'saa | ផ្សារ |

breakfast	m'howp pel pruhk	ម្ហូបពេលព្រឹក
lunch	m'howp pel th'ngay trawng	ម្ហូបពេលថ្ងៃត្រង់
dinner	m'howp pel l'ngiak	ម្ហូបពេលល្ងាច

Eating Out

We'd like a table for five,
please.
> *yæng treuv kaa toh samruhp*   យើងត្រូវការតុសំរាប់ប្រាំនាក់
> *bram niak*

Please bring ...	sohm yohk ... mao	សូមយក...មក
the menu	muhnui/banjii mohk m'howp	ម៉ឺនុយ /បញ្ជីម្ហូប
a glass of water	tuhk muy kaiw	ទឹកមួយកែវ

I can't eat ...	kh'nyohm tawm ...	ខ្ញុំតម...
meat	sait	សាច់
hot (spicy) food	m'howp huhl	ម្ហូបហិរ

No MSG please.
> *sohm kohm dahk bii jeng*   សូមកុំដាក់បីចេង
I'm a vegetarian.
> *kh'nyohm tawm sait*   ខ្ញុំតមសាច់
Please bring the bill.
> *sohm kuht luy*   សូមគិតលុយ

KHMER

Typical Cambodian Dishes

Cambodian meat salad	*phlia*	ផ្លា
spicy sour soup	*samlaw m'juu kreuang*	សម្លម្ជូរគ្រឿង
sour soup	*samlaw m'juu*	សម្លម្ជូរ
spicy beef	*sait kow chaa kreuang*	សាច់គោឆាគ្រឿង
spring rolls	*jaa yaw*	ចាយ៉
pickled vegetables	*j'ruak*	ជ្រក់
crispy rice with spicy sauce	*baay k'dang*	បាយក្ដាំង
fried bread with meat (Cambodian pizza)	*nohm pang jian*	នំប៉័ងជៀន
fermented fish paste (a rural favorite)	*prawhohk*	ប្រហុក
beef soup in clay pot (popular in Phnom Penh)	*soup kow ch'nuhng dei*	ស៊ុបគោឆ្នាំងដី
Yaa hon (like beef soup but with spicy peanut sauce broth)	*yaa hawn*	យ៉ាហន

At the Market

How much is this?
   nih th'lay pohnmaan? — នេះថ្លៃប៉ុន្មាន?
How much is a kg of ...?
   ... muy kilo th'lay pohnmaan? — ...មួយគីឡូថ្លៃប៉ុន្មាន?
A kg of ..., please.
   sohm ... muy kilo — សុំ...មួយគីឡូ
I don't want that one.
   kh'nyohm muhn treuv kaa nuh te — ខ្ញុំមិនត្រូវការនោះទេ
That one please.
   sohm ao-y kh'nyohm aa nooh — សុំឱ្យខ្ញុំអានោះ

Meat

beef	*sait kow*	សាច់គោ
chicken	*sait moan*	សាច់មាន់
duck	*sait tia*	សាច់ទា
goat	*sait pohpae*	សាច់ពពៃ
meat	*sait*	សាច់

Seafood

crab	*k'daam*	ក្ដាម
freshwater fish	*trei tuhk saap*	ត្រីទឹកសាប
lobster	*bawngkawng*	បង្កង
mussels	*krohm*	គ្រុំ
oysters	*ngiw*	ងៀវ
prawn/shrimp	*bawngkia*	បង្គា
saltwater fish	*trei samoht*	ត្រីសមុទ្រ
seafood	*kreuang samoht*	គ្រឿងសមុទ្រ
squid	*meuk*	មឹក

Vegetables

beans	*suhndaik*	សណ្ដែក
cabbage	*spey*	ស្ពៃ
carrot	*karoht*	ការ៉ុត
cauliflower	*ph'kaa spey*	ផ្កាស្ពៃ
corn	*powt*	ពោត
cucumber	*trawsawk*	ត្រសក់
eggplant	*trawp*	ត្រប់
mushrooms	*p'suht*	ផ្សិត
onion	*kh'tuhm baraang*	ខ្ទឹមបារាំង

potato	*damlowng*	ដំឡូង
pumpkin	*l'peuv*	ល្ពៅ
tomato	*peng pawh*	ប៉េងប៉ោះ
vegetables	*buhnlai*	បន្លែ

Fruit

apples	*paom*	ប៉ោម
banana	*jek*	ចេក
coconut	*downg*	ដូង
durian	*thuuren*	ធ្ទុរេន
jackfruit	*kh'nao*	ខ្នុរ
lemon	*krow-it*	ក្រូច
mangosteen	*mangkoht*	មង្ឃុត
mango	*swaay*	ស្វាយ
orange	*krow-it pow sat*	ក្រូចពោធិសាត់
peanuts	*suhndaik dei*	សណ្តែកដី
pineapple	*m'noah*	ម្នាស់
starfruit	*speu*	ស្ពឺ
milkfruit	*phlai tuhk dawh kow*	ផ្លែទឹកដោះគោ

Spices & Condiments

chilli	*m'teh huhl*	ម្ទេសហិរ
cinnamon	*chœ aim*	ឈើអែម
curry	*kaarii*	ការី
fish sauce	*tuhk trei*	ទឹកត្រី
fish paste	*prahok*	ប្រហុក
garlic	*k'tuhm saw*	ខ្ទឹមស
ginger	*kh'nyei*	ខ្ញី
oil	*preng*	ប្រេង
pepper	*m'ret*	ម្រេច

salt	*ambuhl*	អំបិល
soy sauce	*tuhk sii iw*	ទឹកស៊ីអ៊ីវ
sweet soy sauce	*tuhk sii iw p'aim*	ទឹកស៊ីអ៊ីវផ្អែម
sugar	*skaw*	ស្ករ
turmeric	*r'miat*	រមៀត
vinegar	*tuhk kh'meh*	ទឹកខ្មេះ

Drinks

The names of most drinks are preceded by the word 'water' *(tuhk)*.

Cold Drinks

alcohol	*sraa*	ស្រា
beer	*bia*	ប៊ីយែរ
boiled water	*tuhk ch'uhn*	ទឹកឆ្អិន
plain water	*tuhk toamadaa*	ទឹកធម្មតា
citrus juice	*tuhk krow-it pow sat*	ទឹកក្រូចពោធិសាត់
coconut milk	*tuhk downg*	ទឹកដូង
milk	*tuhk dawh kow*	ទឹកដោះគោ
soft drinks	*tuhk drow-it*	ទឹកក្រូច

Hot Drinks

| coffee | *kaafe* | កាហ្វេ |
| tea | *tai* | តែ |

(with/without) milk	
(dahk/kohm dahk) tuhk	
dawh kow	ដាក់/កុំដាក់ទឹកដោះគោ
(with/without) sugar	
(dahk/kohm dahk) skaw	ដាក់/កុំដាក់ស្ករ

Shopping

Where is the ...?	... *neuv ai naa?*	...នៅឯណា?
bookshop	*hahng luak siew pheuv*	ហាងលក់សៀវភៅ
market	*p'saa*	ផ្សារ
tailor	*jiang kaht de*	ជាងកាត់ដេរ

Making a Purchase

How much is it?

nih th'lay pohnmaan?	នេះថ្លៃប៉ុន្មាន?

I'd like to buy ...	*kh'nyohm jawng tein ...*	ខ្ញុំចង់ទិញ...
that statue	*ruup jamlahk nuh*	រូបចំលាក់នោះ
this bottle	*dawp nih*	ដបនេះ
batteries	*th'maw*	ថ្ម
Cambodian scarves	*kramaa*	ក្រមា
mosquito net	*mung*	មុង
needle (sewing)	*m'juhl*	ម្ជុល
rope	*kh'sai*	ខ្សែ
sarong	*sarohng*	សារុង
scissors	*kuhntrai*	កន្ត្រៃ
shoelaces	*kh'sai s'baik jæng*	ខ្សែស្បែកជើង
silverware	*kreuang prahk*	គ្រឿងប្រាក់
thread	*ambawh de*	អំបោះដេរ
towel	*kuhnsaing*	កន្សែង

KHMER

Bargaining

Can I bargain?
kh'nyohm aa-it taw th'lay   ខ្ញុំអាចតថ្លៃបានទេ?
baan te?

That's too much.
th'lay pek   ថ្លៃពេក

I don't have much money.
kh'nyohm mian luy teht tuu-it   មានលុយតិចតួច

Please lower the price.
sohm joh th'lay   សូមចុះថ្លៃ

I'll give you ...
kh'nyohm ao-y ...   ខ្ញុំឱ្យ...

No more than ...
muhn lœh pii ...   មិនលើសពី..

What's your best price?
niak dait pohnmaan?   អ្នកដាច់ប៉ុន្មាន?

Souvenirs

Cambodian scarves	*kramaa*	ក្រមា
gold	*miah*	មាស
handicraft	*sipakam*	សិប្បកម្ម
jewellery	*kreuang ahlahngkaa*	គ្រឿងអលង្ការ
leather	*s'baik kow*	ស្បែកគោ
masks	*mohk*	មុខ
material (cloth)	*krawnaht*	ក្រណាត់
paintings	*ruup kohmnuu*	រូបគំនូរ
pottery	*ch'nuhng*	ឆ្នាំង
silver	*prahk*	ប្រាក់

souvenir	*suuvuhnir/anusawarii*	អនុស្សាវរីយ៍
statue	*ruup jamluhk*	រូបចំលាក់
stone carvings	*ruup jamluhk th'maw*	រូបចំលាក់ថ្ម
woodcarving	*ruup jamluhk chœ*	រូបចំលាក់ឈើ

Toiletries

baby powder	*m'sav trawjeak*	ម្សៅត្រជាក់
condoms	*sraom ahnaamai*	ស្រោមអនាម័យ
contraceptive	*th'nam kaa pia kohm ao-y mian kown*	ថ្នាំការពារកុំឱ្យមានកូន
moisturiser	*kraim s'baik*	ក្រែមស្បែក
mosquito repellent	*th'nam kaa pia muh*	ថ្នាំការពារមុះ
sanitary napkins	*samlei ahnaamai*	សំឡីអនាម័យ
shampoo	*sabuu kawk sawk*	សាប៊ូកក់សក់
shaving cream	*kraim samruhp kao pohk moat*	ក្រែមសំរាប់កោរពុកមាត់
sunblock cream	*kraim kaa pia pohnleu th'ngay*	ក្រែមការពារពន្លឺថ្ងៃ
toilet paper	*krawdah ahnaamai*	ក្រដាស់អនាម័យ
toothbrush	*j'rah doh th'mein*	ច្រាសដុះធ្មេញ
toothpaste	*th'nam doh th'mein*	ថ្នាំដុះធ្មេញ

Photography

I'd like some film for this camera.

    kh'nyohm treuv kaa fil samruhp camaraa nih   ខ្ញុំត្រូវការហ្វីលសំរាប់កាម៉េរ៉ានេះ

When will it be ready?
 wia hao-y awngkal?   វារហើយអង្កាល់?

film	*fil*	ហ្វិល
camera	*camaraa/aaparei*	កាមេរ៉ា /អាប៉ារ៉ុ
B&W film	*fil saw kh'mav*	ហ្វិលសខ្មៅ
colour film	*fil poa*	ហ្វិលពណ៌

Smoking

cigarettes	*baarei*	បារី
matches	*chæ kuh*	ឈើគុស
tobacco	*th'nam juak*	ថ្នាំជក់

A packet of cigarettes, please.
 sohm baarei muy kuhnjawp   សុំបារីមួយកញ្ចប់
Do you have a light?
 niak mian phlæng te?   អ្នកមានភ្លើងទេ?
Please don't smoke.
 sohm kohm juak baarei   សូមកុំជក់បារី

Sizes & Comparisons

big	*thohm*	ធំ
bigger	*thohm jiang*	ធំជាង
biggest	*thohm bamphoht*	ធំបំផុត
too big	*thohm pek*	ធំពេក
very big	*thohm nah*	ធំណាស់
small	*tow-it*	តូច
smaller	*tow-it jiang*	តូចជាង

Health

Where is a ...?	... *neuv ai naa?*	...នៅឯណា?
dentist	*paet th'mein*	ពេទ្យធ្មេញ
doctor	*kruu paet*	គ្រូពេទ្យ
hospital	*mohntrii paet*	មន្ទីរពេទ្យ
medicine	*th'nam*	ថ្នាំ
pharmacy	*kuhnlaing luak th'nam/*	កន្លែងលក់ថ្នាំ/
	ohsawt s'thaan	ឱសថស្ថាន

At the Doctor

I am ill.
  kh'nyohm cheu — ខ្ញុំឈឺ
My ... hurts
  ... r'bawh kh'nyohm cheu — ...របស់ខ្ញុំឈឺ

I feel nauseous.
  kh'nyohm jawng k'uat — ខ្ញុំចង់ក្អួត
I feel weak.
  kh'nyohm awh kamlahng — ខ្ញុំអស់កំលាំង
I keep vomiting.
  kh'nyohm k'uat j'raa-œn — ខ្ញុំក្អួតច្រើន
I feel dizzy.
  kh'nyohm wuhl mohk — ខ្ញុំវិលមុខ

I've been bitten by something.
  mian saht kam kh'nyohm — មានសត្វខាំខ្ញុំ
I'm having trouble breathing.
  kh'nyohm pibaak dawk — ខ្ញុំពិបាកដកដង្ហើម
  dawnghaom

Ailments

Note that the general word for disease is *rowk*, and the general word for sick or pain is *cheu;* if you know the name of your ailment, just put *rowk* before it.

allergy	*rowk muhn treuv thiat*	រោគមិនត្រូវជាតុ
asthma	*rowk huht*	រោគហឺត
cholera	*aasawnarowk*	អាសន្នរោគ
cold	*p'daa saay*	ផ្តាសាយ
constipation	*tohl lia mohk*	ទល់លាមក
diarrhoea	*rowk joh riak*	រោគចុះរាក
dysentery	*rowk mual*	រោគមូល
fever	*krohn/k'dav kh'luan*	ក្រន់/ក្តៅខ្លួន
flu	*krohn p'daa saay th'ngohn*	ក្រន់ផ្តាសាយធ្ងន់
food poisoning	*rowk howp m'howp kow-it*	រោគហូបម្ហូបខូច
gastroenteritis	*rowk r'liak krawpeah*	រោគរលាកក្រពះ
headache	*cheu k'baal*	ឈឺក្បាល
hepatitis	*rowk r'liak th'laom*	រោគរលាកថ្លើម
infection	*me rowk ch'lawng*	មេរោគឆ្លង
malaria	*krohn jain*	ក្រន់ចាញ់
rabies	*rowk ch'kai ch'kuat*	រោគឆ្កែឆ្កួត
sore throat	*cheu kaw*	ឈឺក
stomachache	*cheu puah*	ឈឺពោះ
sunburn	*jain th'ngay*	ចាញ់ថ្ងៃ
typhoid	*krohn puah wian*	ក្រន់ពោះវៀន
venereal disease	*rowk swaay*	រោគស្វាយ
worms	*pruun*	ព្រូន

Women's Health

Could I see a female doctor?
kh'nyohm aa-it juap kruu ខ្ញុំអាចជួបគ្រូពេទ្យដែលជាស្រីបានទេ?
paet dail jia srei baan te?

Could I see a doctor for females?
kh'nyohm aa-it juap paet ខ្ញុំអាចជួបពេទ្យស្រីបានទេ?
s'trei baan te?

I'm pregnant.
kh'nyohm mian p'tey puah ខ្ញុំមានផ្ទៃពោះ

I'm on the (contraceptive) pill.
kh'nyohm lep th'nam awt kown ខ្ញុំលេបថ្នាំអត់កូន

I haven't menstruated for ... weeks.
kh'nyohm awt mian r'deuv ... ខ្ញុំអត់មានរដូវ...អាទិត្យហើយ
aatuht hao-y

sanitary napkins
samlei ahnaamai សំឡីអនាម័យ

Specific Needs

I'm allergic to ... *kh'nyohm muhn* ខ្ញុំមិនត្រូវធាតុ...
treuv thiat...

   penicillin *penicillin* ប៉េនីស៊ីលីន
   antibiotics *awntiibiowtik* អង់ទីប៉ីយោទិក

I have a skin allergy.
kh'nyohm mian rowk s'baik ខ្ញុំមានរោគស្បែក

I have low/high blood
pressure.
kh'nyohm khwah chiam/lœh ខ្ញុំខ្វះឈាម/លើសឈាម
chiam

KHMER

I've been vaccinated.
    kh'nyohm baan jahk th'nam ខ្ញុំបានចាក់ថ្នាំការពាររោគហើយ
    kaa pia rowk hao-y

I have my own syringe.
    kh'nyohm mian siirahng muy ខ្ញុំមានស៊ីរាំងមួយរបស់ខ្ញុំផ្ទាល់
    r'bawh kh'nyohm p'toal

Please use this syringe.
    sohm braa-æ siirahng nih សូមប្រើស៊ីរាំងនេះ

I've had a blood test.
    ke mæl chiam kh'nyohm hao-y គេមើលឈាមខ្ញុំហើយ

I need a blood test.
    kh'nyohm treuv mæl chiam ខ្ញុំត្រូវមើលឈាម

I have health insurance.
    kh'nyohm mian awnsurahn ខ្ញុំមានអាងស៊ូរ៉ង់សុខភាព
    sokaphiap

Parts of the Body

arm/hand	*day*	ដៃ
back	*kh'nawng*	ខ្នង
ear	*trawjiak*	ត្រចៀក
eye	*ph'nek*	ភ្នែក
face	*mohk*	មុខ
finger	*m'riam day*	ម្រាមដៃ
head	*k'baal*	ក្បាល
heart	*beh downg*	បេះដូង
leg/foot	*jæng*	ជើង
mouth	*moat*	មាត់
muscle	*sait dohm*	សាច់ដុំ

nose	j'rawmoh	ច្រមុះ
skin	s'baik	ស្បែក
toes	m'riam jæng	ម្រាមជើង
tooth	th'mein	ធ្មេញ

At the Chemist
I need medicine for ...
> kh'nyohm treuv kaa
> th'nam samruhp...

ខ្ញុំត្រូវការថ្នាំសំរាប់...

How many times a day?
> kh'nyohm treuv lep pohnmaan
> dawng kh'nohng muy th'ngay?

ខ្ញុំត្រូវលេបប៉ុន្មានដងក្នុងមួយថ្ងៃ?

Take these three times a day.
> lep bei dawng kh'nohng
> muy th'ngay

លេបបីដងក្នុងមួយថ្ងៃ

antibiotics	awntiibiowtik	អង់ទីបីយោទិក
antiseptic	th'nam samlahp me rowk	ថ្នាំសំលាប់មេរោគ
aspirin	parasetamol	ប៉ារាសេតាម៉ុល
codeine	codiin	ខូឌីន
medicine	th'nam	ថ្នាំ
penicillin	penicillin	ប៉េនីស៊ីលីន
prescription	wijeah buhnjia	វេជ្ជបញ្ជា
quinine	kiiniin	គីនីន
sleeping pills	th'nam ng'nguy dek	ថ្នាំងងុយដេក
vitamins	viitaamiin	វីតាមីន

KHMER

Time & Dates
Telling the Time

The Khmers divide the day into five parts: morning *(pel pruhk)*, noon *(pel th'ngay trawng)*, afternoon *(pel r'sial)*, evening *(pel l'ngiat)* and night *(pel yohp)*. Asking the time is relatively straightforward, using the same word for 'How much/many' *(pohnmaan)* – literally, 'How many hours?', and answering with the number of hours and minutes. Many Khmers tend to be vague when asked the time, responding 'It's near X o'clock' rather than giving the exact number of minutes until the hour.

hour	*maong*	ម៉ោង
minute	*niatii/minut*	នាទី /មីនុត
second	*winiatii*	វិនាទី
half hour	*kuhnlah maong*	កន្លះម៉ោង

What time is it?
   eileuv nih maong pohnmaan?   ពេលវនេះម៉ោងប៉ុន្មាន?

It's three o'clock.
   maong bei   ម៉ោងបី

It's a quarter to four.
   maong bei saisuhp bram niatii   ម៉ោងបីសែសិបប្រាំនាទី

It's a quarter past four.
   maong buan dawp bram niatii   ម៉ោងបួនដប់ប្រាំនាទី

It's ten past three.
   maong bei dawp niatii   ម៉ោងបីដប់នាទី

It is ten to four.
   maong buan haasuhp niatii   ម៉ោងបួនហាសិបនាទ

o'clock	*maong* (lit: 'hour')	ម៉ោង
in the morning	*pel pruhk*	ពេលព្រឹក

in the afternoon	*pel r'sial*	ពេលរសៀល
in the evening	*pel l'ngiat*	ពេលល្ងាច
at night	*pel yohp*	ពេលយប់

Days of the Week

Names of the days are preceded by the word for 'day', *th'ngay.*

Monday	*th'ngay jahn*	ថ្ងៃចន្ទ
Tuesday	*th'ngay ahngkia*	ថ្ងៃអង្គារ
Wednesday	*th'ngay poht*	ថ្ងៃពុធ
Thursday	*th'ngay prohoah*	ថ្ងៃព្រហស្បតិ៍
Friday	*th'ngay sohk*	ថ្ងៃសុក្រ
Saturday	*th'ngay sav*	ថ្ងៃសៅរ៍
Sunday	*th'ngay aatuht*	ថ្ងៃអាទិត្យ

Months

Names of months are preceded by the word for 'month', *khai.* Many Khmers simply use the number of the month rather than the name, ie *khai bram*, 'month number five', for May.

January	*khai makaraa*	ខែមករា
February	*khai kohmpheah*	ខែកុម្ភៈ
March	*khai minia*	ខែមីនា
April	*khai mesaa*	ខែមេសា
May	*khai ohsaphia*	ខែឧសភា
June	*khai mithohnaa*	ខែមិថុនា
July	*khai kakadaa*	ខែកក្កដា
August	*khai seihaa*	ខែសីហា
September	*khai kanyaa*	ខែកញ្ញា

KHMER

October	*khai tohlaa*	ខែតុលា
November	*khai wijikaa*	ខែវិច្ឆិកា
December	*khai thanuu*	ខែធ្នូ

Present

today	*th'ngay nih*	ថ្ងៃនេះ
this morning	*pruhk nih*	ព្រឹកនេះ
this afternoon	*r'sial nih*	រសៀលនេះ
tonight	*yohp nih*	យប់នេះ
this week	*aatuht nih*	អាទិត្យនេះ
this month	*khai nih*	ខែនេះ
this year	*ch'nam nih*	ឆ្នាំនេះ
now/immediately	*eileuv nih*	ឥឡូវនេះ
just now	*th'mei th'mei nih*	ថ្មីៗនេះ

Past

The Khmer use several words to indicate the past, among them *mein* and *mun;* the former is used for recent periods of time, as in 'this morning' or 'a minute ago', while *mun* (meaning 'before') is used with events occurring in the more distant past, as in *ch'nam mun*, 'last year'. To indicate something done or finished, the word *hao-y* is generally spoken at the end of a sentence.

yesterday	*m'suhl mein*	ម្សិលមិញ
day before yesterday	*m'suhl m'ngay*	ម្សិលម្ងៃ
this morning (speaking later in the same day)	*pruhk mein*	ព្រឹកមិញ
yesterday morning	*pruhk m'suhl mein*	ព្រឹកម្សិលមិញ
this afternoon (speaking later in the same day)	*th'ngay mein*	ថ្ងៃមិញ

yesterday afternoon	*r'sial m'suhl mein*	រសៀលម្សិលមិញ
last night	*yohp mein*	យប់មិញ
last week	*aatuht mun*	អាទិត្យមុន
last month	*khai mun*	ខែមុន
last year	*ch'nam mun*	ឆ្នាំមុន

Future

tomorrow	*th'ngay s'aik*	ថ្ងៃស្អែក
tomorrow morning	*pruhk s'aik*	ព្រឹកស្អែក
tomorrow evening	*yohp s'aik*	យប់ស្អែក
day after tomorrow	*th'ngay khaan s'aik*	ថ្ងៃខានស្អែក
next week	*aatuht krao-y*	អាទិត្យក្រោយ
next month	*khai krao-y*	ខែក្រោយ
next year	*ch'nam krao-y*	ឆ្នាំក្រោយ
ago	*pii mun*	ពីមុន
already	*hao-y*	ហើយ
later	*neuv pel krao-y*	នៅពេលក្រោយ
after	*bawntoap pii*	បន្ទាប់ពី
not yet	*muhn toan*	មិនទាន់

During the Day

sunrise	*preah aatuht reah*	ព្រះអាទិត្យរះ
dawn	*pel proluhm*	ពេលព្រលឹម
noon	*pel th'ngay trawng*	ពេលថ្ងៃត្រង់
sunset	*th'ngay leit*	ថ្ងៃលិច
midnight	*maong dawp pii aatriat*	ម៉ោងដប់ពីរអាធ្រាត្រ
week	*aatuht*	អាទិត្យ
year	*ch'nam*	ឆ្នាំ

KHMER

Numbers

Khmers count in increments of five. Thus, after reaching the number five *(bram)*, the cycle begins again with the addition of one, ie *bram muy* ('five-one') is six, *bram pii* ('five-two') is seven, and so on to 10 *(dawp)*, when a new cycle begins. This system is a bit awkward at first (for example, 18 has three parts: 10, five, and three) but with practice it can be mastered.

You may be confused by a colloquial form of counting which reverses the word order for numbers between 10 and 20 and separates the two words with *duhn: pii duhn dawp* for 12, *bei duhn dawp* for 13, *bram buan duhn dawp* for 19, and so on. This form is often used in markets, so listen keenly.

Cardinal Numbers

0	*sown/zero*	សូន្យ
1	*muy*	មួយ
2	*pii*	ពីរ
3	*bei*	បី
4	*buan*	បួន
5	*bram*	ប្រាំ
6	*bram muy*	ប្រាំមួយ
7	*bram pii/bram puhl*	ប្រាំពីរ
8	*bram bei*	ប្រាំបី
9	*bram buan*	ប្រាំបួន
10	*dawp*	ដប់
11	*dawp muy*	ដប់មួយ
12	*dawp pii*	ដប់ពីរ
16	*dawp bram muy*	ដប់ប្រាំមួយ
20	*m'phei*	ម្ភៃ

KHMER

21	*m'phei muy*	ម្ភៃមួយ
30	*saamsuhp*	សាមសិប
40	*saisuhp*	សែសិប
100	*muy roy*	មួយរយ
1000	*muy poan*	មួយពាន់
a million	*muy lian*	មួយលាន

Ordinal Numbers

Ordinal numbers are formed by adding the prefix *tii* before the number. The adjective 'first', as in 'the first time', can be *tii muy* or *dambowng*.

1st	*tii muy*	ទីមួយ
2nd	*tii pii*	ទីពីរ
3rd	*tii bei*	ទីបី
4th	*tii buan*	ទីបួន
10th	*tii dawp*	ទីដប់

the first bus	*laan tii muy/*	ឡានទីមួយ/
	laan dambowng	ឡានដំបូង
the third building	*aakia tii bei*	អាគារទីបី

Emergencies

Help!	*juay kh'nyohm phawng!*	ជួយខ្ញុំផង!
Stop!	*chohp!*	ឈប់!
Go away!	*teuv ao-y ch'ngaay!*	ទៅឱ្យឆ្ងាយ!
I'll get the police!	*kh'nyohm teuv hav polih!*	ខ្ញុំទៅហៅប៉ូលីស!
Watch out!	*prawyaht!*	ប្រយ័ត្ន!

KHMER

| Thief! | jao! | ចោរ! |
| Fire! | phlæng cheh! | ភ្លើងឆេះ! |

Call the police!
   juay hav polih mao! — ជួយហៅប៉ូលិសមក!
Call an ambulance!
   juay hav laan paet mao! — ជួយហៅឡានពេទ្យមក!
I've been robbed!
   kh'nyohm treuv jao plawn! — ខ្ញុំត្រូវចោរប្លន់!

I've lost ...	kh'nyohm baht ...	ខ្ញុំបាត់...
my money	luy r'bawh kh'nyohm	លុយរបស់ខ្ញុំ
my travellers' cheques	saik r'bawh kh'nyohm	សែករបស់ខ្ញុំ
my passport	pahspor r'bawh kh'nyohm	ប៉ាស្ព័ររបស់ខ្ញុំ

I'm ill.
   kh'nyohm cheu — ខ្ញុំឈឺ
We are lost.
   yæng wohngweng phleuv — យើងវង្វេងផ្លូវ
Could I please use the telephone?
   kh'nyohm braa-æ turasahp baan te? — ខ្ញុំប្រើទូរស័ព្ទបានទេ?
I wish to contact my embassy/
consulate.
   kh'nyohm jawng hav s'thaantuut/kohngsuhl r'bawhprawteh kh'nyohm — ខ្ញុំចង់ហៅស្ថានទូត/ កុងស៊ុលរបស់ប្រទេសខ្ញុំ

I didn't realise I was doing
anything wrong.

   kh'nyohm muhn duhng thaa   ខ្ញុំមិនដឹងថាខ្ញុំមានធ្វើអីខុសទេ
   kh'nyohm mian twæ ei koh te

I didn't do it.

   kh'nyohm muhn baan twæ te   ខ្ញុំមិនបានធ្វើទេ

It's not my fault

   nih muhn maen jia kamhoh   នេះមិនមែនជាកំហុសរបស់ខ្ញុំទេ
   r'bawh kh'nyohm te

I'm sorry. I apologise.

   kh'nyohm sohm toh. kh'nyohm   ខ្ញុំសុំទោស 'ខ្ញុំសុំអភ័យទោស
   sohm aaphei toh

My contact number (next of kin)
is ...

   lek turasahp r'bawh kruasaa   លេខទូរស័ព្ទរបស់គ្រួសារខ្ញុំគឺ...
   kh'nyohm keu ...

My blood group is ....

   chiam kh'nyohm jia krup ...   ឈាមខ្ញុំជាក្រុប...

LAO

Lao

The official language of the Lao People's Democratic Republic (LPDR) is Lao as spoken and written in Vientiane. As an official language, it has successfully become the lingua franca between all Lao and non-Lao ethnic groups in Laos. Of course, native Lao is spoken with differing tonal accents and with slightly differing vocabularies as you move from one part of the country to the next. But it is the Vientiane dialect that is most widely understood.

Modern Lao linguists recognise four basic dialects within the country: Vientiane Lao, Northern Lao, North-Eastern Lao, Central Lao, and Southern Lao. Each of these can be further divided into subdialects.

All dialects of Lao are members of the Thai half of the Thai-Kadai family of languages and are closely related to languages spoken in Thailand, northern Myanmar and pockets of China's Yunnan Province. Standard Lao is indeed close enough to Standard Thai (as spoken in central Thailand) that, for native speakers, the two are mutually intelligible. In fact, virtually all speakers of Lao living in the Maekhong River Valley can easily understand spoken Thai, since the bulk of the television and radio they listen to is broadcast from Thailand. Among educated Lao, written Thai is also easily understood, in spite of the fact that the two scripts differ (to about the same degree that the Greek and Roman scripts differ). This is because many of the textbooks used at the college and university level in Laos are actually Thai texts. Native Thais can't always understand Lao, however, since they've had less exposure.

Even closer to Standard Lao are Thailand's Northern and North-Eastern Thai dialects. North-Eastern Thai (also called Isaan) is virtually 100% Lao in vocabulary and intonation; in fact there are more Lao speakers living in Thailand than in Laos.

Prior to the consolidation of various Lao meuang (principalities) in the 14th century, there was little demand for a written language. When a written language was deemed necessary by the Lan Xang monarchy, Lao scholars based their script on an early alphabet devised by the Thais (which in turn had been created by Khmer scholars who used Mon scripts as models!). The alphabet used in Laos is closer to the original prototype; the original Thai script was later extensively revised (which is why Lao appears 'older' to orthographists than Thai, even though it is newer as a written language).

The Lao script today consists of 30 consonants (but only 20 separate sounds) and 28 vowel and diphthong possibilities (15 separate symbols in varying combinations). Written Lao proceeds from left to right, though vowel-signs may be written before, above, below, 'around' (before, above and after), or after consonants, depending on the sign.

Pronunciation

Vowels

ຍ	i	as in 'it'
ຶ	i	as in 'feet'
ໄຍ, ໃຍ	i	as in 'pipe'
ຍໍ	aa	long 'a' as in 'father'
ຍະ	a	half as long as 'aa' above
ແຍ	ae	as in 'bat'
ເຍະ, ເຍັ	e	as in 'hen'

ເx	**eh**	like 'a' in 'hate'
ເx, ເຶx	**oe**	as in 'rut' but more closed
x̣	**u**	as in 'flute'
x̣	**uu**	as in 'food'
x̂, x̊	**eu**	as in French *deux*, or the 'i' in 'sir'
ເxາ	**ao**	as in 'now'
x̣	**aw**	as in 'jaw'
ໂxະ, x̂	**o**	as in 'phone'
ໂx	**oh**	as in 'toe'
ເxຶ	**eua**	diphthong of **eu** and **a**
xຽx, ເxຍ	**ie**	'i-a' as in the French *rien*
xົວx	**ua**	'u-a' as in 'tour'
xວຍ	**uay**	'u-a-i' ('as in 'Dewey')
x̂ວ, x̂ວ	**iu**	'i-u' (as in 'yew')
xຽວ	**iaw**	a triphthong of 'i-a-w' (as the 'io' in 'Rio')
ແxວ	**aew**	'ae-w'
ເxວ	**ehw**	'eh-w'
ເxົ	**ew**	same as 'ehw' above, but shorter (not as in 'yew')
ເxຍ	**oei**	'oe-i'

Consonants

ກ	**k**	as the 'k' in 'skin'; similar to 'g' in 'good', but unaspirated (no puff of air) and unvoiced
ຂ,ຄ	**kh**	'k' as in 'kite'
ງ	**ng**	as in 'sing'; used as an initial consonant in Lao. Practise by saying 'sing' without the 'si'.

ຈ	**j**	similar to 'j' in 'join' or, more closely, the second 't' in 'stature' (voiceless, unaspirated)
ສ,ຊ	**s/x**	as in 'soap'
ຍ	**ny**	similar to the 'ni' in 'onion'; used as an initial consonant in Lao
ດ	**d**	as in 'dodo' or 'dig'
ຕ	**t**	as the 't' in 'forty' (unaspirated, unvoiced), but not as in 'tea'; similar to 'd'
ທ,ຊ	**th**	't' as in 'tea'
ນ,ໜ	**n**	as in 'nun'
ບ	**b**	as in 'boy'
ປ	**p**	as the 'p' in 'stopper' (unvoiced and unaspirated), not like the 'p' in 'put'
ຜ,ພ	**ph**	'p' as in 'put' (but never as in 'phone')
ຝ, ຟ	**f**	same as in 'fan'
ມ,ໝ	**m**	same as in 'man'
ຢ	**y**	same as in 'yo-yo'
ລ,ຫລ	**l**	as in 'lick'
ວ,ຫວ	**w**	as in 'wing' (often transliterated as 'v')
ຮ,ຫ	**h**	as in 'home'

Tones

Basically, Lao is a monosyllabic, tonal language, like various dialects of Thai and Chinese. Vientiane Lao has six tones (compared with five in Standard Thai, four in Mandarin and up to nine in Cantonese). Three of the tones are level (low, mid and high) while three follow pitch inclines (rising, high falling and

LAO

low falling). All six variations in pitch are relative to the speaker's natural vocal range, so that one person's low tone is not necessarily the same pitch as another person's. So, keen pitch recognition is not a prerequisite for learning a tonal language like Lao.

On a visual curve the tones might look like this:

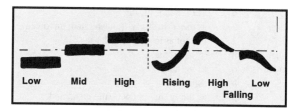

- The low tone is produced at the relative bottom of your conversational tonal range – usually flat and level (though not everyone pronounces it flat and level – some Vientiane natives add a slight rising tone to the end). Example: *dii* (good).

- The mid tone is flat like the low tone, but spoken at the relative middle of the speaker's vocal range. No tone mark used. Example: *het* (do).

- The high tone is flat again, this time at the relative top of your vocal range. Example: *heúa* (boat).

- The rising tone begins a bit below the mid tone and rises to just at or above the high tone. Example: *sãam* (three).

- The high falling tone begins at or above the high tone and falls to the mid level. Example: *sâo* (morning).

- The low falling tone begins at about the mid level and falls to the level of the low tone. Example: *khào* (rice).

Transliteration

The rendering of Lao words into Roman script is a major problem, since many of the Lao sounds, especially certain vowels, do not occur in English. The problem is compounded by the fact that because of Laos' colonial history, transcribed words most commonly seen in Laos are based on the old colonial French system of transliteration, which bears little relation to the way an English speaker would usually choose to write a Lao word.

Since the French don't have a written consonant that corresponds to 'w', they chose to use a 'v' to represent all 'w' sounds, even though the 'v' sound in Lao is closer to an English 'w'. The same goes for 'ch' (or 'j'), which for the French was best rendered 'ti-'.

Since there is no official method of transliterating the Lao language (the Lao government is incredibly inconsistent in this respect, though they tend to follow the old French methods), we have created a transcription system similar to that used in Lonely Planet's *Thai phrasebook*, since the languages have virtually identical phonemes. The public and private sectors in Laos are gradually moving towards a more internationally recognisable system along the lines of the Royal Thai General Transcription (which is fairly readable across a large number of language types).

Pronunciation Hints

In Laos you may come across many instances where the transliteration of vowels and consonants differs significantly, as in 'Louang' for Luang, 'Khouang' for Khuang or 'Xaignabouli' for Sainyabuli. The French spellings are particularly inconsistent in the use of the vowel sound 'ou', which in their transcriptions sometimes corresponds to a 'u' and sometimes to 'w'. An 'o' is often used for a short 'aw', as in 'Bo', which is pronounced more like Baw.

LAO

Instances of 'v' in transcribed Lao words are generally pronounced more like a 'w'. Example: 'Vang Vieng' sounds more like Wang Wieng. In Vientiane, some of the older, educated upper class employ a strong 'v' rather than a 'w' sound.

Many standard place names in Roman script use an 'x' for what in English is 's'. There is no difference in pronunciation of the two; pronounce all instances of 'x' as 's'. Example: 'Xieng' should be pronounced Sieng.

Finally, there is no 'r' sound in modern spoken Lao. When you see an 'r' in transcribed Lao, it is usually an old Lao or a borrowed Thai transliteration; it should be pronounced like an 'l' in this case. Setthathirat (the name of a historic Lao king and common street name), for example, should actually be transcribed with an 'l' instead of an 'r' but usually isn't. Recent government maps have finally started using the spelling 'Luang Phabang' rather than 'Luang Prabang'.

Greetings & Civilities
Greetings & Civilities

Hello.	*sábaai-dii*	ສະບາຍດີ
How are you?	*sábaai-dii baw?*	ສະບາຍດີບ ?
I'm fine.	*sábaai-dii*	ສະບາຍດີ
Thank you.	*khàwp jai*	ຂອບໃຈ
And you?	*jâo dęh?*	ເຈົ້າເດ
Thank you very much.	*khàwp jai lāi lāi*	ຂອບໃຈຫລາຍໆ
It's nothing. (Never mind/Don't bother.)	*baw pęn nyāng*	ບໍ່ເປັນຫຍັງ
Excuse me.	*khāw thôht*	ຂໍໂທດ

Traditionally the Lao greet each other not with a handshake but with a prayer-like palms-together gesture known as a *wâi*. If someone *wâis* you, you should *wâi* back (unless *wâi*-ed by a child). In Vientiane and large cities a light version of the Western-style handshake is commonly offered to foreigners.

A smile and *sábąai-dįi* goes a long way toward calming the initial trepidation that locals may feel upon seeing a foreigner, whether in the city or the countryside.

Forms of Address

The Lao generally address each other using their first names with a kinship term or other title preceding it. Other formal terms of address include *náai* (Mr) and *náang* (Miss or Mrs). Friends often use nicknames or kinship terms like *âai/êuay* (elder brother/sister), *nâwng* (younger sibling) or *lúng/pâa* (uncle/aunt) depending on the age difference. Young children can be called *lāan* ('nephew' or 'niece').

The following list includes kinship terms commonly used as forms of address for non-relatives, based on relative age difference from the speaker. For more kinship terms, see Family, page 187.

elder sister	*êuay*	ເອື້ອຍ
elder brother	*âai*	ອ້າຍ
younger sibling	*nâwng*	ນ້ອງ
uncle	*lúng*	ລຸງ
aunt	*pâa*	ປ້າ
grandfather	*phaw tháo*	ພໍ່ເຖົ້າ
grandmother	*mae thào*	ແມ່ເຖົ້າ
niece/nephew	*lāan*	ຫລານ

LAO

Pronouns
First Person

I/me (to most people)	*khàwy*
I/me (to elders or people of high status)	*kha-nâwy*
we/us	*phûak háo* or *phûak khàwy*

Second Person

you (singular)	*jâo*
you (plural)	*phûak jâo*

Another pronoun meaning 'you' is *thaan* but this is reserved for persons in high social positions such as monks or government officials or for Laos who are substantially older than you to show respect, The all-purpose 'you', *jâo,* is sufficient, however. *Tǫh* is used between lovers and in other intimate relationships.

Third Person

he/she (most people)	*khão*
he/she (elders)	*phoen*
he/she (people you know)	*láo*
he/she (people of high status)	*thaan*
they	add *phûak* before *láo,* *khão* or *phoen* as with 'you' (plural) above
it (inanimate objects and animals)	*mán*

LAO

Body Language

Nonverbal behaviour or 'body language' is very important in Laos, perhaps more important than in most Western countries.

When walking indoors in front of someone who's sitting down, you should stoop a little as a sign of respect.

The feet are the lowest part of the body (spiritually as well as physically) so don't point your feet at people or things with your feet. In the same context, the head is regarded as the highest part of the body, so don't touch people on the head.

Temples

Correct behaviour in temples entails several guidelines, the most important of which is to dress neatly (no shorts or sleeveless shirts) and to take your shoes off when you enter any building that contains a Buddha image. Buddha images are sacred objects, so don't pose in front of them for pictures and definitely do not clamber upon them.

Monks are not supposed to touch or be touched by women. If a woman wants to hand something to a monk, the object should be placed within his reach, not handed directly to him.

When sitting in a religious building, keep your feet pointed away from any Buddha images or monks. The usual way to do this is to sit in the 'mermaid' pose in which your legs are folded to the side, with the feet pointing backwards.

LAO

Language Difficulties

Can you speak English?
    jâo páak pháasaa angkít
    dâi baw?
    ເຈົ້າປາກພາສາອັງກິດໄດ້ບໍ່?
Please speak slowly.
    kálunaa wâo sâa-sâa
    ກະລຸນາເວົ້າຊ້າໆ

Please repeat.
   kálunaa wâo mai boeng dµu   ກະລຸນາເວົ້າໃໝ່ເບິ່ງດູ
Do you understand?
   jâo khào jai baw?   ເຈົ້າເຂົ້າໃຈບໍ່ ?
(I) don't understand.
   baw khào jai   ບໍ່ເຂົ້າໃຈ
Forgive me, I don't
understand.
   khãw thôht, kháwy baw khào   ຂໍໂທດ - ຂ້ອຍບໍ່ເຂົ້າໃຈ
What?
   nyãng?   ຫຍັງ ?

Small Talk
Meeting People
What is your name?
   jâo seu nyãng?   ເຈົ້າຊື່ຫຍັງ ?
My name is ...
   kháwy seu ...   ຂ້ອຍຊື່ ...
Pleased to meet you.
   dµi-jai thii hûu káp jâo   ດີໃຈທີ່ຊູ້ກັບເຈົ້າ

Nationalities
Where do you come from?
   jâo máa tae sai?   ເຈົ້າມາແຕ່ໃສ ?

I come from ...   *kháwy m a tae ...*   ຂ້ອຍມາແຕ່ ...
I am a/an ...   *kháwy pęn khón ...*   ຂ້ອຍເປັນຄົນ ...
  Australia   *aw-sátęh-lía*   ອໍສະເຕເລຍ
  Canada   *kąanáadąa*   ການາດາ
  China   *jµin*   ຈີນ

England	*angkít*	ອັງກິດ
Holland	*háwlándaa*	ຮໍລັງດາ
Italy	*ítaalíi*	ອິຕາລີ
Japan	*yii-pun*	ຍີ່ປຸ່ນ
Laos	*páthêht láo*	ປະເທດລາວ
New Zealand	*níu síiláen*	ນິວຊີແລນ
Singapore	*sīnga-pôh*	ສິງກະໂປ
Spain	*sápehn*	ສະເປນ
Taiwan	*tâiwān*	ໄຕ້ຫວັນ
USA	*améhlikaa*	ອະເມລິກາ

Age

Asking someone's age is a common question in Laos. It's not considered rude to ask strangers their age.

How old are you?
   jâo aanyuu jákápii?   ເຈົ້າອາຍຸຈັກປີ ?
I'm ... years old.
   kháwy aanyuu ... pii   ຂ້ອຍອາຍຸ ...ປີ
Very young!
   num laai!   ໜຸ່ມຫລາຍ
Very old!
   tháo laai!   ເຖົ້າຫລາຍ

Occupations

I am a/an ...	*kháwy pen ...*	ຂ້ອຍເປັນ ...
actor	*sīn-lapin*	ສິນລະປິນ
businessperson	*nak thulakít*	ນັກທຸລະກິດ
diplomat	*nak kaan-thûut*	ນັກການທູຕ
doctor	*phâet*	ແພດ

engineer	*witsáwakawn*	ວິສະວະກອນ
farmer	*sáo-náa*	ຊາວນາ
journalist	*nak khao*	ນັກຂາວ
lawyer	*thanái-khwáam*	ທະນາຍຄວາມ
military	*thahāan*	ທະຫານ
musician	*nak dôntii*	ນັກດົນຕີ
pilot/flyer	*nak-bin*	ນັກບີນ
secretary	*léhkhāanukan*	ເລຂານຸການ
student	*nak-séuksāa*	ນັກສຶກສາ
teacher	*khúu*	ຄູ
traveller/tourist	*nak thawng thiaw*	ນັກທ່ອງທ່ຽວ
volunteer	*qasaasámak*	ອາສາສມັກ
worker	*khón ngáan*	ຄົນງານ

(I'm) unemployed.
    waang ngáan   ຫວ່າງງານ

Religion

My religion is ...	*kháwy thēu ...*	ຂ້ອຍຖື ...
Buddhism	*sáatsánaa phut*	ສາດສະໜາພຸດ
Christianity	*sáatsánaa khlit*	ສາດສະໜາຄລິດ
Judaism	*sáatsánaa nyíw*	ສາດສະໜາຍິວ
Hinduism	*sáatsánaa hínduu*	ສາດສະໜາຮິນດູ
Islam	*sáatsánaa*	ສາດສະໜາ
	ít-sáláam	ອິດສະລາມ

Family

How many in your family?
    míi khâwp khúa ják khón?   ມີຄອບຄົວຈັກຄົນ ?

LAO

I have ... (in my family).
  míi ... khón   ມີ...ຄົນ

Are you married (yet)?
  taeng-ngáan lâew lēu baw?   ແຕ່ງງານແລ້ວຫລືບໍ ?

Yes, I'm married.
  taeng-ngáan lâew   ແຕ່ງງານແລ້ວ

Not yet.
  yáng baw taeng-ngáan   ຍັງບໍ່ແຕ່ງງານ

(I'm) single.
  pen sòht   ເປັນໂສດ

Do you have any children (yet)?
  míi lûuk lâew baw?   ເຈົ້າມີລູກແລ້ວບໍ ?

Not yet.
  yang baw míi lûuk   ຍັງບໍ່ມີລູກ

I have ... child/children.
  míi lûuk ... khón lâew   ມີລູກ...ຄົນແລ້ວ

family	*khâwp khúa*	ຄອບຄົວ
child/children	*lûuk*	ລູກ
daughter	*lûuk sāo*	ລູກສາວ
son	*lûuk sáai*	ລູກຊາຍ
younger sister	*nâwng sāo*	ນ້ອງສາວ
younger brother	*nâwng sáai*	ນ້ອງຊາຍ
older sister	*êuay*	ເອື້ອຍ
older brother	*âai*	ອ້າຍ
parents	*phaw-mae*	ພໍ່-ແມ່
mother	*mae*	ແມ່
father	*phaw*	ພໍ່
wife	*mía*	ເມັຍ
husband	*phūa*	ຜົວ

Making Conversation

We're friends.
   háo pẹn pheuan kạn   ເຮົາເປັນເພື່ອນກັນ

We're relatives.
   háo pẹn phii-nâwng kạn   ເຮົາເປັນພີ່ນ້ອງກັນ

I've come on business.
   kháwy máa het thulakít   ຂ້ອຍມາເຮັດທຸລະກິດ

Nice weather, isn't it?
   aakáat dịi maen baw?   ອາກາດດີ ແມ່ນບໍ່ ?

I like it here.
   kháwy mak yuu nîi   ຂ້ອຍມັກຢູ່ນີ້

I think that ...
   khàwy khit waa ...   ຂ້ອຍຄິດວ່າ ...

I agree.
   nyín nyáwm   ຍິນຍອມ

I disagree.
   baw nyín nyáwm   ບໍ່ຍິນຍອມ

May I have (ask for) your address?
   khaw bawn-yuu khawng   ຂໍບອນຢູ່ຂອງເຈົ້າໄດ້ບໍ່ ?
   jâo dâi baw?

This is my address.
   nîi maen bawn-yuu   ນີ້ແມ່ນບອນຢູ່ຂອງຂ້ອຍ
   khāwng khàwy

Getting Around
Finding Your Way

I want to go to ...
   khàwy yàakápại ...   ຂ້ອຍຢາກໄປ ...

I'm looking for ...
   khàwy sâwk haa ...   ຂ້ອຍຊອກຫາ ...

Where is the ...	... yùu sāi?	... ຢູ່ໃສ ?
bus station	sathāanii lót pájam tháang	ສະຖານີລົດປະຈຳ ,ທາງ
bus stop	bawn jàwt lot pájam tháang	ບອນຈອດລົດປະຈຳ ທາງ
taxi stand	bawn jàwt lot thaek-sîi	ບອນຈອດລົດ ແທກຊີ້
map	phāen thii	ແຜນທີ່

What time will the ... leave?	... já àwk ják móhng?	...ຈະອອກຈັກໂມງ
boat	heúa	ເຮືອ
minivan	lot tûu	ລົດຕູ້
airplane	héua bin	ເຮືອບິນ

Directions

How many kilometres from here?
   ják kí-lóh-mâet jàak nîi?   ຈັກກິໂລແມດ ຈາກນີ້ ?

Go straight ahead.	pai seu-seu	ໄປຊື່ໆ
Turn left/right.	lîaw sâai/khwāa	ລ້ຽວ ຊ້າຍ/ຂວາ
Turn around.	îaw káp	ວ້ຽວກັບ
Turn back. (return)	káp máa	ກັບມາ
How far?	kai thao dai?	ໄກເທົ່າໃດ ?
far/not far	kai/baw kai	ໄກ / ບໍ່ໄກ
near/not near	kâi/baw kâi	ໃກ້ / ບໍ່ໃກ້

north	thit nēua	ທິດເໜືອ
south	thit tâi	ທິດໃຕ້
east	thit tạawán àwk	ທິດຕາເວັນອອກ
west	thit tạawán tók	ທິດຕາເວັນຕົກ

Buying Tickets

I'd like a ticket.
   khàwy yàak dâi pîi   ຂ້ອຍຢາກໄດ້ປີ້

I'd like two tickets.
   khàwy yàak dâi pîi sāwng bại   ຂ້ອຍຢາກໄດ້ປີ້ສອງໃບ

How much per 'place' (seat,
deck space, etc)?
   bawn-la thao dại?   ບ່ອນລະເທົ່າໃດ ?

We'd like to reserve ... places.
   phuak háo yàak jawng   ພວກເຮົາຢາກຈອງ
   bawn ... bawn   ບ່ອນ ... ບ່ອນ

I'd like to change my ticket.
   khàwy yàak pian pîi   ຂ້ອຍຢາກປ່ຽນປີ້

I'd like a refund on my ticket.
   khàwy yàak khéun pîi   ຂ້ອຍຢາກຄືນປີ້

How many depar-tures are there ...?	... *míi ják thîaw?*	... ມີຈັກກ້ຽວ ?
today	*mêu nîi*	ມື້ນີ້
tomorrow	*mêu eun*	ມື້ອື່ນ

Air

airlines	*kạan-bịn*	ການບິນ
Lao Aviation	*Kạan-bịn Láo*	ການບິນລາວ
airplane	*héua bịn*	ເຮືອບິນ
airplane tickets	*pîi héua bịn*	ປີ້ເຮືອບິນ
departures/flights	*thîaw*	ກ້ຽວ
airport	*doen bịn*	ເດີນບິນ

What time will the plane leave?
   ják móhng héua bịnsi àwk?   ຈັກໂມງເຮືອບິນຊິອອກ ?

Bus

Because of road conditions in Laos, intercity buses are limited to the areas around provincial capitals while inter-province bus service is virtually non-existent. Outside the Mekong River Valley, Soviet, Vietnamese or Japanese trucks are often converted into passenger carriers. These passenger trucks are called *thâek-síi* ('taxi') or in some areas *sãwng-thãew*, which means 'two rows' in reference to the benches in the back.

bus station	*sathāanii lót*	ສະຖານີລົດປະ
	pájạm tháang	ຈຳທາງງ
	(khíu lot méh)	(ຄິວລົດເມ)

How many departures are
there today/tomorrow?
   mêu-nîi/mêu-eun míi   ນີ້ນີ້ / ນີ້ອື່ນມີຈັກກ້ຽວ
   ják thîaw?

What time will the bus leave?
   lot já àwk ják móhng?   ລົດຈະອອກຈັກໂມງ ?

Taxi

Each of the country's three largest towns – Vientiane, Luang Phabang and Savannakhet – has a handful of car taxis that are used by foreign businesspeople and the occasional tourist. The only place you'll find these taxis is at the airports (arrival times only) and in front of the larger hotels.

Samlors & Jumbos

Three-wheeled motorcycle taxis are common in large cities. This type of vehicle can be called 'taxi' *(thâek-síi)* or *sāam-lâw* ('samlor' or 'three-wheels'). The larger ones are called 'jumbos' *(jạmbôh)* and can hold four to six passengers. In Vientiane they

LAO

are sometimes called *túk-túk* as in Thailand, while in the south they may be called *sakai-làep* ('Skylab') because of the perceived resemblance to a space capsule! They go anywhere a regular taxi can go, but aren't usually hired for distances greater than 20 km.

How much to ...?
  pai ... thao dại?   ໄປ ... ເທົ່າໃດ ?
Too expensive. How about ... kìip?
  pháeng phôht. ... kìip   ແພງໂພດ ... ກີບໄດ້ບໍ ?
  dâi baw?
Agreed. Let's go.
  tók-lóng lâew pai   ຕົກລົງແລ້ວ. ໄປ
Drive slowly please.
  kálunaa kháp sâa-sâa dae   ກະລຸນາຂັບຊ້າໆແດ່
Stop here.
  jàwt yuu nîi   ຈອດຢູ່ນີ້

Boat

For long distances, large diesel ferries with overnight accommodation are used. For shorter river trips it's best to hire a river taxi since the large ferries only ply their routes a couple of times a week. The long-tail boats *(héua hãang nyáo)* with engines gimbal-mounted on the stern are the most typical, though for a really short trip, ie crossing a river, a rowboat *(héua phái)* can be hired.

boat	*héua*	ເຮືອ
boat taxi ('hire boat')	*héua jâang*	ເຮືອຈ້າງ
cross-river ferry	*héua khàam fâak*	ເຮືອຂ້າມຟາກ
'longtail' boat	*héua hãang nyáo*	ເຮືອຫາງຍາວ
row boat	*héua phái*	ເຮືອພາຍ
speed boat	*héua wái*	ເຮືອໄວ

Where do we get on the boat?
lóng heua yuu sāi?   ລົງເຮືອຢູ່ໃສ?

What time does the boat leave?
héua já àwk ják móhng?   ເຮືອຈະອອກຈັກໂມງ?

What time does the boat arrive?
héua já máa hâwt ják   ເຮືອຈະມາຮອດຈັກໂມງ?
móhng?

Useful Phrases

I'd like to rent a ...   *khàwy yàak sao ...*   ຂ້ອຍຢາກເຊົ່າ ...
  car   *lot (ôh-tôh)*   ລົດ(ໂອໂຕ)
  motorcycle   *lot ják*   ລົດຈັກ

How much ...?   *... thao dại?*   ... ເທົ່າໃດ?
  per hour   *sua-móhng-la*   ຊົ່ວໂມງລະ
  per day   *mêu-la*   ມື້ລະ

Does the price include insurance?
láakháa huam náam   ລາຄາຮວມນຳປະກັນໄພບໍ່?
pákạn phài baw?

What time do we/does it
leave here?
já àwk tae yuu nîi ják   ຈະອອກແຕ່ຢູ່ນີ້ຈັກໂມງ?
móhng?

What time do we/does it
arrive there?
já máa hâwt yuu phûn   ຈະໄປຮອດພຸ້ນຈັກໂມງ?
ják móhng?

Where does the vehicle
depart from?
lot àwk tae yuu sāi?   ລົດອອກແຕ່ຢູ່ໃສ?

May I sit here?
nang bawn nîi dâi baw?   ນັ່ງບ່ອນນີ້ໄດ້ບໍ?

Can I put my bag here?
wáang thõng yuu nîi dâi baw?   ວາງກົງຢູ່ນີ້ໄດ້ບໍ?

Can you wait for me?
thàa khàwy dâi baw?   ຖ້າຂ້ອຍໄດ້ບໍ?

Where are you going?
pại sãi?   ໄປໃສ?

I'll get out here.
khàwy si long bawn nîi   ຂ້ອຍຊິລົງບ່ອນນີ້

Which vehicle goes to ...?
lot khan dại pại ...?   ລົດຄັນໃດໄປ ...?

When we arrive in ..., please tell me.
wéhláa hâwt ... bàwk khàwy dae   ເວລາຮອດ ...ບອກຂ້ອຍແດ່

Stop here.
jàwt bawn nîi   ຈອດບ່ອນນີ້

Accommodation

Traditionally, a 'single' means a room with one large bed that will sleep two, while a 'double' has two large beds. The price is usually set according to the number of beds a room has, not the number of people who will be using it. At newer, Western-style hotels, rates increase according to the number of guests per room.

An 'ordinary room' *(hàwng thámadạa)* usually means a less expensive room with a fan rather than with air-conditioning.

In villages where there are no hotels or guesthouses you may be able to stay with local residents. Sometimes this entails money, sometimes not, but you should always offer a useful gift – food or something needed in the household – to your host family.

Finding Accommodation

hotel	*hóhng háem*	ໂຮງແຮມ
guesthouse	*hāw hap kháek*	ຫໍຮັບແຂກ

Excuse me, is there a hotel
nearby?
  *khāw thôht, mii hóhng
  háem yuu kâi nîi baw?*   ຂໍໂທດ. ມີໂຮງແຮມຢູ່ໃກ້ນີ້ບໍ່?

Is this a hotel?
  nîi maen hóhng háem baw?   ນີ້ແມ່ນໂຮງແຮມບໍ່?

Is this a guesthouse?
  *nîi maen hāw hap kháek
  baw?*   ນີ້ແມ່ນຫໍຮັບແຂກບໍ່?

Is there a place to stay here?
  míi bawn phak yuu nîi baw?   ມີບ່ອນພັກຢູ່ນີ້ບໍ່?

Can (I/we) stay here?
  phak yuu nîi dâi baw?   ພັກຢູ່ນີ້ໄດ້ບໍ່?

Checking In

Do you have a room?
  míi hàwng baw?   ມີຫ້ອງບໍ່?

one person	*neung khón* *(khon diaw)*	ນຶ່ງຄົນ (ຄົນດຽວ)
two persons	*sāwng khón*	ສອງຄົນ

How much ...?	*... thao dại?*	... ເທົ່າໃດ?
per night	*khéun-la*	ຄືນລະ
per week	*qathit-la*	ອາທິດລະ
per month	*dèuan-la*	ເດືອນລະ
for three nights	*sāam khéun*	ສາມຄືນ

LAO

Too expensive.
pháeng phôht   ແພງໂພດ

Can you lower the price?
lut láakháa dâi baw?   ຫລຸດລາຄາໄດ້ບໍ່ ?

Can (I/we) look at the room?
khaw boeng hàwng dâi baw?   ຂໍເບິ່ງຫ້ອງໄດ້ບໍ່ ?

Do you have any other rooms?
míi hàwng ìik baw?   ມີຫ້ອງອີກບໍ່ ?

(I/we) will stay two nights.
si phak sāwng khéun   ຊິພັກຢູ່ສອງຄືນ

We need a ...	*phûak háo tâwng-*	ພວກເຮົາຕ້ອງການ
room than this.	*kaan hàwng ... nîi*	ຫ້ອງ...ນີ້
cheaper	*théuk-kwaa*	ຖືກກວ່າ
larger	*nyai-kwaa*	ໃຫຍ່ກວ່າ
smaller	*nâwy-kwaa*	ນ້ອຍກວ່າ
quieter	*mit-kwaa*	ມິດກວ່າ

Requests & Complaints

Is there ...	*míi ... baw*	ມີ...ບໍ່
telephone	*thóhlasáp*	ໂທຣະສັບ
hot water	*nâam hâwn*	ນ້ຳຮ້ອນ

(I/we) need (a) ...	*tâwng-kaan ...*	ຕ້ອງການ ...
another bed	*tịang ìik*	ຕຽງອີກ
blanket	*phàa hom*	ຜ້າຫົມ
key	*kájae*	ກະແຈ
pillow	*māwn*	ໝອນ
sheet	*pháa pụu bawn náwn*	ຜ້າປູບ່ອນນອນ

Can you clean the room?
   *het khwáam sá-áat
   hàwng dâi baw*   ເຮັດຄວາມສະອາດ ຫ້ອງໄດ້ບໍ ?

This room isn't clean.
   hàwng nîi baw sá-áat   ຫ້ອງນີ້ບໍ່ສະອາດ

There is no hot water.
   baw míi nâam hâwn   ບໍ່ມີນ້ຳຮ້ອນ

Can you repair it?
   jâo sàwm dâi baw?   ເຈົ້າສ້ອມໄດ້ບໍ ?

Can I store my bags here?
   *fàak kheuang yuu nîi
   dâi baw?*   ຝາກເຄື່ອງຢູ່ນີ້ໄດ້ບໍ ?

Can you wash these clothes?
   sak séua pháa nîi dâi baw?   ຊັກເສື້ອຜ້ານີ້ໄດ້ບໍ ?

Where can I wash my clothes
(myself)?
   *kháwy sak séua pháa
   ehng dâi yuu sãi?*   ຂ້ອຍຊັກເສື້ອຜ້າເອງໄດ້ຢູ່ໃສ ?

Is there a laundry near here?
   *míi hàwng sak lîit kâi
   yuu nîi baw?*   ມີຫ້ອງຊັກລິດໄກ້ຢູ່ນີ້ບໍ ?

LAO

Useful Words

air-con	*ae yen*	ແອເຢັນ
bathroom	*hàwng nâam*	ຫ້ອງນ້ຳ
bed	*tiang náwn*	ຕຽງນອນ
electricity	*kaan fái fâa*	ການໄຟຟ້າ
elevator (lift)	*lif*	ລິຟ
entrance	*thaang khào*	ທາງເຂົ້າ
exit	*tháang àwk*	ທາງອອກ
fan	*phat lóm*	ພັດລົມ

room	hàwng	ຫ້ອງ
soap	sábuu	ສະບູ
toilet	sùam	ສ້ວມ
towel	phàa set tôh	ຜ້າເຊັດໂຕ

Around Town

Where is the ...?	... yùu sāi?	...ຢູ່ໃສ ?
How far is ...?	... kại thao dại?	... ໄກເທົ່າໃດ ?
I'm looking for the ...	khàwy sâwk hāa ...	ຂ້ອຍຊອກຫາ
bank	thanáakháan	ທະນາຄານ
post office	pại-sá-níi (hóhng sāai)	ໄປສະນີ (ໂຮງສາຍ)

At the Post Office

Is this the post office?
nîi maen pại saníi baw?   ນີ້ແມ່ນໄປສະນີບໍ່ ?

I want to send a ...	khàwy yàak song ...	ຂ້ອຍຢາກສົ່ງ
letter	jót-māai	ຈົດໝາຍ
postcard	pại saníi bát	ໄປສະນີບັດ
parcel	haw kheuang	ຫໍ່ເຄື່ອງ
telegram	thóhlalêhk	ໂທລະເລກ

May I have (a/an/some) ...	khăw ...	ຂໍ ...
stamps	sataem	ສະແຕມ
envelope	sáwng jót-māai	ຊອງຈົດໝາຍ
insurance	pákạn phái	ປະກັນໄພ
registered receipt	bại lóng thabịan	ໃບລົງທະບຽນ

LAO

Is there any mail for me?
  míi jót-māai sāmláp
  khàwy baw?

ບີ່ຈິດໝາຍສົ່ງຫລັບຂ້ອຍບໍ່?

air (mail)	*tháang ǫakàat*	ທາງອາກາດ
surface (mail)	*thámadǫa*	ທຳມະດາ
express (mail)	*tháang duan*	ທາງດວນ

Telephone

The best place to make international calls is the International Telephone Office (Cabines T,l,communiques Internationales) on Thanon Setthathirat in Vientiane, which is open 24 hours a day. In provincial capitals, international telephone service is available at the GPO.

telephone	*thóhlasáp*	ໂທລະສັບ
international call	*thóhlasáp rawaang* *páthêt*	ໂທລະສັບລະຫວ່າງ ປະເທດ
long distance (domestic)	*tháang kʉi*	ທາງໄກ

How much does it cost to call ...?
  thóhlasáp thõeng ...
  láakháa thao dại?

ໂທລະສັບບຸ່ງໄປ... ລາຄາເທົ່າໃດ?

I'd like to speak for 10 minutes.
  khàwy yàak wâo síp
  náa-thíi

ຂ້ອຍຢາກເວົ້າສິບນາທີ

LAO

Telecommunications

Fax, telex and telegraph services are handled at the GPO in each provincial capital. Larger hotels with business centres offer the same telecommunication services but always at higher rates.

| fax | *fáek* | ແຟກ໌ |
| telegraph | *thóhlalêhk* | ໂທລະເລກ |

How much per page?
phaen-la thao dại? ແຜ່ນລະເທົ່າໃດ ?
How much per word?
khám-la thao dại? ຄຳລະເທົ່າໃດ ?

At the Bank

Outside Vientiane most provincial banks accept only US dollars or Thai baht. Many hotels, upscale restaurants and gift shops in Vientiane accept Visa or MasterCard credit cards. A few also accept American Express.

Can (I/we) change money here?
pian ngóen yuu nîi dâi baw? ປ່ຽນເງິນຢູ່ນີ້ໄດ້ບໍ່ ?
What is the exchange rate?
tạa pian thao dịi? ອັຕຕາປ່ຽນເທົ່າໃດ ?
Can I get smaller change?
khãw pian ngóen nâwy dâi baw? ຂໍ້ຍປ່ຽນເງິນນ້ອຍໄດ້ບໍ່ ?

I have ... *khàwy míi ...* ຂ້ອຍມີ ...
    US$ *dôh-láa améhlikạa* ໂດລາອະເມລິກາ
    UK£ *pạwn ạngkít* ພາວອັງກິດ
    A$ *dôh-láa awsáteh-lía* ໂດລາອອສະເຕເລຍ

HK\$	*dôh-láa hong kông*	ໂດລາຮົງກົງ
German marks	*mâak yôe-lamán*	ມາກເຢ້ຍລະມັນ
Japanese yen	*nyéhn nyiipun*	ເຢັນ ຍີ່ປຸ່ນ

Sightseeing

Do you have a local map?
jâo mîi phāen thii thâwng thiin bau? ເຈົ້າມີແຜນທີ່ທ້ອງກີ່ນບໍ່?

What time does it open/close?
man pòet/pít jak móhng? ມັນເປີດ/ປິດຈັກໂມງ?

May I take photographs?
kháwy khāw thaay huub dâi bau? ຂ້ອຍຂໍ່ກ່າຍຮູບໄດ້ບໍ່?

cemetery	*baa sâa*	ປ່າຊ້າ
church	*sim khlit*	ສິມຄລິດ
museum	*phiphithaphán*	ພິພິທະພັນ
park (garden)	*sūan*	ສວນ
stupa	*thâat*	ທາດ
Buddhist temple/ monastery	*wat*	ວັດ

Paperwork

name	*xeu laea naam sáa kuun*	ຊື່ແລະນາມສະກຸນ
address	*thii yùu*	ທີ່ຢູ່
date of birth	*wán deuan pii koet*	ວັນເດືອນປີເກີດ
place of birth	*sa thaan thii koet*	ສະຖານທີ່ເກີດ
age	*aanyuu*	ອາຍຸ

sex	*peht*	ເພດ
nationality	*xeua sâat*	ເຊື້ອຊາດ
religion	*sáatsánaa*	ສາສນາ
profession	*aaxiib*	ອາຊີບ
marital status	*sáthaanapaab*	ສະຖານະພາບ
passport number	*lêhk năng seu phaan daen*	ເລກໜັງສືຜ່ານແດນ
visa	*jaeng auuk/khào*	ແຈ້ງອອກ/ເຂົ້າ
driving licence	*bai khap khii nyaan nyon*	ໃບຂັບຂີ່ຍານຍົນ
purpose of visit	*jut pa xong khăwng khaan yiem yaam*	ຈຸດປະສົງຂອງ ການຢ້ຽມຢາມ

In the Country

Weather

How's the weather?
aakáat pẹn jang-dại? ອາກາດເປັນຈັ່ງໃດ ?

(It's) very cold.
nāao lāai ໜາວຫລາຍ

(It's) very hot.
hâwn lāai ຮ້ອນຫລາຍ

(It's) raining hard.
fõn tók nak ຝົນຕົກໜັກ

(It's) flooding.
náam thûam ນ້ຳຖ້ວມ

weather	*aakàat*	ອາກາດ
fog	*nâam màwk*	ນ້ຳໝອກ
lightning	*sãi fâa mâep*	ສາຍຟ້າແມບ
monsoon	*máw-la-sũm*	ມໍລະສຸມ

Geographical Terms

cave	*thàm*	ຖ້ຳ
cliff	*phāa*	ຜາ
countryside	*bâan nâwk*	ບ້ານນອກ
rice field (wet)	*náa*	ນາ
field (dry)	*hai*	ໄຮ່
forest	*paa*	ປ່າ
hill	*phúu nâwy*	ພູນ້ອຍ
jungle	*dông*	ດົງ
mountain	*phúu khāo*	ພູເຂົ້າ
river	*mae nâam*	ແມ່ນ້ຳ
sea	*thaléh*	ທະເລ
swamp	*beung*	ບຶງ
trail/footpath	*tháang thíaw/*	ທາງທ່ຽວ /
	tháang nyaang	ທາງຍ່າງ
waterfall	*nâam tók tàat*	ນ້ຳຕົກຕາດ

Flora

bamboo	*phai*	ໄຜ່
flower	*dàwk mâi*	ດອກໄມ້
grass/herb	*nyàa*	ຫຍ້າ
dipterocarp	*yaang*	ຍາງ
pine	*tôn sōn*	ຕົ້ນສົນ
tree	*tôn mâi*	ຕົ້ນໄມ້
teak	*tôn sák*	ຕົ້ນສັກ

Fauna

banteng (type of wild cattle)	*ngúa dàeng*	ງົວແດງ
barking deer	*fáan*	ຟານ

bird	*nok*	ນົກ
cow	*ngúa*	ງົວ
civet	*samot*	ສະໝົດ
crocodile	*khàe*	ແຂ້
dog	*māa*	ໝາ
fish	*pqa*	ປາ
fishing cat	*sēua pqa*	ເສືອປາ
fly	*máng wán*	ແມງວັນ
gaur	*káthíng*	ກະທິງ
horse	*mâa*	ມ້າ
monkey	*líng*	ລີງ
rabbit	*kátqi*	ກະຕ່າຍ
snake	*ngúu*	ງູ
snake (venomous)	*ngúu phit*	ງູພິດ
water buffalo	*khwáai*	ຄວາຍ

Camping

Can (I/we) put a tent here?
(kháwy/phuak háo) wang tùup phàa yuu nîi dâi baw?
(ຂ້ອຍ/ພວກເຮົາ)ວາງ
ຕູບຜ້າຢູ່ນີ້ໄດ້ບໍ່ ?

Is it safe?
pàwt phái baw?
ປອດໄພບໍ່ ?

Is drinking water available?
míi nâam deum baw?
ມີນ້ຳດື່ມບໍ່ ?

blanket	*phàa hom*	ຜ້າຫົ່ມ
sleeping bag	*thõng náwn*	ຖົງນອນ
tent	*tùup phàa*	ຕູບຜ້າ

Useful Words & Phrases

(I/we) would like to hire a guide.
   yàak jâang khón nám thiaw ຢາກຈ້າງຄົນນຳທ່ຽວ

How many hours per day
will we walk?
   já nyaang mêu-la ják จะย่างมื้ລะจักຊົ່ວໂມງ ?
   sua-móhng?

Is it a difficult walk?
   tháang nyaang pại nyâak ທາງຢ່າງໄປຍາກບໍ ?
   baw?

hill tribe	*sáo khāo*	ຊາວເຂົາ
(High Lao)	*(láo sūung)*	(ລາວສູງ)
lodging	*bawn phak*	ບ່ອນພັກ
medicine	*yạa*	ຢາ
mosquitoes	*nyúng*	ຍຸງ
mosquito coil	*yạa kạn nyúng*	ຢາກັນຍຸງ
	(bàep jút)	(ແບບຈຸດ)
mosquito net	*mûng*	ມຸ້ງ
opium	*yạa fīn*	ຢາຝິ່ນ
raft	*pháe*	ແພ
village headman	*phùu nyai bân*	ຜູ້ໃຫຍ່ບ້ານ
water	*nâam*	ນ້ຳ

LAO

Food

Lao cuisine is very similar to Thai cuisine in many ways. But the Lao eat a lot of what could be called Chinese food which is generally, but not always, less spicy. Rice is the foundation for all Lao meals, as elsewhere in South-East Asia.

Eating Out

Please bring (a) ...	*khǎw ... dae*	ຂໍ...ແດ່
menu	*láai-kạan ạahāan*	ລາຍການອາຫານ
plate	*jạan*	ຈານ
bowl	*thùay*	ກ້ວຍ
glass	*jàwk*	ຈອກ
spoon	*buang*	ບວງ
fork	*sâwm*	ສ້ອມ
chopsticks	*mâi thuu*	ໄມ້ທູ
knife	*mîit*	ມີດ
bill	*sék*	ເຊັກ

(I) don't like it hot and spicy.
baw mak phét   ບໍ່ມັກເຜັດ

What do you have that's special?
míi nyǎng phi-sèt?   ມີຫຍັງພິເສດ

I didn't order this.
khàwy baw dâi sang   ຂ້ອຍບໍ່ໄດ້ສັ່ງແນວນີ້
náew nîi

I eat only vegetables.
khàwy kịn tae phák   ຂ້ອຍກິນແຕ່ຜັກ

I can't eat pork.
khàwy kịn mūu baw dâi   ຂ້ອຍກິນໝູບໍ່ໄດ້

I can't eat beef.
khàwy kịn sìn ngúa baw dâi   ຂ້ອຍກິນຊີ້ນງົວບໍ່ໄດ້

Please don't use raw fish sauce.
kalunáa baw sai pạa dàek   ກະລຸນາບໍ່ໃສ່ປາແດກ

Please don't use MSG.
kalunáa baw sai phông   ກະລຸນາບໍ່ໃສ່ຜົງຊູລົດ
súu-lot (aji-no-moh-toh)

Typical Lao Dishes

steamed white rice   *khào nèung*   ເຂົ້ານຶ້ງ
sticky rice   *khào nīaw*   ເຂົ້ານຽວ

fõe   ເຝີ
> Rice noodle soup with vegetables and meat. The many varieties of rice noodle soup are popular snacks or even breakfasts, and they are almost always served with a plate of fresh lettuce, mint, coriander, mung-bean sprouts, lime wedges and sometimes basil for adding to the soup as desired.

mii hàeng   ໝີ່ແຫ້ງ
> yellow wheat noodles with vegetables and meat

khào pûn   ເຂົ້າປຸ້ນ
> white flour noodles served with sweet-spicy sauce

làap sìn   ລາບຊີ້ນ
> minced meat tossed with lime juice, garlic, powdered sticky rice, green onions, mint leaves and chillies.

kaeng jèut   ແກງຈືດ
> mild soup with vegetables and pork

tôm yám pạa   ຕົ້ມຍຳປາ
> fish and lemongrass soup with mushrooms

kai phát khĩng   ໄກ່ຜັດຂີງ
> chicken with ginger

mūu sòm-wāan   ໝູສົ້ມຫວານ
> sweet and sour pork

pîng kûng   ປີ້ງກຸ້ງ
> grilled prawns

pạa sòm-wāan   ປາສົ້ມຫວານ
> sweet and sour fish

phát phák   ຜັດຜັກ
> stir-fried mixed vegetables

LAO

khào-nŏm màw kǫeng   ເຂົ້າໜົມໝໍ້ແກງ
  egg custard
khào nĩaw màak muang   ເຂົ້າໜຽວໝາກມ່ວງ
  sticky rice in coconut cream and ripe mango

At the Market
Meat
chicken	*kai*	ໄກ່
beef	*sìn ngúa*	ຊີ້ນງົວ
pork	*mũu*	ໝູ

Seafood
carp	*pǫa pàak*	ປ່າປາກ
catfish	*pǫa dúk*	ປ່າດຸກ
eel	*ian*	ອຽນ
fish	*pǫa*	ປ່າ
giant Mekong catfish	*pǫa béuk*	ປ່າບຶກ
serpent fish	*pǫa khaw*	ປ່າຄໍ່
sheatfish	*pǫa sa-ngùa*	ປ່າສະງົ້ວ
shrimp/prawns	*kûng*	ກຸງ
freshwater stingray	*pǫa fãa lái*	ປ່າຝາໄລ

Vegetables
bamboo shoots	*naw mâi*	ໜໍ່ໄມ້
bean	*thua*	ຖົ່ວ
bean sprouts	*thua ngâwk*	ຖົ່ວງອກ
bitter melon	*máaláa-jĩin (màak ha)*	ມະລະຈີນ(ໝາກກະ)
cabbage	*ká-lam pị̂*	ກະຫລ່ຳປີ

cauliflower	*dàwk ká-lam*	ດອກກະຫລ່ຳ
Chinese radish *(daikon)*	*phák kàat hūa*	ຜັກກາດຫົວ
corn	*khào sāalíi*	ເຂົ້າສາລີ
cucumber	*màak tạeng*	ໝາກແຕງ
eggplant	*màak khēua*	ໝາກເຂືອ
garlic	*hūa phák thíam*	ຫົວຜັກທຽມ
lettuce	*phák sálat*	ຜັກສະລັດ
long green beans	*thua nyáo*	ຖົ່ວຍາວ
lotus root	*tôn bụa*	ຕົ້ນບົວ
onion (bulb)	*hūa phák bua*	ຫົວຜັກບົວ
onion (green) ('scallions')	*tôn phák bua*	ຕົ້ນຜັກບົວ
potato	*mán falang*	ມັນຝະລັ່ງ
pumpkin	*màak éu (màak fak)*	ໝາກອຶ (ໝາກຟັກ)
tomato	*màak len*	ໝາກເຫລັ້ນ
vegetables	*phak*	ຜັກ

Fruit

apple	*màakápohm*	ໝາກໂປ່ມ
banana	*màak kûay*	ໝາກກ້ວຍ
coconut	*màak phâo*	ໝາກພ້າວ
custard-apple	*màak khìap*	ໝາກຂຽບ
durian	*thulían*	ທຸລຽນ
guava	*màak sīi-dạa*	ໝາກສີດາ
jackfruit	*màak mîi*	ໝາກມີ້
lime	*màak náo*	ໝາກນາວ
longan	*màak nyám nyái*	ໝາກຍ່ຳໃຍ

LAO

lychee	màak lînjii	ໝາກລີ້ນຈີ່
mandarin orange	màak kîang	ໝາກກ້ຽງ
mango	màak muang	ໝາກມວງ
mangosteen	màak máng-khut	ໝາກມັງຄຸດ
papaya	màak hung	ໝາກຫຸງ
pineapple	màak nat	ໝາກນັດ
rambutan	màak ngaw	ໝາກເງາະ
rose-apple	màak kiang	ໝາກກຽງ
sugarcane	âwy	ອ້ອຍ
tamarind	nâam màak khāam	ນ້ຳໝາກຂາມ
watermelon	màak móh	ໝາກໂມ

Condiments, Herbs & Spices

chilli	màak phét	ໝາກເຜັດ
coconut extract	nâam màak phâo	ນ້ຳໝາກພ້າວ
	(nâam ká-tí)	(ນ້ຳກະທິ)
coriander (cilantro)	phàk hāwm	ຜັກຫອມ
dried shrimp	kûng hàeng	ກຸ້ງແຫ້ງ
fish sauce	nâam pạa	ນ້ຳປາ
ginger	khĩng	ຂີງ
lime juice	nâam màak náo	ນ້ຳໝາກນາວ
sesame	ngáa	ງາ
soy sauce	nâam sáyûu	ນ້ຳສະອີ້ວ
salt	kẹua	ເກືອ
sugar	nâam-tạan	ນ້ຳຕານ
sweet basil	bại hóhlapháa	ໃບໂຫລະພາ
tamarind	màak khāam	ໝາກຂາມ
vinegar	nâam sòm	ນ້ຳສົ້ມ

Drinks
Nonalcoholic

drinking water	nâam deum	ນ້ຳດື່ມ
boiled water	nâam tôm	ນ້ຳຕົ້ມ
ice	nâam kâwn	ນ້ຳກ້ອນ
weak Chinese tea	nâam sáa	ນ້ຳຊາ
hot water	nâam hâwn	ນ້ຳຮ້ອນ
cold water	nâam yén	ນ້ຳເຢັນ
Lao tea with sugar	sáa hâwn	ຊາຮ້ອນ
Lao tea with milk & sugar	sáa nóm hâwn	ຊານົມຮ້ອນ
iced Lao tea with milk & sugar	sáa nóm yén	ຊານົມເຢັນ
No sugar.	baw sai nâam-taan	ບໍ່ໃສ່ນ້ຳຕານ
Lao coffee with milk & sugar	kạa-féh nâam hâwn	ກາເຟນົມຮ້ອນ
Ovaltine	oh-wantin	ໂອວັນຕິນ
orange juice (or orange soda)	nâam máak kîang	ນ້ຳໝາກກ້ຽງ
plain milk	nâam nóm	ນ້ຳນົມ
yoghurt	nóm sòm	ນົມສົ້ມ

Alcoholic

beer	bia	ເບຍ
draught beer	bia sót	ເບຍສົດ
rice whisky	lào láo	ເຫຼົ້າລາວ
soda water	nâam sah-dạa	ນ້ຳໂສດາ
glass	jàwk	ຈອກ
bottle	kâew	ແກວ

Shopping

bookshop	hàan khǎai nǎng sěu	ຮ້ານຂາຍໜັງສື

How much is it?
   thao dại?   ເທົ່າໃດ ?

Do you have any ...?
   mịi ... baw?   ມີ ... ບໍ່ ?

Making a Purchase

What is this made of?
   nîi het dûay nyǎng?   ນີ້ເຮັດດ້ວຍຫຍັງ ?

Do you have any more?
   mịi ìik baw?   ມີອີກບໍ່ ?

I'd like to see another style.
   khǎw beeng ìik bàep neung   ຂໍເບິ່ງອີກແບບນຶ່ງ

Do you have any- thing ... than this?	*mịi ... nîi baw?*	ມີ ... ນີ້ບໍ່ ?
larger	*nyai-kwaa*	ໃຫຍ່ກວ່າ
smaller	*nâwy-kwaa*	ນ້ອຍກວ່າ

Bargaining

Bargaining is common practice and will become easier the more you indulge. Anything bought in a market should be bargained for. Prices in department stores and most non-tourist shops are fixed, however. Use some discretion when going for the bone on a price. There's a fine line between bargaining and niggling – getting hot under the collar over a few kìp makes both seller and buyer lose face.

Do you have something cheaper?
míi thèuk-kwaa nîi baw?   ມີຖືກກວ່ານີ້ບໍ່ ?

The price is very high.
láakháa pháeng lãai   ລາຄາແພງຫລາຍ

I think that's too much.
khit waa phaeng phôht   ຄິດວ່າແພງໂພດ

Can you bring the price down?
lut láakháa dâi baw?   ຫລຸດລາຄາໄດ້ບໍ່ ?

Can you lower it more?
lut ìik dâi baw?   ຫລຸດອີກໄດ້ບໍ່ ?

How about ... kìip?
... kìip dâi baw?   ...ກີບໄດ້ບໍ່ ?

I don't have much money.
baw míi ngóen thao dại   ບໍ່ມີເງິນເທົ່າໃດ

The quality is not very good.
khúnaphâap baw dịi pạan dại   ຄຸນະພາບບໍ່ດີປານໃດ

Souvenirs

baskets	*ká-taa*	ກະຕ່າ
embroidery	*phàa thák saew*	ຜ້າຖັກແສ່ວ
handicrafts	*kheuang fĩi-méu*	ເຄື່ອງຟີມື
ikat-style, tie-dyed cloth	*mat-mĩi*	ມັດມີ
pottery/ceramics	*kheuang dìn/ kheuang thùay*	ເຄື່ອງດິນ/ ເຄື່ອງຖ້ວຍ
gems	*phet pháwy*	ເພັດ - ພອຍ
gold (pure)	*tháwng khám*	ທອງຄຳ
silver	*ngóen*	ເງິນ

Toiletries

brush	*paeng*	ແປງ
condoms	*thãng yaang anáamái*	ກ້ງຢາງອະນະໄມ
deodorant	*yaa kan kin tua*	ຢາກັນກິນຕົວ
mosquito repellant	*yaa kan nyúng*	ຢາກັນຍຸງ
razor	*mîit thãe*	ມີດແຖ
razor blades	*bai mîit thãe*	ໃບມີດແຖ
sanitary napkins	*phàa anáamái*	ຜ້າອະນາໄມ
shampoo	*nâam yaa sá phõm*	ນ້ຳຢາສະຜົມ
soap	*sá-buu*	ສະບູ
toilet paper	*jîa hong nâam*	ເຈ້ຍຫ້ອງນ້ຳ
toothbrush	*paeng thũu khàew*	ແປງຖູແຂ້ວ
toothpaste	*yaa thũu khàew*	ຢາຖູແຂ້ວ

Photography

camera	*kâwng thaai hûup*	ກ້ອງຖ່າຍຮູບ
film	*fĩm hûup*	ຟິມຮູບ
colour	*sĩi*	ສີ
B&W	*khão dam*	ຂາວ-ດຳ
lens	*léhn*	ເລັນ
slide film	*fĩm sálái*	ຟິມສະໄລ

Smoking

Do you mind if I smoke?
jâo mîi banhaa bau thaa kháwy sùup yaa

ເຈົ້າມີບັນຫາບໍ່ກ້າຂ້ອຍສູບຢາ?

Please don't smoke.
ka lu naa yaa sùup yaa

ກະລຸນາຢ່າສູບຢາ

| cigarettes | *yáa sùup* | ຢາສູບ |
| matches | *káp fái* | ກັບໄຟ |

Sizes & Comparisons

size	*khanàat*	ຂະຫນາດ
too small	*nâwy phôht*	ນ້ອຍໂພດ
too large	*nyai phôht*	ໃຫຍ່ໂພດ

Health

Where is a ...?	... *yùu sāi?*	... ຢູ່ໃສ ?
dentist	*māw pұa khàew*	ໝໍປົວແຂ້ວ
doctor	*māw*	ໝໍ
hospital	*hóhng māw*	ໂຮງໝໍ
pharmacy	*hâan khāai yạa*	ຮ້ານຂາຍຢາ

At the Doctor

I am ill.	*khàwy baw sábạai*	ຂ້ອຍບໍ່ສະບາຍ
It hurts here.	*jép yuu nîi*	ເຈັບຢູ່ນີ້
(I) cant sleep.	*náwn baw lap*	ນອນບໍ່ຫລັບ
I'm tired.	*khàwy meuay*	ຂ້ອຍເມື່ອຍ
(I've) a fever.	*pẹn khài*	ເປັນໄຂ້

(I've) vomited several times.
   hàak lāai theua   ຮາກຫລາຍເທື່ອ

Ailments

AIDS	*lôhk éht*	ໂລກເອດ
anaemia	*lôhk lêuat nâwy*	ໂລກເລືອດໜ້ອຍ
asthma	*lôhk hèut*	ໂລກຫືດ

cancer	*maleng*	ມະເລັງ
cholera	*ahíwáa*	ອະຫິວາ
cramps	*pân (phùuk)*	ປັ້ນ (ພູກ)
dengue fever	*khài sàa*	ໄຂ້ສ່າ
diabetes	*lôhk bạo wān*	ໂລກເບົາຫວານ
diarrhoea	*lóng thâwng*	ລົງທ້ອງ
dysentery	*lôhk thâwng bít*	ໂລກທ້ອງບິດ
headache	*pùat hūa*	ປວດຫົວ
influenza	*khài wát nyai*	ໄຂ້ຫວັດໃຫຍ່
itch	*khán*	ຄັນ
malaria	*khài paa*	ໄຂ້ປ່າ
pneumonia	*lôhk pàwt bụam*	ໂລກປອດບວມ
rabies	*lôhk pẹn wâw*	ໂລກເປັນວ້ໍ
sprain	*pùat khat*	ປວດຂັດ
stomachache	*pùat thâwng*	ປວດທ້ອງ
toothache	*jép khàew*	ເຈັບແຂ້ວ
veneral disease	*kạama lôhk*	ກາມໂລກ

Women's Health

I want to see a female doctor.
 khǎwy tāwng kaan phâet nyíing   ຂ້ອຍຕ້ອງການແພດຍິ່ງ
I'm pregnant.
 khǎwy theu paa   ຂ້ອຍຖືພາ
I'm on the (contraceptive) pill.
 khǎwy xay yaa khuum kam noet   ຂ້ອຍໃຊ້ຢາຄຸມກຳເນີດ
I haven't had my period for … weeks.
 khǎwy baw pehn la du dâi …   ຂ້ອຍບໍ່ເປັນລະດູໄດ້…
 aathit lâew   ອາທິດແລວ

Parts of the Body

arm	*khāen*	ແຂນ
back	*lăng*	ຫລັງ
ear	*hŭu*	ຫູ
eye	*tąa*	ຕາ
face	*nàa*	ໜ້າ
finger	*nîu méu*	ນິ້ວມື
hand	*méu*	ມື
head	*hŭa*	ຫົວ
heart	*hŭa jai*	ຫົວໃຈ
leg	*khăa*	ຂາ
mouth	*pàak*	ປາກ
tooth/teeth	*khàew*	ແຂວ

At the Chemist

How many times a day?
  mêu-la ják theua?   ມື້ລະຈັກເທື່ອ ?

four times a day
  mêu-la sii theua   ມື້ລະສີ່ເທື່ອ

How much per tablet/pill?
  met-la thao dąi?   ເມັດລະເທົ່າໃດ ?

insulin	*yąa kâe lôhk bąo wāan*	ຢາແກ້ໂລກເບົ້າຫວານ
painkiller	*yąa kâe pùat*	ຢາແກ້ປວດ
pill/tablet	*yą met*	ຢາເມັດ
sleeping medication	*yąa náwn láp*	ຢານອນຫລັບ
vitamin	*witąamín*	ວິຕາມິນ

LAO

Useful Words

addict	*khón tít yạa*	ຄົນຕິດຢາ
allergic (to)	*phâe*	ແພ້
bandage	*phàa haw bàat*	ຜ້າຫໍບາດ
blood	*lêuat*	ເລືອດ
bone	*kádùuk*	ກະດູກ
ill	*puay*	ປ່ວຍ
pain	*khwáam jép-puàt*	ຄວາມເຈັບປວດ

Time & Dates
Telling the Time

The Lao tell time using a 12-hour system which divides the day into four sections *(tạwn)*:

6 am to midday	*tạwn sâo*	ຕອນເຊົ້າ
midday to 3 or 4 pm	*tạwn baai*	ຕອນບ່າຍ
3 or 4 pm to 6 pm	*tạwn láeng*	ຕອນແລງ
6 to 11 pm	*tạwn khám*	ຕອນຄ່ຳ

After 11 pm is *kạang khéun*. When speaking of specific clock times, use *móhng* (hour) and *náa-thíi* (minutes), plus one of these five times of day. *Baai* (afternoon) comes before the hour quote; all the other times of day come after. Noon is *tạwn thiang*, midnight *thiang khéun*.

9 am	*kâo móhng sâo*	ເກົ້າໂມງເຊົ້າ
midday	*thiang*	ທ່ຽງ
1 pm	*baai móhng*	ບ່າຍໂມງ
2.15 pm	*baai sãwng móhng síp-hàa*	ບ່າຍສອງໂມງ ສິບຫ້າ

8.20 pm	*bàet móhng sáo tạwn khám*	ແປດໂມງຊາວຕອນຄ່ຳ
midnight	*thiang khéun*	ທ່ຽງຄືນ

If expressing time in terms of number of hours, use *sua-móng*:

three hours	*sãam sua-móhng*	ສາມຊົ່ວໂມງ

Days of the Week

Sunday	*wán ạathit*	ວັນອາທິດ
Monday	*wán jạn*	ວັນຈັນ
Tuesday	*wán ạngkháan*	ວັນອັງຄານ
Wednesday	*wán phut*	ວັນພຸດ
Thursday	*wán phahát*	ວັນພະຫັດ
Friday	*wán súk*	ວັນສຸກ
Saturday	*wán sáo*	ວັນເສົາ

Months

January	*dẹuan mángkạwn*	ເດືອນມັງກອນ
February	*dẹuan kụmpháa*	ເດືອນກຸມພາ
March	*dẹuan mináa*	ເດືອນມີນາ
April	*dẹuan méhsãa*	ເດືອນເມສາ
May	*dẹuan pheutsá pháa*	ເດືອນພຶດສະພາ
June	*dẹuan mithúnáa*	ເດືອນມິຖຸນາ
July	*dẹuan kạwlakót*	ເດືອນກໍລະກົດ
August	*dẹuan sĩnghãa*	ເດືອນສິງຫາ
September	*dẹuan kạnyáa*	ເດືອນກັນຍາ
October	*dẹuan túláa*	ເດືອນຕຸລາ
November	*dẹuan phajík*	ເດືອນພະຈິກ
December	*dẹuan thánwáa*	ເດືອນທັນວາ

Seasons

hot season/dry season (Mar-May)
  leuduu hâwn/leuduu lâeng   ລະດູຮ້ອນ / ລະດູແລ້ງ
rainy season (Jun-Oct)
  leuduu fõn   ລະດູຝົນ
cool season (Nov-Feb)
  leuduu não   ລະດູໜາວ

Dates

The traditional Lao calendar is a solar-lunar mix. The year is reckoned by solar phases, the months by lunar phases (unlike the Gregorian calendar in which months as well as years are reckoned by the sun). Year one of the Lao Buddhist Era (BE) calendar is 638 BC, so subtract 638 from the Lao calendar year to arrive at the Gregorian calendar year (eg 1999 AD is 2637 BE). Most educated Lao are also familiar with the 'Christian era' (*khit sák-álâat*) calendar.

2637 (BE)
  (pháw sãw) sãwng phán   ພໍ ສ ສອງ ພັນ ຫົກ ຮ້ອຍ ສາມ
  hók hâwy sãam-síp jét   ສິບ ເຈັດ
1999 (AD)
  (kháw sãw) neung phán   ກໍ ສ ນຶ່ງ ພັນ ເກົ້າ ຮ້ອຍ ເກົ້າ
  kâo hâwy kâo-síp-kâo   ສິບ ເກົ້າ

Days of the month are numbered according to the familiar Gregorian calendar.

13th of January
  wán thíi síp-sãam deuan   ວັນທີ ສິບສາມ ເດືອນມັງກອນ
  mángkawn

Present

today	*mêu nîi*	ມື້ນີ້
this evening	*láeng nîi*	ແລງນີ້
tonight	*khéun nîi*	ຄືນນີ້
this morning	*sâo nîi*	ເຊົ້ານີ້
this afternoon	*baai nîi*	ບ່າຍນີ້
this month	*dẹuan nîi*	ເດືອນນີ້
all day long	*talàwt mêu*	ຕລອດມື້
now	*diaw nîi/tạwn nîi*	ດຽວນີ້/ຕອນນີ້

Past

yesterday	*mêu wáan nîi*	ມື້ວານນີ້
the day before yesterday	*mêu séun*	ມື້ຊືນ
last week	*qathit thii lâew*	ອາທິດທີ່ແລ້ວ
two weeks ago	*sãwng qathit thii lâew*	ສອງອາທິດທີ່ແລ້ວ

Future

tomorrow	*mêu eun*	ມື້ອື່ນ
day after tomorrow	*mêu héu*	ມື້ຮື
next week	*qathit nàa*	ອາທິດໜ້າ
next month	*dẹuan nàa*	ເດືອນໜ້າ
two more months	*ìik sãwng dẹuan*	ອີກສອງເດືອນ

During the Day

dawn	*táwán khèun*	ຕາເວັນຂຶ້ນ
daytime	*kạang wán*	ກາງວັນ
evening	*láeng*	ແລງ
night	*khéun*	ຄືນ

LAO

Numbers

Cardinal Numbers

0	*sŭun*	ສຸນ
1	*neung*	ນຶ່ງ
2	*sǎwng*	ສອງ
3	*sǎam*	ສາມ
4	*sii*	ສີ່
5	*hàa*	ຫາ
6	*hók*	ຫົກ
7	*jét*	ເຈັດ
8	*pàet*	ແປດ
9	*kâo*	ເກົ້າ
10	*síp*	ສິບ
11	*síp-ét*	ສິບເອັດ
12	*síp-sǎwng*	ສິບສອງ
13	*síp-sǎam*	ສິບສາມ
14	*síp-sii*	ສິບສີ່
...-teen	*síp ...*	ສິບ...
20	*sáo*	ຊາວ
21	*sáo-ét*	ຊາວເອັດ
30	*sǎam-síp*	ສາມສິບ
40	*sii-síp*	ສີ່ສິບ
100	*hâwy*	ຮອຍ
200	*sǎwng hâwy*	ສອງຮອຍ
1000	*phán*	ພັນ
million	*lâan*	ລານ

Classifiers (Counters)

To state a quantity of something in Lao, you first name the thing you want, then the number and then add the classifier (or counter) of the item. So five oranges is *sòm ha lûuk* ('orange five fruit'). Every noun in Lao that's countable must take a classifier.

• glasses (of water etc)	*jàwk*
• vehicles	*khán*
• people	*khón*
• pairs of items (people, things)	*khuu*
• plates (food)	*jaan*
• letters, newspapers (flatsheets)	*sábáp*
• slices (cakes, cloth)	*phaen*
• sets of things	*sut*
• animals, furniture, clothing	*tǫh*
• round hollow objects, leaves	*bai*
• rolls (toilet paper, film)	*mûan*
• pills, seeds, small gems	*kaen*
• monks, Buddha images	*hùup*
• fruit, balls	*nuay*
• candles, books	*hŭa*
• houses	*lãng*
• small objects, miscellaneous	*tǫh*

If you don't know (or forget) the appropriate classifier, *tǫh* may be used for almost any small thing. Alternatively the Lao sometimes repeat the noun rather than not use a classifier at all.

Ordinal Numbers

These are formed by adding *thíi* before the cardinal numbers.

first	*thíi neung*	ທີນຶ່ງ
second	*thíi sǎwng*	ທີສອງ

Emergencies

Help!	suay dae	ຊ່ວຍແດ່
Stop!	yút	ຢຸດ !
Go away!	pai dǫe	ໄປເດີ້
Watch out!	lawáng	ລະວັງ
Thief!	khá-móhy	ຂະໂມຍ
Fire!	fái mài	ໄຟໃໝ້

Call a doctor!
  suai tǫam hǎa mǎw hài dae   ຊ່ວຍຕາມຫາໝໍໃຫ້ແດ່
Call an ambulance!
  suay ôen lot hóhng mǎw dae   ຊ່ວຍເອີ້ນລົດໂຮງໝໍໃຫ້ແດ່
Call the police!
  suay ôen tam-lùat dae   ຊ່ວຍເອີ້ນຕຳຫລວດແດ່
I've been robbed.
  khàwy thèuk khá-móhy   ຂ້ອຍຖືກຂະໂມຍ
I've been raped.
  khàwy thèuk khòm khēun   ຂ້ອຍຖືກຂົ່ມຂືນ
I am ill.
  khawy puay   ຂ້ອຍປ່ວຍ
I am lost.
  khàwy lóng tháang   ຂ້ອຍຫລົງທາງ

My ... was stolen.	khá-móhy ... khāwng khàwy	ຂະໂມຍ...ຂອງຂ້ອຍ
I've lost my ...	... hǎai lêew	...ຫາຍແລ້ວ
bags	kǫng khāwng	ກົງຂອງ
money	ngóen	ເງິນ
travellers' cheques	sek dǫen tháang	ເຊັກເດິນທາງ
passport	nǎng sēu phaan dǫen	ໜັງສືຜ່ານແດນ

Where is the police station?
sathāaníi tam-lùat yuu sāi? ສະຖານີຕຳຫລວດຢູ່ໃສ?

Where are the toilets?
hàwng sùam yuu sāi? ຫ້ອງສ້ວມຢູ່ໃສ?

Could I please use the telephone?
sâi thóhlasáp dâi baw? ໃຊ້ໂທລະສັບໄດ້ບໍ່?

I wish to contact my embassy/
consulate.
*yàak tít taw sathāan-thûut
khāwng khàwy* ຢາກຕິດຕໍ່ສະຖານທູດຂອງຂ້ອຍ

I didn't realise I was doing
anything wrong.
*khàwy baw hûu dâi het
nyāng phít* ຂ້ອຍບໍ່ຮູ້ໄດ້ເຮັດຫຍັງຜິດ

I didn't do it.
khàwy baw dâi het ຂ້ອຍບໍ່ໄດ້ເຮັດ

I'm sorry, I apologise.
khāw thôht, sīa jai ຂໍໂທດ. ເສຍໃຈ

Contact number in case of
emergency (next of kin) ...
*khâwp khúa thii já hài tít
taw nái kálaníi súk sōen ...* ຄອບຄົວທີ່ຈະໃຫ້ຕິດ
ຕໍ່ໃນກໍລະນີ ສຸກເສີນ ...

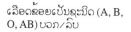

My blood group is (A,B,O,AB)
positive/negative.
*lêuat khàwy pęn sànit
(A, B, O, AB) bùak/lop* ເລືອດຂ້ອຍເປັນຊະນິດ (A, B,
O, AB) ບວກ/ລົບ

TAGALOG (PILIPINO)

Tagalog (Pilipino)

Tagalog, along with English, is the official language of the Philippines. In 1937, when it was declared the national language of the Philippines, it was officially called Pilipino, but Tagalog is the traditional name and the name which is used in colloquial speech. It is spoken as the mother tongue or as a second language by up to 50 million people in the Philippines.

Tagalog was declared the national language for a number of reasons. It is native to the southern part of the island of Luzon and so was the dialect spoken in the capital city, Manila. It is the most widely spoken and understood language in the Philippines. It was the language of the revolution against Spain late last century and became synonymous with Philippine pride and identity.

Tagalog is a member of the Philippine branch of the Austronesian language family. It incorporates words from other Philippines languages and shows elements of Sanskrit and Arabic. It has also been influenced by Chinese and by Spanish, due to over three centuries of colonial domination of the Philippines by Spain.

Tagalog has spread widely throughout the Philippines because of official government policy mandating its study in schools, but also because of the economic and social importance of the Manila area and because of the influence of Tagalog films, broadcasts, and reading materials. Furthermore, in many areas where migration patterns have led to populations with a great deal of ethnic and linguistic variety, Tagalog has become the means of intergroup communication. Thus Tagalog is now the main language not only in its home base but in some of the major cities of Palawan and Mindanao and has become the second language everywhere except in the most isolated regions.

Abbreviations Used in This Chapter

fam	familiar
f	feminine
m	masculine
n	noun
pol	polite
sg	singular
pl	plural

Pronunciation
Vowels

Vowels can be long or short. They are not usually indicated in written Tagalog but in this chapter, long vowels are indicated by an acute accent.

a	as in 'f**a**ther'
e	as in 'l**e**t'
i	as in 'm**ee**t'
o	as in 'h**o**t'
u	as in 't**oo**'

Diphthongs

ay	as in 'h**igh**'
oy	as in 'b**oi**l'
uy	sounds like 'ph**ooey**'
iw	a sound beginning with 'ee' and moving to 'oo'; as in 'f**ue**l'
aw	as in 'h**ou**se'
ey	as in 'h**ay**'

Vowels in Sequence

If several vowels are written in a sequence, each is pronounced distinctly, separated by a glottal stop.

Consonants

Most consonants in Tagalog are pronounced in the same way as their English counterparts, with the exception of the following:

g   hard, as in 'get', never as in 'gin'
h   always aspirated, never silent
ng   as in 'sing'; it can occur at the beginning of a word
r   like a rolled 'r', but the tongue only taps against the roof of the mouth once
s   as in 'sit', never as in 'wisdom'

Glottal Stop

A glottal stop is the halting 'sound' you hear in the middle of 'Oh-oh!'. It is also the sound that replaces 'tt' in 'bottle' when said by a cockney. The glottal stop, represented here by a grave accent placed over the vowel which precedes it, occurs only before a pause, eg *walà*, 'there isn't any'. If something is placed after *walà*, the glottal stop is dropped, and the preceding vowel is lengthened, eg *walá na*, 'there isn't any more'.

Stress

Stress is on the last long vowel in the word. If the word contains no long vowels, stress is on the final syllable:

mánunulat	writer
nagwáwalang-ba**hál**à	not care
nag**bá**basa	be reading
pagbaba**sa**	a reading
kuma**ká**in	be eating

Spelling Conventions

The particle *nang* (used to indicate possession) is written as *ng* even though it is still pronounced 'nang'. The particle *manga* (placed before a noun to indicate the plural) is written as *mga* but is pronounced 'mah-ngá'. They are both written as separate words.

The house belonging to the teachers.
> *Ang báhay ng mga títser.*
> (pronounced: *ang báhay nang manga títser*)

Greetings & Civilities
Greetings & Goodbyes

Good morning.	*Magandang umága.*
Good day (noon).	*Magandang tangháli.*
Good afternoon.	*Magandang hápon.*
Good evening.	*Magandang gabi.*
Hello/Hi.	*Hoy/Uy.* (fam)
Goodbye.	*Paálam.*
Bye.	*Síge.* (fam)

Civilities

'Thank you' is not used as much in Tagalog as it is in English. Saying 'Thank you' for a service you'd expect sounds sarcastic in Tagalog.

Thank you (very much).	*(Maráming) salámat.*
You're welcome.	*Walang anuman.*
	(literally 'it's nothing')
Excuse me/Sorry. (pol)	*Ipagpaumanhin ninyo ako*
May I/Do you mind?	*Pupwéde ba?*

Yes.	*Óo.*
No.	*Hindì*

To say 'Please' attach the prefix *paki* to the verb and use the word for 'you' – *mo* (fam) or *hó ninyo* (pol) – after the verb.

Please pass the bread.   *Pakipása hó ninyo ang tinápay.*

Forms of Address

You can use the common forms of address in English – 'Mr, Miss, Ms, Mrs, Dr, etc' – when addressing people.

• Use the title *mámà* for a man who is a stranger:

How much are the atis?   *Magkáno hó ba ang átis, mámà?*

• but use *sir* for a professional man:

May I ask you a question?   *Pwéde hó bang magtanong sir?*

• The more friendly and familiar term *páre* can also be used for a man who is a stranger:

Excuse me, my friend.   *Ekskyus lang páre.*

• For women, a friendly but respectful term of address is *ále* (literally 'auntie'):

How much is a kilogram of mangos?   *Magkáno hó ba ang kílo ng mangga ále?*

- When addressing people of high status or older people the particle *hó* should be used together with the pronoun *kayo* ('you'). The particle *pò* is also used, but it connotes great respect and is not as common.

How are you?   *Kumusta hó kayo?*

Pronouns

I	*ako*	we (including you)	*táyo*
		we (exluding you)	*kami*
you (sg & fam)	*ka/ikaw*	you (pl & pol)	*kayo*
he, she, it	*siya*	they	*sila*

Body Language

Filipinos signify 'Yes' by raising the eyebrows or lifting the head upwards slightly. The hand movements which mean 'Go away' to us signify 'Come here' in the Philippines.

The thumb and middle finger are not used to indicate numbers. Instead of pointing with your finger, indicate discreetly by pointing pursed lips in the direction you want.

One hisses to gain attention, for example, when calling a waiter in a restaurant. When you want to pay the bill, draw a rectangle in the air with your index finger and thumb.

If Filipinos don't understand a question, they open their mouths.

Language Difficulties

Do you speak English?	*Nagsásalitá ka ba ng Ingles?*
Yes, I do.	*O, nakákapagsalitá ako.*
No, I don't.	*Hindí ako marúnong.*
Does anyone speak English?	*May nakákapagsalitá ng Ingles díto?*
I speak a little.	*Marúnong akong magsalitá ng kóntì.*
Do you understand?	*Náiintindihan mo ba?*
I (don't) understand.	*(Hindí) ko náiintindihan.*
Could you speak more slowly?	*Pwéde mo bang bagálan ang iyong pagsasalità?*
Could you repeat that?	*Pakiúlit mo yon.*
Please write it down.	*Pakisúlat mo naman.*
How do you say ...?	*Paáno mo sásabíhin ...?*
What does ... mean?	*Ano'ng íbig sabíhin ng ...?*

Small Talk
Meeting People

How are you?	*Kumusta hó kayo?* (pol)
Hi Ting, how are you?	*Hoy Ting, kumusta ka?* (fam)
Fine. And you?	*Mabúti naman. Ikaw?* (fam)
What is your name?	*Ano ang pangálan mo?*
My name is ...	*Ako ay ...*
I'd like to introduce you to ...	*Gusto kitang ipakilála kay ...*
I'm pleased to meet you.	*Ikinatútuwá kong nákilála ko kayo.*

Nationalities

Where are you from?	*Tagasaan ka?*
I'm from ...	*Taga ... ako.*
Australia	*Awstralya*
Canada	*Kanada*
England	*Inglatera*
Europe	*Yurópa*
Ireland	*Irlandia*
Japan	*Hapon*
the Philippines	
the USA	*Isteyts (Amerika)*

Age

How old ...?	*Ilang taon ...?*
are you (to a child)	*ka na*
are you (to an adult)	*hó kayo*
is your son/daughter	*hó ang anak ninyo*
I'm ... years old.	*May ... ng taon na ako.*

(See Numbers & Amounts, page 269, for your age.)

Occupations

What (work) do you do?	*Ano ang trabáho mo?*
I am a/an ...	*... ako.*
artist	*pintor*
businessperson	*mángangalakal*
doctor	*doktor*
engineer	*inhinyéro*

farmer	*magsasaka*
journalist	*peryodista*
lawyer	*abogádo*
mechanic	*mekaniko*
nurse	*nars*
office worker	*kawáni*
scientist	*sayintist*
student	*estudyánte*
teacher	*títser (gúrò)*
waiter	*wéyter* (m)/*wéytres* (f)
writer	*mánunulat*

I'm unemployed.   *Walá akong trabáho.*

Religion
What is your religion?   *Ano ang relihiyon mo?*
I'm not religious.   *Hindí ako relihiyóso.*

I'm ...   *... hó ako.*
  Buddhist   *budist*
  Christian   *kristiyáno*

The Tagalog terms for Hindu, Muslim and Jewish are considered
to be derogatory. It is, on the other hand, quite acceptable to use
the English terms. Most people will understand these.

Family
Are you married?   *May asáwa ka na ba?*
I am single.   *Walá pa akong asáwa.*
I am married.   *May asáwa na ako.*

How many children do you have?	*Ilan ang anak ninyo?*
We don't have any children.	*Walá pa kaming anak.*
I have a ...	*Méron akong ...*
How many siblings do you have?	*Ilan kayong magkakapatid?*
Is your husband/wife here?	*Nandíto ba ang asáwa mo?*
Do you have a (boyfriend/girlfriend)?	*May (nóbyo/nóbya) ka na ba?*

brother/sister	*kapatid*
children	*mga anak*
family	*pamílya*
father	*tátay*
husband/wife	*asáwa*
mother	*nánay*
older brother	*kúya*
older sister	*áte*
son/daughter	*anak*

Interests

I like ...	*Gusto kong ...*
I don't like ...	*Áyaw kong ...*
going out	*magpasyal*
playing games	*maglaró*
playing soccer	*maglaró ng soccer*
playing sport	*maglaró ng isport*
reading books	*magbasa ng mga libro*
shopping	*mamili*
travelling	*magbiyáhe*
watching TV	*manood ng TV*

Do you like ...?	*Gusto mo ng ....?*
film	*pelikula*
music	*musika*

Making Conversation

Do you live here?	*Ito ba ang báhay ninyo?*
Where are you going?	*Saan ka púpunta?*
What are you doing?	*Ano' ng ginágawá mo?*
What do you think (about ...)?	*Ano ang palagay mo (sa ...)?*
Can I take a photo (of you)?	*Pwéde ba kitang kúnan nang retráto?*
What is this called?	*Ano' ng pangálan nito?*
Beautiful, isn't it!	*Ang ganda pala!*
It's very nice here.	*Maganda díto e.*
We love it here.	*Nagúgustuhan námin itong lugar.*
What a cute baby!	*Ang kyut ng bátá.*
Are you waiting too?	*Naghíhintay ba rin kayo?*
That's strange!	*Nakapagtátaka yon.*
That's funny (amusing)	*Nakatátáwa yon.*

Useful Phrases

Sure.	*Óo ba.*
Just a minute.	*Téka múna.*
It's OK.	*OK lang yan.*
It's important.	*Importánte yon.*
It's not important.	*Hindí importánte.*
It's possible.	*Pwéde.*
It's not possible.	*Hindí pwéde.*
Look!	*Tingnan mo!*
Listen/Listen to this!	*Makinig ka/Pakinggan mo ito!*

TAGALOG (PILIPINO)

I'm ready.	*Handá na ako.*
Are you ready?	*Handá ka na ba?*
Good luck!	*Swertehin ka nawà!*
Just a second!	*Sandalí lang!*

Getting Around
Finding Your Way

Where is the ...?	*Násaan ang ...?*
bus station	*terminal ng bus*
train station	*terminal ng tren*
road to Bontoc	*daan papuntang Bontoc*
What time does the ... leave/arrive?	*Anong óras áalis/dárating ang ...?*
aeroplane	*eropláno*
boat	*bapor*
bus	*bus*
train	*tren*

Directions

How do we get to ...?	*Paáno tayo makákapunta sa ...?*
Is it far from/near here?	*Maláyó (malápit) ba díto?*
Can we walk there?	*Pwéde bang lakarin?*
Can you show me (on the map)?	*Pwéde mo bang ipakíta (sa mápa)?*
Are there other means of getting there?	*May iba pa bang paraan papunta doon?*

What … is this?	*Anong .... hó ba ito?*
street	*daan*
city	*lunsod*
village	*baryo*

Turn ...	*Likó ...*
at the next corner	*sa súsunod na kánto*
at the traffic lights	*sa ílaw*

Straight ahead.	*Dirétso lámang.*
To the right.	*Papakánan.*
To the left.	*Papakaliwà.*
behind	*sa likod ng ...*
in front of	*sa harap ng ...*
far	*maláyò*
near	*malápit*
opposite	*katapat ng ...*

north	*nórte*
south	*sur*
east	*éste*
west	*wéste*

Buying Tickets

Excuse me, where is the ticket office?	*Ikskyus hó, násaan ang ticket office?*
Where can I buy a ticket?	*Saan ako pwédeng bumili ng ticket?*
We want to go to ...	*Gusto náming pumunta sa ...*
Do I need to book?	*Kailángan bang magreserba ng lugar?*

I'd like to book a seat to ...	*Gusto kong magreserba ng úpúan papuntang ...*
It is full.	*Punó na.*
Can I get a stand-by ticket?	*Mayroon bang stand-by?*

I'd like ...	*Gusto kong kumúha ng ...*
a one-way ticket	*ticket na papunta doon lang*
a return ticket	*bálíkang paglalakbay*
two tickets	*dalawang ticket*
a student's fare	*ticket pára sa estudyánte*
a child's/pensioner's fare	*ticket na pára sa bátà/ pensionádo*

| 1st class | *priméra kláse* |
| 2nd class | *segunda kláse* |

Air

Is there a flight to Ormoc?	*May flight ba pára sa Ormoc?*
When is the next flight to Cebu?	*Anong óras ang súsunod na flight pára sa Cebu?*
How long does the flight take?	*Anong katagal ang flight?*
What time do I have to check in at the airport?	*Anong óras ako dápat magcheck-in sa airport?*
Where is the baggage claim?	*Saan ko pwédeng kúnin ang áking bagáhe?*

Bus

| Where is the bus stop? | *Násaan ang parahan ng mga bus?* |
| Which bus goes to ...? | *Aling bus ang púpunta sa ...?* |

Does this bus go to ...?	*Púpunta ba itong bus na ito sa ...?*
How often do buses come?	*Gaano kadalas dumádaan ang mga bus?*

What time is the ... bus?   *Anong óras dárating ang ... bus?*

next	*ang súsunod na*
first	*ang únang*
last	*ang huling*

Could you let me know when we get to ...?	*Pwéde hó bang sabíhin nyo sa ákin kung táyo'y nása ... na?*
I want to get off at ...	*Gusto kong bumabá sa ...*
Does this bus leave soon?	*Malápit na bang umalis itong bus?*
Where do I get the bus for ...?	*Saan hó ang sákáyan papuntang ...?*

Train

What station is this?	*Anong istasyon na ito?*
What is the next station?	*Ano ang súsunod na istasyon?*
Does this train stop at Naga?	*Naghíhinto ba ang tren na ito sa Nága?*
The train is delayed/cancelled.	*Nahuli/nakansel ang tren.*
How long will it be delayed?	*Gaano katagal ang mahuli?*

Taxi

Is this taxi free?	*Pwéde bang masakyan ang taksing ito?*
Please take me to ...	*Pwéde ninyo akong dalhin sa ...*

How much does it cost to go to ...?	Magkáno hó papuntang ...?
How much is the fare?	Magkáno hó ang pamasáhe?
Do we pay extra for luggage?	May extrang báyad ang bagáhe?

Instructions

Continue!	Dirétso lang!
The next street to the left/right.	Pakaliwá/Pakánan sa súsunod na kánto.
Please slow down.	Pakibagálan lang hó ang pagtakbo.
Please wait here.	Pakihintay hó ríto
Stop here!	Pára na hó díto!
Stop at the corner.	Pára na hó sa kánto!

Boat

Where does the boat leave from?	Saan umalis ang bárko?
What time does the boat arrive?	Anong óras dárating ang bárko?
Is it unsafe to get off the boat while it is dark?	Delikádo bang bumabá ng bárko hanggang madilim pa?

Useful Phrases

How long does the trip take?	Anong katagal ang biyáhe?
Is it a direct route?	Dirétso ba ang paglalakbay?
Is that seat taken?	May nakaupó na riyan?
I want to get off at ...	Gusto kong bumabá sa ...
Where can I hire a bicycle?	Saan hó ako pwédeng magarkila ng bisikléta?

Accommodation
Finding Accommodation

I'm looking for a ...	*Nagháhanap ako ng ...*
camping ground	*kampingan*
guesthouse	*báhay pára sa mga turist*
hotel	*hotel*
motel	*motel*
youth hostel	*hotel pàra sa mga binátà*

Where can I find a ...?	*Saan hó pwédeng mákíta ang isang ...?*
good hotel	*magaling na hotel*
nearby hotel	*hotel na malápit díto*
clean hotel	*malínis na hotel*

Where is the ... hotel?	*Saan hó ba díto ang ... hotel?*
best	*pinakamagandang*
cheapest	*pinakamúrang*

What is the address?	*Ano ang adres?*
Could you write the address, please?	*Pwéde hó bang pakisúlat ang adres?*

Checking In

Do you have any rooms available?	*May bakánte hó ba kayo?*
Sorry, we're full.	*Sorry hó, punó na kami.*
Do you have a room with two beds?	*Méron hó ba kayong kwártong mé dalawang káma?*

Do you have a room with a double bed?	*Méron hó ba kayong kwártong mé kámang pangdalawahan?*

I'd like ...
    to share a dorm
    a single room
	Gusto kong ...
	    makipag-share ng kwárto
	    ng pangisahang kwárto

We want a room with a ...
 	
    bathroom
    shower
    TV
    window
	Gusto námin ng kwártong may saríling ...
	    bányo
	    dutsa
	    TV
	    kwártong may bintánà

Can I see it? Are there any others? Where is the bathroom? Is there hot water all day?	*Pwéde hó bang patingin?* *Méron pang iba?* *Násaan hó ba díto ang bányo?* *May maínit na túbig ba buong áraw?*

How much for ...?
 	
    one night
    a week
    two people
	Magkáno hó ba ang báyad pára sa ...?
	    isang gabi
	    isang linggo
	    dalawang táo

Is there a discount for children/students? It's fine. I'll take it.	*May táwad ba ang mga bátà/estudyánte?* *Síge. Kúkúnin ko.*

Requests & Complaints

I need a (another) ...

Pwéde hó bang makahingí ng (isa pang) ...

bar of soap	*sabon*
face cloth	*bimpo*
bottle of water	*bóte ng túbig*
lamp	*lámsyed*
mosquito coil	*katol*
towel	*twalya*

Do you have a safe where I can leave my valuables?

Mayroon ba kayong káha na pwéde kong paglagyan ng áking mga mahalagang bágay?

Could I have a receipt for them?

Pwéde hó bang pahingí ng resíbo?

Is there somewhere to wash clothes?

Saan pwédeng maglaba ng damit?

Can we use the telephone?

Makíkigámit hó kami ng telepono.
or *Pwéde hó bang pagámit ng telepono.*

Please put some drinking water in my room.

Pakidala ngá hó ng túbig na inumin díto sa kwarto.

My room is too dark

Madilim hó yáta itong áking kwárto.

It's too cold/hot.

Ang ginaw/alinsángan díto.

It's too noisy.

Ang íngay díto.

I can't open/close the window.

Hindí mabuksan/masarhan ang bintánà.

This ... is not clean.	*Madumi hó yáta itong ...*
blanket/sheet	*kúmot*
pillow case	*punda*
pillow	*únan*

| Please change them/it. | *Pwéde hó bang pakipalitan?* |

Checking Out

Can I pay with a travellers' cheque?	*Tumátanggap hó ba kayo ng travellers' cheque?*
Could I have the bill please?	*Magkáno hó ang bábayáran ko?*
There's a mistake in the bill.	*Méron hó yátang malí díto sa kwénta.*

Useful Words

air-con	*érkon*
clean	*malínis*
key	*súsì*
lock	*kandádo*
soap	*sabon*
toilet	*kubéta/CR*
toilet paper	*tisyu*
towel	*twalya*
water (cold/hot)	*malamig/maínit na túbig*

Around Town

Where is a ...?	*Násaan hó mérong ...?*
bank	*bangko*
consulate	*konsuládo*
embassy	*embaháda*

TAGALOG (PILIPINO)

post office	*post office*
public telephone	*telepono*
public toilet	*kubéta*
town square	*plása*

At the Post Office

If you're not sure how to ask for something, use the English term and you are likely to be understood.

I want to buy ...	*Pabili hó ako ng ...*
postcards	*tarhéta postal*
stamps	*sélyo*

I want to send a ...	*Gusto kong magpadala ng ...*
letter	*súlat*
parcel	*pakéte*
telegram	*telegráma*

Please send it by ...	*Pakipadala hó ito ng ...*
How much does it cost to send this to ...?	*Magkáno ito kung ipápadala ko sa ...?*
Please weigh this letter.	*Pakitimbang itong súlat.*

| aerogram | *aerogram* |
| envelope | *sóbre* |

Telephone

| Could I please use the telephone? | *Pwéde hong pagámit ng telepono?* |
| I want to call ... | *Gusto kong tawágan ang ...* |

The number is ...	*... ang numero niyon.*
How much does a three-minute call eost?	*Magkáno ang táwag na tatlong minúto?*
I want to make a long-distance call to Australia.	*Gusto kung tumáwag sa long-distance sa Australia.*
I want to make a reverse-charges/collect call.	*Gusto kong tumáwag ng collect.*
Hello, is ... there?	*Helo, nandíto hò ba si ...*
Yes, he/she is here.	*Nárito hò siya.*
One moment, (please).	*Sandalí lang (hò).*

At the Bank

You'll find that English terms are often used in banks.

I want to change ...	*Gusto kong magpapalit ng ...*
cash/money	*péra*
a cheque	*cheque*
a travellers' cheque	*travellers cheque*
What time does the bank open?	*Anong óras magbúbukas ang bangkong ito?*
Where can I cash a travellers' cheque?	*Saan hò pwédeng magpapalit ng travelers' check?*
What is the exchange rate?	*Magkáno hò ang halagá ng pálítan?*
Can I transfer money here from my bank?	*Pwéde hò ba akong maglípat ng péra díto gáling sa áking bangko?*
How long will it take to arrive?	*Gaano katagal bágo ito dumating?*

Sightseeing

Where is the tourist office?	*Násaan hó ba ang opisína ng turismo?*
Do you have a local map?	*Mé mápa hó ba kayo ng lugar na ito?*
I'd like to see ...	*Gusto kong tingnan ...*
What time does it open?	*Anong óras ito magbúbukas?*
What time does it close?	*Anong óras ito magsásara?*
What is that building?	*Ano hó ba ang gusáli na iyon?*
What is this monument?	*Ano ba ang monuméntong ito?*
Who lived there?	*Síno ang tumira doon?*
May we take photographs?	*Pwéde ba kaming kumúha ng litráto?*
I'll send you the photograph.	*Padádalhan kita nitong litráto.*
Could you take a photograph of me?	*Pwéde mo akong kúnan ng litráto?*

castle	*kastilyo*
church/cathedral	*simbahan*
cinema	*sinehan*
concert	*konserto*
crowded	*masikip*
museum	*museum*
nice	*maganda*
park	*párke*
statue	*istátwa*
university	*unibersidad*
nightclub	*naitclub*

TAGALOG (PILIPINO)

Paperwork

name	*pangálan*
address	*tiráhan*
date of birth	*petsang isinílang*
place of birth	*lugar na sinilángan*
age	*edad/gulang*
sex	*kasarian/kasarían*
nationality	*nasionalidad*
religion	*relihiyon*
profession/work	*propesyon/trabáho*
reason for travel	*dahilan sa paglakbay*
marital status	*kasádo ba hindì*
single	*binátà* (m)/*dalága* (f)
married	*kasádo*
divorced	*diborsyádo*
widow/widower	*báo*
identification	*ID*
passport number	*bilang ng pasaporte*
visa	*bísa*
baptismal certificate	*partído de bautismo*
driving licence	*lisensiya sa pagmamaného*
customs	*adwána*
immigration	*imigrasyon*
purpose of visit	*dahilan ng paglakbay*
holiday	*magbakasyon*
business	*mangalákal*
visiting relatives	*magbisíta ng kamag-ának*
visiting the homeland	*balikbáyan*

TAGALOG (PILIPINO)

In the Country
Weather

What's the weather like?   *Anong kláse ang panahon?*

Today it is ...   *... ngayon.*
  cloudy   *maúlap*
  cold   *maginaw*
  hot   *maínit*
  warm   *medyo maínit*
  windy   *mahángin*

It's raining heavily.   *Matindig ang ulan.*
It's raining lightly.   *Umáambon.*
It's flooding.   *Bumábahà.*

dry season   *tag-áraw*
rainy season   *tag-ulan*
storm   *bagyo*
sun   *áraw*

Geographical Terms

beach   *apláya*
cave   *kwéba*
forest   *gubat*
hill   *bundok*
hot spring   *bukal ng maínit na túbig*
island   *pulò*
lake   *lawà*
mountain   *bundok*
river   *ílog*

sea	*dágat*
valley	*lambak*
waterfall	*talon*

Flora & Agriculture

coconut palm	*púnó ng niyog*
corn	*mais*
flower	*bulaklak*
harvest (verb)	*áni*
irrigation	*patúbig*
leaf	*dáhon*
planting/sowing	*pagtatanim*
rice field	*páláyan*
sugar cane	*tubo*
terraced land	*baíbaítang na lúpà*
tobacco	*tabákò*
tree	*káhoy*

Fauna

bird	*íbon*
buffalo	*kalabaw*
cat	*púsà*
chicken	*manok*
cockroach	*ípis*
cow	*báka*
crocodile	*buáya*
dog	*áso*
fish	*isdà*
fly	*lángaw*
horse	*kabáyò*

leech	*lintà*
lion	*leon*
monkey	*unggoy*
mosquito	*lamok*
pig	*báboy*
sheep	*túpa*
snake	*áhas*
spider	*gagamba*
tiger	*tígre*

Camping

camping	*pagkakampo/pagkakamping*
campsite	*kampuhan/kampingan*
rope	*léteng*
tent	*tolda*
torch (flashlight)	*pláslait*

Useful Words & Phrases

Are there any tourist attractions near here?	*May mga lugar na pangturista ba na malápit díto?*
Is it safe to swim here?	*Hindí ba delikádong lumangoy díto?*
Where is the nearest village?	*Násaan ang pinakamalápit na baryo?*
Is it safe to climb this mountain?	*Hindí ba delikádong umáhon sa bundok na ito?*
Is there a hut up there?	*May kúbo ba doon sa táas?*
Do we need a guide?	*Kailángan ba námin ng kasáma?*

TAGALOG (PILIPINO)

diving	*pagsisísid*
fishing	*pangingisdà*
hiking	*paglalakad ng mahábà*
hunting	*pangangáso*
mountain climbing	*pamumundok*
surfing	*paglalaró sa dalúyong*
swimming	*paglangoy*

Food

breakfast	*almusal/agáhan*
lunch	*tanghalían*
dinner	*hapúnan*

Eating Out

Table for (five), please.	*Kailángan hó námin nang mésang (panlima).*
May we see the menu?	*Pwéde hó bang mákíta ang menu?*
Please bring some ...	*Pwéde hó bang magdala nang ...*
Do I get it myself or do they bring it to us?	*Ako na lang ba ang kúkúha o sila ang magdádala díto sa átin?*
I'm a vegetarian.	*Gúlay lámang ang kinákáin ko.*
I can't eat dairy products.	*Hindí ako makakáin nang mga produktong gawá sa gátas.*
Please bring ...	*Pakidala hó ang*
an ashtray	*siniséro*
the bill	*kwénta/chit*
a fork	*tinidor*

a glass of water (with/without ice)	*isang básong túbig (mé yélo/walang yélo)*
a knife	*kutsilyo*
a plate	*pláto*

No ice in my beer, please.   *Walang yélo sa áking beer.*
Is service included in the bill?   *Kasáli ba ang serbisyo sa kwénta?*

Typical Filipino Dishes

Adobo
    popular dish made from chicken and pork and cooked with vinegar, pepper, garlic and salt or soy sauce

Ampaláya con Carne
    beef with bitter melon, prepared with onions, garlic, soy sauce and some sesame oil; served with rice

Atsára
    a very healthy and vitamin rich side dish, the Philippine sauerkraut – unripe papayas

Batchoy
    beef, pork and liver in noodle soup

Calderéta
    a stew of goat's meat or beef, peas and paprika

Dinuguan
    finely chopped pork offal stewed in fresh blood, usually seasoned with hot peppers

Halo-Hálò
    dessert made from crushed ice mixed with coloured sweets and fruits, smothered in evaporated milk and mixed together. It tastes better with a little rum.

Kiláwin
  small pieces of raw fish lightly roasted, then marinated in
  vinegar and other spices
Lapu-Lápong Iníhaw
  grilled grouper, seasoned with salt, pepper, garlic and soy
  sauce. It is the most popular fish dish in the country, but is
  expensive.
Lechon
  suckling pig served with a thick liver sauce. It is an important dish at fiestas.
Lumpià
  spring rolls filled with vegetables or meat. They are served
  with soy sauce, vinegar or a slightly sweet sauce.
Pancit Canton
  noodle dish made with thick noodles which are baked, then
  combined with pork, shrimps and vegetables
Sinigang
  sour vegetable soup with fish or pork; it can be served with
  rice

At the Market
Meat

beef	*báka*
meat	*kárne*
pork	*báboy*
goat	*kambing*

Seafood

clams	*tulya*
lobster	*ulang*
mussels	*tahong*

TAGALOG (PILIPINO)

oysters	*talaba*
sea crabs	*alimásag*
shrimp	*hípon*
swamp crabs	*alimángo*

Vegetables

bean sprouts	*tawgi*
beans with edible pods	*bátaw*
bitter melon	*ampaláya*
cassava	*kamóteng káhoy*
Chinese string beans	*sítaw*
eggplant	*talong*
lima beans	*patánì*
mild radish-type vegetable	*singkamas*
ramie leaves	*salúyot*
spinach-like vegetable	*kangkong*
squash	*kalabása*
sweet potatoes	*kamóte*
vegetables	*gúlay*

Fruit

avocado	*abokádo*
calamondon	*kalamundí*
cantaloupe	*milon*
custard apple	*átis*
lansium	*lansónes*
mango	*mangga*
orange	*lukban*
papaya/pawpaw	*papáya*
pineapple	*pínya*
sandor	*santol*

TAGALOG (PILIPINO)

sapodilla	*tsíko*
shaddock fruit	*pomélo*
soursop	*gwayabano*
Spanish plum	*sinigwélas*
star apple	*kaimíto*

Spices & Condiments

coconut milk	*gatà*
garlic	*áhos*
ginger	*lúya*
onions	*sibóyas*
red peppers	*sili*
salt	*asin*

Drinks

avocado drink	*abokádo dyus*
mango drink	*mango dyus*
lemonade	*lemonáda*
coffee	*kape*
(cup of) tea	*(isang tásang) tsá*
with/without milk	*may/walang gátas*
with/without sugar	*may/walang asúkal*

Useful Words

cup	*tása*
fresh	*saríwà*
spicy	*maanghang*
stale/spoiled	*sirá na*
sweet	*matamis*
toothpick	*tutpik*

TAGALOG (PILIPINO)

Shopping

barber	*barbéro*
bookshop	*tindáhan ng mga libro*
camera shop	*tindáhan ng mga kamera*
chemist/pharmacy	*botíkà*
clothing store	*tindáhan ng mga damit*
general store	*tindáhan*
laundry	*labandería*
market	*paléngke*
souvenir shop	*tindáhan ng pasalúbong*

Making a Purchase

I'd like to buy ...	*Gusto kung bumili ng ...*
Do you have others?	*May iba pa?*
I don't like it.	*Áyaw ko ito.*
Can I look at it?	*Pwédeng patingin?*
I'm just looking.	*Tumítingin lang ako.*
How much is this?	*Magkáno hó ito?*
Can you write down the price?	*Pwéde isulat ang présyo?*
Do you accept credit cards?	*Tumátanggap hó kayo ng credit card?*
Please wrap it.	*Pwéde hó bang pakibálot?*

Bargaining

I think it's too expensive.	*Sa palagay ko masyádo itong mahal.* or *Ang mahal naman niyan!*
It's too much for us.	*Hindí námin káyang bilhin.*
Can you lower the price?	*May táwad ba iyan?*

TAGALOG (PILIPINO)

Prices

The Philippine currency is the *peso*, from the Spanish. In Tagalog it is the *píso*. Prices over 10 are given in Spanish numbers:

three pesos	*tatlong píso*
15 pesos	*kínse pésos*

For quantities, Tagalog numbers are used up to 10, but above 10 Spanish numbers are mainly used.

How much for ...?	*Magkáno ang ...?*
a hundred	*isandaan (syénto)*
a dozen	*isang doséna (doséna)*

Souvenirs

baskets	*mga basket*
brassware	*kasangkápang tansò*
cane ware/furniture	*sulíhiya/mwébles gawá sa úway*
handicraft	*mga bágay na yárí ng kamay*
woodcarved figure	*statuwang inúkit*
souvenirs made of shell	*subenir gawá sa kabíbi*

Toiletries

condoms	*condoms*
deodorant	*deodorant*
moisturising cream	*krim na pambasà*
razor	*pang-áhit*
sanitary napkins	*tampon*
shampoo	*syampu*
shaving cream	*sabon pára mag-áhit*
soap	*sabon*
sunblock	*sunblock*

tampons	*tampons*
toilet paper	*tisyu*

Photography

How much is it to process this film?	*Magkáno hó magpadibélop nitong film?*
When will it be ready?	*Kailan hó makúkúha?*
I'd like a film for this camera.	*Gusto ko ng film pára díto sa kamera.*

B&W film	*film na putí at itim*
camera	*kamera*
flash/flash bulb	*kislap/bombilyang kislap*
lens	*lénte*

Smoking

A packet of cigarettes, please.	*Isang káhang yosi ngà.*
Are these cigarettes strong or mild?	*Malakas ba itong sigarilyos o hindì?*
Do you have a light?	*May panindi ka ba?*
Please don't smoke.	*Pwéde bang huwag kang manigarilyo?*
Do you mind if I smoke?	*Okey lang ba sa iyo kung manigarilyo ako?*
I'm trying to give up.	*Sinúsubúkan kung tumígil.*

cigarettes	*sigarilyo/yósi*
cigarette papers	*papel pára sigarilyo*
matches	*pospóro*
pipe	*kwáko*
tobacco	*tabákò*

Sizes & Comparisons

small	*maliit*
big	*malaki*
heavy	*mabigat*
light	*magaan*
more	*mas marámi*
little (amount)	*kokóntì*
too much/many	*masyádong marámi*
many	*marámi*
enough	*táma lang*
also	*din*
a little bit	*kokóntí*

Health

Where is the ...?	*Násaan ang ...?*
doctor	*doktor*
hospital	*ospital*
chemist	*botíkà*
dentist	*dentista*

I'm sick.	*May sakit ako.*
My friend is sick.	*May sakit ang kasáma ko.*

At the Doctor

Where does it hurt?	*Saan sumásakit?*
It hurts there.	*Masakit díto.*
I feel nauseous.	*Naalibadbaran ako.*
I've been vomiting.	*Nagsúsuka ako.*
I feel better/worse.	*Mabúti na/mas masamá ang pakiramdam ko.*

Ailments

burn	*sunog*
cold	*sipon*
constipation	*tibi*
diarrhoea	*pagtatae ng malakas*
fever	*lagnat*
gastroenteritis	*sumásakit ang tsikmúrá*
headache	*sakit ng úlo*
heart condition	*sakit sa púsó*
infection	*impeksyon*
pain	*sakit*
sore throat	*pagkasakit ng lalamúnan*
stomach ache	*pagkasakit ng tiyan*
toothache	*pagkasakit ng ngipin*
urinary infection	*impeksyon ng pantog*
venereal disease	*pagkasakit ng panlaman*

Women's Health

Could I see a female doctor?	*Pwédeng makipagkíta sa babáeng doktor.*
I'm pregnant.	*Buntis ako.*
I'm on the pill.	*Ako'y nagpípills.*
I haven't had my period for ... weeks.	*... linggo na akong hindí nagkákarégla.*

Specific Needs

I'm ...	*May ... ako.*
diabetic	*diabitis*
asthmatic	*híkà*
anaemic	*anemya*

I'm allergic to antibiotics/ penicillin.	*Alerdyik ako sa antibiotika/ penicillin*
I have a skin allergy.	*Naáalerdyik ang balat ko.*
I've had my vaccinations.	*Nagpabakúna na ako.*
I have my own syringe.	*May saríli akong ineksiyon.*
I'm on medication for ...	*Umíinom ako ng ...*
I need a new pair of glasses	*Kailángan ko ng bágong salamin.*

addiction	*pagkágúmon*
bite	*kagat*
blood test	*pagsurí ng dugò*
contraceptive	*contraceptive*
injection	*ineksiyon*
injury	*kapinsaláan*
vitamins	*bitamína*
wound	*súgat*

Parts of the Body

arms	*bráso*
chest	*dibdib*
ears	*ténga*
eye	*mga mata*
foot	*páa*
hand	*kamay*
head	*úlo*
legs	*binti*
ribs	*tadyang*
skin	*balat*
stomach	*tiyan*
teeth	*ngípin*

TAGALOG (PILIPINO)

At the Chemist

I need something for ...	*Kailángan ko ng gamot pára sa ...*
Do I need a prescription for ...?	*Kailángan ko ba ng reséta pára makabili ng ...?*
How many times a day?	*Ilang béses sa isang áraw?*

antibiotics	*antibayótik*
antiseptic	*antiséptiko*
aspirin	*aspirin*
bandage	*bendáhe*
Band-aids	*korítas*
cotton balls	*búlak*
gauze	*gása*
rubbing alcohol	*alkohol na panghaplos*

Time & Dates
Telling the Time

Spanish numers (with Tagalog spellings) are used to tell the time. Terms for 'am' and 'pm' are not used.

What time is it?	*Anong óras na?*
(It's) one o'clock.	*Ala úna na.*
(It's) ten o'clock.	*Alas diyes na.*

'Half past' is expressed by the word *imédya*:

Half past one.	*Ala úna imédya.*
Half past three.	*Alas trés imédya.*

Times can be expressed as so many minutes past the hour:

One fifteen.   *Ala úna kínse.*

Times can also be expressed as the next hour minus *(ménos)* so many minutes.

Quarter to five.   *Ménos kínse pára alas síngko.*

Days of the Week

Monday	*Lúnes*
Tuesday	*Mártes*
Wednesday	*Myérkules*
Thursday	*Hwébes*
Friday	*Byérnes*
Saturday	*Sábado*
Sunday	*Linggo*

Months

January	*Enéro*
February	*Pebréro*
March	*Márso*
April	*Abril*
May	*Máyo*
June	*Húnyo*
July	*Húlyo*
August	*Agósto*
September	*Setyémbre*
October	*Októbre*
November	*Nobyémbre*
December	*Disyémbre*

TAGALOG (PILIPINO)

Seasons

summer	*summer*
autumn	*autumn*
winter	*winter*
spring	*spring*
dry season	*tag-áraw*
rainy season	*tag-ulan*

Dates

What date it is today?	*Anong pétsa ngayon?*
It's 18 October.	*Ngayon ang akínse Októbre.*

Present

today	*ngayon*
this morning	*ngayong umága*
tonight	*ngayong gabi*
this week	*ngayong linggo*
this year	*ngayong taon*
now	*ngayon*

Past

yesterday	*kahápon*
day before yesterday	*nang isang áraw*
yesterday morning	*kahápon ng umága*
last night	*kagabi*
last week	*noong isang linggo*
last year	*noong isang taon*

Future

tomorrow	*búkas*
day after tomorrow	*búkas makalawa*

tomorrow morning/	*búkas sa umága/*
afternoon/evening	*hápon/gabi*
next week	*sa isang linggo*
next year	*sa isang taon*

During the Day

afternoon	*hápon*
dawn	*madaling áraw*
day	*áraw*
early	*maága*
midnight	*hátinggabi*
morning	*umága*
night	*gabi*
noon	*tanghálì*
sunrise	*pagsíkat ng áraw*
sunset	*paglubog ng áraw*

Numbers

There are two sets of numbers: the native Tagalog and the Spanish. Spanish numbers are used for times, dates and with prices above 10 pesos. English numbers are also widely used.

Cardinal Numbers

	Spanish	Tagalog
1	*úno*	*isa*
2	*dos*	*dalawa*
3	*tres*	*tatlo*
4	*kwátro*	*ápat*
5	*síngko*	*lima*
6	*sais/seis*	*ánim*

7	*siéte*	*pito*
8	*ótso*	*walo*
9	*nwébe*	*siyam*
10	*diyes*	*sampò*
11	*ónse*	*labing isa*
12	*dóse*	*labing dal'wa*
13	*trése*	*labing tatlo*
14	*katórse*	*labing apat*
15	*kínse*	*labing lima*
16	*diyesiseis*	*labing anim*
17	*diyesisyéte*	*labing pito*
18	*diyesiótso*	*labing walo*
19	*diyesinwébe*	*labing siyam*
20	*béynte/bénte*	*dalawampò*
21	*béynteúno*	*dalawampu't isa*
22	*béyntedos*	*dalawampu't dal'wa*
30	*tréynta/trénta*	*tatlumpò*
40	*kwarénta*	*apatnapò*
50	*singkwénta*	*limampò*
60	*sisénta*	*ánimnapò*
70	*siténta*	*pitumpò*
80	*otsénta*	*walumpò*
90	*nobénta/nubénta*	*siyamnapò*
100	*syénto*	*isandaan*
1000	*mil*	*isang líbo*
one million	*un million*	*isang milyon*

Ordinal Numbers

1st	*úna*
2nd	*ikalawa*
3rd	*ikatlo*

Emergencies

ISTASIYON NG PULIS   POLICE STATION

Help!	*Saklólo!*
Stop!	*Pára!*
Go away!	*Umalis ka!*
Thief!	*Magnanákaw!*
Fire!	*Súnog!*
Watch out!	*Bantay!*

Call the police!	*Tumáwag ka ng pulis!*
Call a doctor!	*Tumáwag ka ng doktor!*
Call an ambulance!	*Tumáwag ka ng ambulans!*

I've been raped.	*Ginahásá ako!*
I've been robbed.	*Ninakáwan ako!*
I am ill.	*May sakit ako.*
My friend is ill.	*May sakit ang kasáma ko.*
I have medical insurance.	*May insurance akong nagbábáyad ng pagpapagamot.*
I'm lost.	*Nawáwalá ako.*

I've lost my ...   *Nawalan ako ng áking ...*
   bags   *bagáhe*
   money   *péra*
   travellers' cheques   *travelers cheques*
   passport   *pasapórte*

My possessions are insured.   *May insurance ang áking mga gámit.*

TAGALOG (PILIPINO)

Where are the toilets?

Násaan hó ang CR?

I'm sorry/I apologise.
I didn't realise I was doing
anything wrong.
I didn't do it.

Sorry hò.
Hindí ko namaláyan na may
ginágawá pala akong malì.
Hindí ko ginawá iyan.

I wish to contact my
embassy/consulate.

Gusto kong tawágan ang
embaháda/konsuládo ko.

THAI

Thai

Thailand's official language is Thai (also known as Siamese) as spoken and written in central Thailand. While native Thai is spoken with various tonal accents and with slightly differing vocabularies as you move from one part of the country to the next, especially in a north to south direction, the central dialect has successfully become the lingua franca between all Thai and non-Thai ethnic groups in the kingdom, and provides the language used in this chapter.

All Thai dialects are members of the Thai half of the Thai-Kadai family of languages, and are closely related to languages spoken in Laos, northern Myanmar, north-western Vietnam, Assam and pockets of southern China. Thai-Kadai itself is part of the larger Austro-Thai group, one of the oldest language families in the world.

Experts disagree as to the exact origins of Thai script, but it was apparently developed around 800 years ago and was based on the Mon and possibly Khmer writing systems, both of which were in turn inspired by South Indian scripts. Like these languages, Thai is written from left to right, though vowel signs may be written before, above, below, 'around' (before, above and after), or after consonants, depending on the sign.

Most of the difficulty in mastering basic Thai comes from getting used to the new and different sounds. Once your ears become accustomed to the overall phonetic system the rest is fairly easy. The grammar is very straightforward; words do not change to signify tense, gender or plurality, and there are no articles.

So if you put aside your trepidations and take the plunge, you'll soon be getting by without. Listen closely to the way Thais themselves speak. Half the struggle in learning is discovering the spirit of the language. Thais will often laugh at your pronunciation, but this is usually an expression of their appreciation for your efforts rather than a mocking sort of criticism.

Abbreviations Used in This Chapter

f	spoken by females
m	spoken by males

Pronunciation
Vowels

Most Thai vowels have approximate English equivalents. Those that do not will require careful listening and practice; a cursory knowledge of French and Italian vowels will help.

Take care to distinguish between long and short vowels, signified by doubling the vowel or addition of 'h': the distinction can change the meaning (just as 'ship' and 'sheep' depend on vowel length for meaning in English).

a	like the 'u' in 'but'
aa	as the 'a' in 'father'; twice as long as **a**
ae	as the 'a' in American 'bat'
ai	as the 'i' in 'pipe'
ao	as the 'ow' in 'now'
aw	as the 'aw' in 'jaw'
e	as the 'e' in 'hen'
eh	like 'a' in 'hay' but flat; twice as long as **e**
eu	as the 'i' in 'sir'
eua	**eu**+ **a**

i	as the 'i' in 'it'
ii	as the 'ee' in 'feet'; twice as long as **i**
ia	**i** + **a** as in 'Fiat'
iaw	**i** + **a** + **w** as the 'io' in 'Rio'
iu	**i** + **u** as in 'new'
o	as the 'o' in 'bone' but shorter
oh	as the 'o' in 'toe'; twice as long as **o**
oe	as the 'u' in 'hut' but more closed
oei	**oe** + **i**
u	as the 'u' in 'flute', but shorter
uu	as the 'oo' in 'food'; longer than **u**
ua	**u** + **a**
uay	**u** + **a** + **i**

Consonants

If you hold your finger in front of your mouth as you make the English sounds 'k', 'p' and 't' you'll feel a slight puff of air. In Thai, you can produce each of these with or without breath to make different sounds. For example, the *k* in *lék* has no breath; you have to 'swallow' the ending.

Breath is signified by the letter *h*. For example, the *k* in *khão* is pronounced with breath. So don't be confused by *ph* (which means *p* with breath, *not* the 'f' sound in 'photo'). Note, however, that the combination *ch* is like in English 'chop'.

Other consonants which may cause difficulty are:

ng	as the 'ng' in 'sing'; used as an initial consonant in Thai (practise by saying 'singer' without the 'si')
j	similar to 't' in 'rapture'
r	similar to the 'r' in 'run' but flapped (tongue touches the palate); in everyday speech often pronounced as 'l'

Tones

Thai has five different tones: level or mid, low, falling, high and rising. The range of all five tones is relative to each speaker's vocal range; there is no fixed musical pitch intrinsic to the language. Words in Thai that appear to have more than one syllable are usually compounds made up of two or more word units, each with its own tone. They may be words taken directly from Sanskrit, Pali or English, in which case each syllable must still have its own tone. Sometimes the tone of the first syllable is not as important as that of the last, so for these the tone mark has been omitted.

- The level or mid tone is pronounced 'flat' (ie doesn't move up or down) at the relative middle of the speaker's vocal range. No tone mark is used. Example: *dii* 'good'.
- The low tone is 'flat' like the mid tone, but pronounced at the relative bottom of one's vocal range. Example: *bàat* 'baht'
- The falling tone is pronounced as if you were emphasising a word, or calling someone's name from afar. Example: *mâi* 'no' or 'not'.
- The high tone is usually the most difficult for Westerners. It is pronounced near the relative top of the vocal range, as level as possible. Example: *níi* 'this'.
- The rising tone sounds like the inflection English speakers generally give to a question 'Yes?' Example: *sǎam* 'three'.

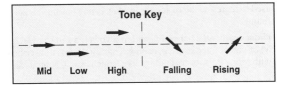

Tone Key

Mid　Low　High　Falling　Rising

Transliteration

Writing Thai in Roman script is a perennial problem; no truly
satisfactory system has yet been devised to assure both consisten-
cy and readability. The Thai government uses the Royal Thai
General System of Transcription for official government documents in English and for most highway signs. However, this
system was not designed for people trying to learn Thai! It doesn't
represent distinctions which are important for accurate pronunciation.

The following is a brief summary of common pitfalls you may
encounter trying to pronounce transliterated words in Thailand.

- There is no 'v' sound in Thai, so 'Sukhumvit' is pronounced
  sukhumwit and 'Vieng' sounds like *wiang*.

- The letters 'l' and 'r' at the end of a word are always
  pronounced like an *n*; hence, Satul is pronounced *satun* and
  Wihar, *wihaan*. The exception to this is when 'er' or 'ur' is used
  to indicate the sound *oe*, as in 'ampher' (*amphoe*); or when 'or'
  is used for the sound *aw* as in Porn (*phawn*).

- The sounds *l* and *r* are often used interchangeably in speech,
  and this shows up in some transliterations. For example, *naliga*
  (clock) may appear as 'nariga' and *lâat nâa* (a type of noodle
  dish) might be rendered 'raat naa' or 'rat na'.

- The letter 'u' is often used to represent the short *a* sound, as in
  tam or *nam*, which may appear as 'tum' and 'num'. It is also
  used to represent the *eu* sound, as when *beung* (swamp) is spelt
  'bung'.

- Phonetically all Thai words end in a vowel, a semi-vowel (*y*,
  w) or one of three stops: *p*, *t* and *k*. That's it. Words transcribed
  with 'ch', 'j', 's' or 'd' endings like Panich, Raj, Chuanpis and

Had should be pronounced as if they end in *t*, as in *panit*, *rat*, *chuanpit* and *hat*. Likewise 'g' should be pronounced *k* (Ralug is actually *raluk*) and 'b' is pronounced *p* (Thab becomes *thap*).

Greetings & Civilities
khráp/khâ

As a normal courtesy, Thai speakers end their sentences with a 'politening syllable': *khráp* (if the speaker is male) or *khâ* (if the speaker is female). You should follow this convention or you may appear abrupt and aggressive. Always use *khráp/khâ* after *sawàt-dii* ('Hello'), *khàwp khun* ('Thank you') and small talk. However, if your conversation is a long one (let's be ambitious!), you can drop the *khráp/khâ* after a few lines.

These words are also used to answer 'Yes' to a question, to show agreement, or simply to acknowledge that you're listening. (Thai has an equivalent of 'uh-huh', *anh*, but it's not nearly as polite.)

In everyday speech, the 'r' in *khráp* is dropped to produce the simplified *kháp*.

Women should pronounce their *kha* with a high tone *kh* instead of the usual falling tone (*khâ*) when forming questions:

Greetings

The all-purpose Thai greeting (and farewell) is *sawàt-dii (khráp/khâ)*. It's often accompanied by a *wâi*, the prayer-like, palms-together gesture of respect. Its literal meaning derives from the Sanskrit words *su* ('happiness') plus *asti* ('is'), hence it has the general meaning of wishing happiness or wellbeing on the listener.

If someone says *sawàt-dii (khráp/khâ)* to you, you should reply with the same phrase.

Other common greetings are *pai nãi?* ('Where are you going?') and *thaan khâo láew rẽu yang?* ('Have you eaten yet?'). As with the English 'How are you?', the answer doesn't usually matter. If you're just out for a stroll, a common reply to *pai nãi?* is *pai thîaw*, which roughly translates as 'I'm just out for fun'. The greeting *thaan khâo láew rẽu yang?* carries an implicit invitation to dine together (even for just a quick bowl of noodles), hence you choose the reply based on whether you'd like to spend time with the person. Answer *yang* ('Not yet') if you're willing to accept a possible meal invitation; answer *thaan láew* ('I've eaten already') if you'd rather be on your way.

Traditionally Thais greet each other not with a handshake but with a *wâi*. If someone *wâis* you, you should *wâi* back (unless *wai*ed by a child). In Bangkok and large cities the Western-style handshake is commonly offered to foreigners.

Civilities

How are you?

| *pen yang-ngai?* or | เป็นยังไง? |
| *sabaai-dii rẽu?* | สบายดีหรือ? |

I'm fine.

| *sabàay dii* | สบายดี |

Thank you.

| *khàwp khun* | ขอบคุณ |

Thank you very much.

| *khàwp khun mâak* | ขอบคุณมาก |

It's nothing (Never mind.)

| *mâi pen rai* | ไม่เป็นไร |

Excuse me.

| *khãw thôht* | ขอโทษ |

Forms of Address

Thais often address each other using their first names with the honorific *khun* or other title preceding it. Other formal terms of address include *naai* (Mr) and *naang* (Ms/Miss/Mrs). Friends often use nicknames or kinship terms like *phîi* (elder sibling), *náwng* (younger sibling), *mâe* (mother) or *lung* (uncle) depending on the age differencel. Young children can be called *lāan* ('nephew' or 'niece').

Pronouns

I/me (males)	*phõm*
I/me (females)	*dìi-chǎn*
we/us	*rao*
you	*khun/thâan/thoe*
he/him/she/her/they/them	*khǎo*
it (inanimate objects/animals)	*man*

Body Language

Nonverbal behaviour or 'body language' is more important in Thailand than in most Western countries.

If you're inside and you walk in front of someone who's sitting down you should stoop a little as a sign of respect.

The feet are the lowest part of the body (spiritually as well as physically) so don't point your feet at people or point at things with your feet. In the same context, the head is regarded as the highest part of the body, so don't touch Thais on the head.

Temples

To enter a temple you must be neatly dressed (no shorts or sleeveless shirts) and you must take your shoes off when you enter any building that contains a Buddha image. Buddha images are sacred objects, so don't pose in front of them for pictures and definitely do not clamber upon them.

Monks are not supposed to touch or be touched by women. If a woman wants to hand something to a monk, the object should be placed within reach of the monk, not handed directly to him.

When sitting in a religious edifice, keep your feet pointed away from any Buddha images or monks. The usual way to do this is to sit in the 'mermaid' pose in which your legs are folded to the side, with the feet pointing backwards.

Language Difficulties

I can't speak Thai.

phŏm (m)/*dìi-chān* (f) *phûut phaasăa thai mâi dâi*

ผม/ดิฉันพูดภาษาไทยไม่ได้

Can you speak English?

khun phûut phaasăa angkrìt dâi măi?

คุณพูดภาษาอังกฤษได้ไหม?

Please repeat.

phûut ìik thii sí

พูดอีกทีซิ

Sorry, I don't understand.

khăw thôht phŏm (m)/ *dìi-chān* (f) *mâi khâo jai*

ขอโทษ–ผม/ดิฉันไม่เข้าใจ

Do you understand?

khun khâo jai măi?

คุณเข้าใจไหม?

What?

a-rai ná?

อะไรนะ?

What do you call this in Thai?

níi phaasăa thai rîak wâa arai?

นี่ภาษาไทยเรียกว่าอะไร?

Small Talk
Meeting People
Hello/Greetings.
   sawàt-dii (khráp/khâ)　　สวัสดี (ครับ/ค่ะ)
Are you well?
   sabaai-dii rēu? or　　สบายดีหรือ?
   pen yang-ngai?
I'm fine.
   sabaai-dii　　สบายดี
What is your name?
   khun chêu arai?　　คุณชื่ออะไร?
My name is ...
   phōm chêu ... (m)　　ผมชื่อ...
   dìi-chān chêu ... (f)　　ดิฉันชื่อ...
Pleased to meet you.
   yin-dii thîi dâi rúujàk　　ยินดีที่ได้รู้จัก

Nationalities
Where do you come from?
   maa jàak thîi nāi?　　มาจากที่ไหน?

I come from ...	*phōm* (m)/*dìi-chān* (f) *maa jàak ...*	ผม/ดิฉันมาจาก...
Africa	*afríkaa*	อัฟริกา
Australia	*aw-sàtreh-lia*	ออสเตรเลีย
Canada	*khaenaadaa*	แคนาดา
China	*jiin*	จีน
England	*angkrìt*	อังกฤษ
Europe	*yúrohp*	ยุโรป

India	*india*	อินเดีย
Japan	*yîi-pùn*	ญี่ปุ่น
Latin America	*laa-tin amehrikaa*	ลาตินอเมริกา
the Middle East	*tawan-àwk-klaang*	ตะวันออกกลาง
Singapore	*sīnga-poh*	สิงคโปร์
Thailand	*prathêt thai*	ประเทศไทย
the USA	*sàhàrát amehrikaa*	สหรัฐอเมริกา

Age

How old are you?
khun aayúu thâo rai? คุณอายุเท่าไร?

I'm ... years old.
phõm (m)/dìi-chān (f) ผม/ดิฉันอายุ...ปี
aayúu ... pii

| Very young! | *nùm mâak!* | หนุ่มมาก |
| Very old! | *kàe mâak!* | แก่มาก |

Occupations

I am a/an ...   *phõm (m)/dìi-*   ผม/ดิฉันเป็น...
                chān (f) pen ...

actor	*nák-sadāeng*	นักแสดง
businessperson	*nák thúrákìt*	นักธุรกิจ
diplomat	*nák kaan-thûut*	นักการทูต
doctor	*phâet*	แพทย์
engineer	*wítsàwakawn*	วิศวกร
farmer	*chao-naa*	ชาวนา

journalist	nák nãng sẽu phim	นักหนังสือพิมพ์
lawyer	thanai-khwaam	ทนายความ
military	thahãan	ทหาร
missionary	phûu sãwn sàat-sanãa	ผู้สอนศาสนา
musician	nák dontrii	นักดนตรี
student	nák-sèuksãa	นักศึกษา
teacher	khruu	ครู
traveller/tourist	nák thâng thîaw	นักท่องเที่ยว

(I'm) unemployed.
  wâang ngaan   ว่างงาน

Religion

My religion is ...   phõm (m)/dì-chãn   ผม/ดิฉันนับถือ...
                      (f) náp thẽu ...
  Buddhism   sàatsànãa phút   ศาสนาพุทธ
  Christianity   sàatsànãa khrít   ศาสนาคริสต์
  Hinduism   sàatsànãa hinduu   ศาสนาฮินดู
  Judaism   lát-thí yiw   ลัทธิยิว
  Islam   sàatsànãa it-salaam   ศาสนาอิสลาม

Family

How many brothers and sisters
do you have?
  mii phîi-náwng kìi khon?   มีพี่น้องกี่คน?
I have ... brothers and sisters.
  mii phîi-náwng ... khon   มีพี่น้อง...คน

Are you married (yet)?

 tàeng-ngaan láew rēu yang? แต่งงานแล้วหรือยัง?

Yes, I'm married.

 tàeng láew แต่งแล้ว

Not yet.

 yang mâi tàeng-ngaan ยังไม่แต่งงาน

(I'm) single.

 penòsht เป็นโสด

Do you have any children (yet)?

 mii lûuk láew rēu yàng? มีลูกแล้วหรือยัง?

Not yet.

 yang mâi mii lûuk ยังไม่มีลูก

I have ... child/children.

 mii lûuk ... khon làew มีลูก...คนแล้ว

family	khrâwp khrua	ครอบครัว
child/children	lûuk	ลูก
daughter	lûuk săo	ลูกสาว
son	lûuk chaai	ลูกชาย
younger sister	náwng săo	น้องสาว
younger brother	náwng chaai	น้องชาย
older sister	phîi săo	พี่สาว
older brother	phîi chaai	พี่ชาย
mother	mâe	แม่
father	phâw	พ่อ
husband	phŭa	ผัว
wife	mia	เมีย

Making Conversation

I think that ...		
phŏm (m)/*dì-chăn* (f)		ผม/ดิฉันคิดว่า...
khít wâa ...		
I feel that ...		
phŏm/dì-chăn rúusèuk wâa ...		ผม/ดิฉันรู้สึกว่า...
I agree.		
hĕn dûay		เห็นด้วย
I disagree.		
mâi hĕn dûay		ไม่เห็นด้วย
(In) my opinion ...		
khwaam khít-hĕn khăwng		ความคิดเห็นของผม/ดิฉัน...
phŏm (m)/*dì-chăn* (f) ...		
(It's) not important.		
mâi sămkhan		ไม่สำคัญ
(This is) fun!		
sanùk dii		สนุกดี

Getting Around
Finding Your Way

Where is the ...	... *yùu thîi nǎi?*	...อยู่ที่ไหน?
bus station	*sathăanii rót meh*	สถานีรถเมล์
bus stop	*thîi jàwt rót*	ที่จอดรถประจำ
	pràjam	
map	*phaen thîi*	แผนที่
railway station	*sathăanii rót fai*	สถานีรถไฟ
taxi stand	*thîi jàwt rót*	ที่จอดรถแท็กซี่
	tháek-sîi	

Which ... is this?	*thîi nîi ... a-rai?*	ที่นี่...อะไร?
alley	*tràwk*	ตรอก
province	*jang-wàt*	จังหวัด
street/road/avenue	*thanõn*	ถนน
village	*mùu bâan*	หมู่บ้าน

Directions

Excuse me, I'm looking for ...

| | *khãw thôht phõm* (m)/ | ขอโทษ–ผม/ดิฉันหา... |
| | *dìi-chān* (f) *hãa ...* | |

Turn ...	*líaw ...*	เลี้ยว...
left	*sáai*	ซ้าย
right	*khwãa*	ขวา

Turn around.	*thawy klàp*	ถอยกลับ
Turn back (return)	*klàp*	กลับ
Straight ahead.	*trong pai*	ตรงไป
How far?	*klai thâo rai?*	ไกลเท่าไร?
far/not far	*klai/mâi klai*	ไกล/ไม่ไกล
near/not near	*klâi/mâi klâi*	ใกล้/ไม่ใกล้

north	*thít nēua*	ทิศเหนือ
south	*thít tâi*	ทิศใต้
east	*thít tawan àwk*	ทิศตะวันออก
west	*thít tawan tòk*	ทิศตะวันตก

Buying Tickets

I'd like a ticket.

   yàak dâi tŭa   อยากได้ตัว

Are there any tickets to ...?

   mii tŭa pai ...?   มีตัวไป...ไหม

How much per 'place' (seat, berth, etc)?

   thîi-lá thâo rai?   ที่ละเท่าไร

We would like to reserve ... places (seats, berths etc).

   rao yàak jà jawng thîi nâng เราอยากจองที่นั่ง...ที่
   ... thîi

How many departures are there ...?	*... mii kìi thîaw?*	...มีกี่เที่ยว
today	*wan níi*	วันนี้
tomorrow	*phrûng níi*	พรุ่งนี้

I'd like to change my ticket.

   yàak plian tŭa   อยากเปลี่ยนตัว

I'd like a refund on my ticket.

   yàak kheun tŭa   อยากคืนตัว

Air

aeroplane	*khrêuang bin*	เครื่องบิน
aeroplane tickets	*tŭa khrêuang bin*	ตัวเครื่องบิน
airline	*kaan-bin*	การบิน
airport	*sanăam bin*	สนามบิน
departures/flights	*thîaw*	เที่ยว

What time will the plane leave?
kìi mohng khrêuang bin jà   กี่โมงเครื่องบินจะออก?
àwk?

Bus

air-con bus	*rót ae (rót thua)*	รถแอร์ (รถทัวร์)
first class	*chán nèung*	ชั้นหนึ่ง
government bus station	*sathāanii baw khāw sāw*	สถานีบ.ข.ส.
ordinary bus	*rót thamadaa*	รถธรรมดา
second class	*chán sāwng*	ชั้นสอง
'VIP' bus	*rót nawn (rót wii-ai-phii)*	รถนอน (รถวีไอพี)

What time will the bus leave?
kìi mohng rót jà àwk?   กี่โมงรถจะออก?

Train

express train	*rót dùan*	รถด่วน
ordinary train	*rót thamadaa*	รถธรรมดา
rapid train	*rót rehw*	รถเร็ว
sleeper	*rót nawn*	รถนอน
sleeping berth	*thîi nawn*	ที่นอน
stationmaster	*nai sathāanii*	นายสถานี
train station	*sathāanii rót fai*	สถานีรถไฟ
lower	*lâang*	ล่าง
upper	*bon*	บน

What time will the train leave?
    kìi mohng rót jà àwk?   กี่โมงรถจะออก?
What time will the train arrive?
    kìi mohng rót jà thĕung?   กี่โมงรถจะถึง?

Taxi

taxi	*rót tháek-sîi*	รถแท็กซี่
metered taxi	*tháek-sîi mii-toe*	แท็กซี่มิเตอร์

Turn on the meter.
    pòet mii-toe sí   เปิดมิเตอร์ซิ
How much to ...?
    pai ... thâo rai?   ไป...เท่าไร?
Too expensive. How about ...
baht?
    phaeng pai ... bàat dâi mãi?   แพงไป...บาทได้ไหม?
Agreed. Let's go.
    tòklong láew pà   ตกลงแล้ว ปะ
Drive slowly please.
    karunaa khàp rót   กรุณาขับรถช้าๆหน่อย
    cháa-cháa nàwy
Stop here.
    jàwt thîi nîi   จอดที่นี่

Boat

boat	*reua*	เรือ
boat taxi ('hire boat')	*reua jâang*	เรือจ้าง

Chinese junk	*reua sām phao*	เรือสำเภา
cross-river ferry	*reuan khâam fâak*	เรือข้ามฟาก
express boat	*reua dùan*	เรือด่วน
'longtail' boat	*reua hāang yao*	เรือหางยาว
sampan	*reua sāmpân*	เรือสำปั้น

Where do we get on the boat?
long reua thîi nāi?   ลงเรือที่ไหน?

What time does the boat leave?
kìi mohng reua jà àwk?   กี่โมงเรือจะออก?

What time does the boat arrive?
kìi mohng reua jà thĕung? กี่โมงเรือจะถึง?

Songthaews, Samlors & Tuk-Tuks

Outside Bangkok, the most common form of public city transport
is the songthaew (*sāwng-thāew*), literally 'two rows'. Often there
are two kinds: the *rót pràjam* which run along regular routes like
buses and the *rót mǎo* which must be chartered for each trip. On
the *rót pràjam* you pay a flat per-person fare while for a *rót mǎo*
you must negotiate a fee.

The samlor (*sāam-láw*), literally 'three wheels', is a pedicab in
which one or two passengers ride in a small carriage behind the
front half of a bicycle. In most places you must negotiate the fare.

A *túk-túk*, named for the sound of its two-stroke engine, is a
motorised, somewhat larger version of the samlor that can carry
three to eight passengers. Typically you must negotiate a fare,
though in some cities (Ayuthaya, for example) tuk-tuks which run
along regular routes may be available for set fares.

Useful Phrases

When will the ... leave?	... jà àwk mêua-rai?	...จะออกเมื่อไร?
aeroplane	khrêuang bin	เครื่องบิน
aircon bus	rót ae	รถแอร์
boat	reua	เรือ
minivan	rót tûu	รถตู้
ordinary bus	rót thammadaa	รถธรรมดา
train	rót fai	รถไฟ

I'd like to rent a ...	phŏm (m)/dìi-chǎn (f) yàak châo ...	ผม/ดิฉันอยากเช่า...
car	rót yon	รถยนต์
motorcycle	rót maw-toe-sai	รถมอเตอร์ไซค์
bicycle	rót jàkràyaan	รถจักรยาน

How much ...?	... thâo rai?	...เท่าไร?
per day	wan-lá	วันละ
per week	aathít-lá	อาทิตย์ละ

Does the price include insurance?
raakhaa ruam kap pràkan ราคารวมกับประกันไหม?
mǎi?

What time does the first vehicle
leave?
khan râek jà àwk kìi คันแรกจะออกกี่โมง?
mohng?

What time does the last vehicle
leave?

> *khan sùt-thai jà àwk kìi*
> *mohng?*   ศันสุดท้ายจะออกกี่โมงฯ

Where does the vehicle (bus,
songthaew, etc) depart from?

> *rót àwk jàak thîi nãi?*   รถออกจากที่ไหนฯ

Where are you going?

> *pai nãi?*   ไปไหนฯ

Which vehicle goes to ...?

> *rót nãi pai ...?*   รถไหนไป...ฯ

Accommodation
Finding Accommodation

| guesthouse | *bâan phák (kèt háo)* | บ้านพัก (เกสต์เฮาส์) |
| hotel | *rohng raem* | โรงแรม |

Excuse me, is there a hotel
nearby?

> *khãw thôht mii rohng raem*   ขอโทษ–
> *klâi thîi nîi mãi?*   มีโรงแรมใกล้ที่นี่ไหมฯ

Is this a hotel?

> *nîi pen rohng raem mãi?*   นี่เป็นโรงแรมไหมฯ

Is this a guesthouse?

> *nîi pen bâan phák mãi?*   นี่เป็นบ้านพักไหมฯ

Is there a place to stay here?

> *mii thîi phák thîi nîi mãi?*   มีที่พักที่นี่ไหมฯ

Can (I/we) stay here?

> *phák thîi nîi dâi mãi?*   พักที่นี่ได้ไหมฯ

Checking In

vacant	*wâang*	ว่าง
not vacant	*mâi wâang*	ไม่ว่าง

Do you have a room?
  mii hâwng mǎi?   มีห้องไหม?
How many (persons)?
  kìi khon?   กี่คน?
one person
  nèung khon (khon diaw)   หนึ่งคน(คนเดียว)
two persons
  sǎwng khon   สองคน

How much ...?	... *thâo rai?*	...เท่าไร?
per night	*kheun-lá*	คืนละ
per week	*aathít-lá*	อาทิตย์ละ
per month	*deuan-lá*	เดือนละ
for three nights	*sâam kheun*	สามคืน

Too expensive.
  phaeng pai   แพงไป
(I/we) will stay two nights.
  jà phák sǎwng kheun   จะพักสองคืน
Can (I/we) look at the room?
  duu hâwng dâi mǎi?   ดูห้องได้ไหม?
Do you have any other rooms?
  mii hâwng ìik mǎi?   มีห้องอีกไหม?

We need a ... room	rao tâwng-kaan	เราต้องการห้อง...นี้
than this.	hâwng ... níi	
cheaper	tùuk-kwàa	ถูกกว่า
larger	yài-kwàa	ใหญ่กว่า
smaller	lék-kwàa	เล็กกว่า
quieter	ngîap-kwàa	เงียบกว่า

Requests & Complaints

(I/we) need (a) ...	tâwng-kaan ...	ต้องการ...
another bed	tiang ìik	เตียงอีก
blanket	phâa hòm	ผ้าห่ม
pillow	māwn	หมอน
sheet	phâa puu thîi nawn	ผ้าปูที่นอน
soap	sabùu	สบู่
towel	phâa chéht tua	ผ้าเช็ดตัว

Please clean the room.
  tham khwaam-sa-àat hâwng dâi māi?   ทำสะอาดห้องได้ไหม?

This room isn't clean.
  hâwng níi mâi sa-àat   ห้องนี้ไม่สะอาด

There is no hot water.
  mâi mii náam ráwn   ไม่มีน้ำร้อน

Can you fix it?
  sâwm dâi māi?   ซ่อมได้ไหม?

Can you wash these clothes?
  sák sêua phâa nîi dâi māi?   ซักเสื้อผ้านี้ได้ไหม?

Where can I wash my clothes
(myself)?

phŏm/dìi-chān sák sêua   ผม/ดิฉันซักเสื้อผ้าเองได้ที่ไหน?
phâa ehng dâi thîi nãi?

Checking Out

(I/we) will return in two weeks.

iìk sãwng aathít jà klàp   อีกสองอาทิตย์จะกลับ

Can I store my bags here?

fàak kràbão wái thîi nîi dâi   ฝากกระเป๋าไว้ที่นี่ได้ไหม?
mãi?

Useful Words

bed	*tiang nawn*	เตียงนอน
electricity	*kaan fai fáa*	การไฟฟ้า
fan	*phát lom*	พัดลม
food	*aahãan*	อาหาร
key	*kun-jae*	กุญแจ
lift (elevator)	*líf*	ลิฟต์
lights	*fai*	ไฟ
toilet	*sûam*	ส้วม

Around Town

Where is the ...?	*... yùu thîi nãi?*	...อยู่ที่ไหน?
bank	*thanaakhaan*	ธนาคาร
post office	*thîi tham-kaan*	ที่ทำการ
	praisanii	ไปรษณีย์

At the Post Office

Is this the post office?

nîi pen thîi-tham-kaan
praisanii châi mãi?

นี่เป็นที่ทำการไปรษณีย์ใช่ไหม?

I want to send
(a/an) ...

phõm (m)/*dìi-
chãn* (f) *yàak sòng ...*

ผม/ดิฉันอยากส่ง...

aerogram	*jòt-mãai aakàat*	จดหมายอากาศ
letter	*jòt-mãai*	จดหมาย
postcard	*praisanii bàt*	ไปรษณียบัตร
parcel	*phátsàdù*	พัสดุ
telegram	*thohrálêhk*	โทรเลข

How much to send this letter
to England?

sòng jòt-mãai níi pai
angkrìt raakhaa thâo rai?

ส่งจดหมายนี้ไปอังกฤษรา
คาเท่าไร?

I want to send this package by
airmail.

phõm/dìi-chãn yàak sòng
hàw níi thaang aakàat

ผม/ดิฉันอยากส่งจดหมายนี้ทาง
อากาศ

I want a registered receipt.

phõm (m)/*dìi-chãn* (f) *yàak*
dâai bai thábian

ผม/ดิฉันอยากได้ใบทะเบียน

Is there any mail for me?

mii jòt-mãai sãmràp phõm
(m)/dìi-chãn (f) *mãi?*

มีจดหมายสำหรับผม/ดิฉัน
ไหม?

air (mail)	*thaang aakàat*	ทางอากาศ
envelope	*sawng jòt-māai*	ซองจดหมาย
express (mail)	*thaang dùan*	ทางด่วน
stamps	*sataem*	แสตมป์
surface (mail)	*thamadaa*	ธรรมดา

Telecommunications

reverse-charges/ collect call	*kèp plaai thaang*	เก็บปลายทาง
international call	*thohr sàp ráwàang pràthêt*	โทรศัพท์ ระหว่างประเทศ
long distance (domestic)	*thaang klai*	ทางไกล
telephone	*thohr sàp*	โทรศัพท์

I'd like to make an international collect call.

    phōm (m)/*dìi-chān* (f) *yàak thohr sàpáráwàang pràthêt kèp plai thaang*

ผม/ดิฉันอยากโทรศัพท์ระหว่าง ประเทศเก็บปายทาง

How much does it cost to call ...?

    thoh pai ... raakhaa thâo rai?

โทรไป...ราคาเท่าไร?

I'd like to speak for 10 minutes.

    phōm (m)/*dìi-chān* (f) *yàak phûut sìp naa-thii*

ผม/ดิฉันอยากพูดสิบนาที

| fax | *fáek* | แฟ็คส์ |
| telegraph | *thorálêhk* | โทรเลข |

How much per page?
phàen-lá thâo rai?   แผ่นละเท่าไรฯ
How much per word?
kham-láthâo rai?   คำละเท่าไรฯ

At the Bank

Can (I/we) change money here?
lâek ngoen thîi nîi dâi mǎi?   แลกเงินที่นี่ได้ไหมฯ

I have ...	*phǒm* (m)/	ผม/ดิฉันมี...
	dì-chǎn (f) *mii ...*	
US $	*dawn-lâa sàhàrát*	ดอลล่าสหรัฐ
UK £	*pawn angkrìt*	ปอนด์อังกฤษ
Australian $	*dawn-lâa*	ดอลล่าออสเตรเลีย
	aw-satreh-lia	

What is the exchange rate?
àtraa lâek plian thâo rai?   อัตราแลกเปลี่ยนเท่าไรฯ
Can I get smaller change?
khǎw lâek ngoen plìik dâi   ขอแกเงินปีกได้ไหมฯ
mǎi?

| money | *ngoen* | เงิน |
| exchange rate | *àtraa lâek plìan* | อัตราแลกเปลี่ยน |

Sightseeing

Do you have a local map?
mii phǎenthǐi nǐi mǎi rēu   มีแผนที่ของท้องที่นี่ไหมฯ
séu phǎenthǐi khǎwng   หรือซื้อแผนที่นี่ได้
thongthǐi nǐi dâi thǐinǎi

What time does it open/close?
ráan bèut mēurai/ pìt mēurai   ร้านเปิดเมื่อไร/ปิดเมื่อไร

May I take photographs?
thai rūub dâi mái   ถ่ายรูปได้ไหม?

Buddhist temple/ monastery	*wát*	วัด
cemetery	*sùsāan*	สุสาน
church	*bòht khrít*	โบสถ์คริสต์
cinema	*rohng phâaphayon (rohng nāng)*	โรงภาพยนตร์ (โรงหนัง)
monument	*anú-sāa-wárii*	อนุสาวรีย์
museum	*phíphíth phan*	พิพิธภัณฑ์
national park	*won-ù-th yaan hàeng châat*	วนอุทยานแห่ง ชาติ
park (garden)	*sūan*	สวน
shrine (usually Chinese)	*sāan jâo*	ศาลเจ้า
tourist office	*sāmnák-ngaan thâwng thîaw*	สำนักงานท่อง เที่ยว
zoo	*sūan sàt*	สวนสัตว์

Paperwork

name	*chêua*	ชื่อ
address	*thîiyuù*	ที่อยู่
date of birth	*wankeut*	วันเกิด
place of birth	*thìikeut*	ที่เกิด

age	*aayú*	อายุ
sex	*phèt*	เพศ
nationality	*sānchâat*	สัญชาติ
religion	*saatsanaa*	ศาสนา
profession	*aachîip*	อาชีพ
marital status	*phaawásōmrót*	ภาวะสมรส
passport number	*lekthîi*	เลขที่หนังสือ
	nāngsēudeun-thaang	เดินทาง
visa	*wiisàa*	วีซ่า
driving licence	*baikhàpkhìi*	ใบขับขี่
customs	*sūnlakakawn*	ศุลกากร
immigration	*truatkhon khâo meuang*	ตรวจคนเข้าเมือง
purpose of visit	*wátthuuprasōng nai kaan deun thaang*	วัตถุประสงค์ในการเดินทาง

In the Country
Weather

What's the weather like?
　aakàat pen yang-ngai?　อากาศเป็นยังไง?

(It's) windy.	*lom pht*	ลมพัด
(It's) very cold.	*nāo mâak*	หนาวมาก
(It's) very hot.	*ráwn mâak*	ร้อนมาก

| (It's) raining hard. | *fŏn tòk nàk* | ฝนตกหนัก |
| (It's) flooding. | *náam tûam* | นงท่วม |

fog	*màwk*	หมอก
hot weather	*aakàat ráwn*	อากาศร้อน
monsoon	*maw-rá-sūm*	มรสุม

Geographical Terms

bay/gulf	*ào*	อ่าว
beach	*chai-ha'at*	ชายหาต
cave	*thâm*	ถง
cliff	*phǎa*	ผา
coral	*hǐn pàkaarang*	หินปะการัง
countryside	*chonabòt*	ชนบท
creek	*lam-thaan*	ลำธาร
field	*naa*	นา
forest	*pàa*	ป่า
hill	*noen*	เนิน
mountain	*phuu khǎo*	ภูเขา
mountain peak	*doi*	ตอย
nature	*thamachâat*	ธรรมชาติ
ocean	*samùt*	สมุทร
river	*mâe náam*	แมนง
river rapids	*kàeng*	แก่ง
sea	*thaleh*	ทะเล
spring/well	*bàw*	บ่อ
stream	*hûay*	ห้วย

swamp	*beung*	บึง
trail/footpath	*thaang doen*	ทางเดิน
waterfall	*náam tòk*	นงตก

Flora

bamboo	*phài*	ไผ่
dipterocarp	*yaang*	ยาง
flower	*dàwk mái*	ดอกไม้
grass/herb	*yâa*	หญ้า
pine	*tôn sõn*	ต้นสน
teak	*tôn sàk*	ต้นสัก
tree	*tôn mái*	ต้นไม้

Fauna

ant	*mót*	มด
banteng (type of wild cattle)	*wua daeng*	วัวแดง
barking deer	*ii-kêhng*	อีเก้ง
bear	*mĩi*	หมี
bee	*phêung*	ผึ้ง
bird	*nók*	นก
butterfly	*phĩi sêua*	ผีเสื้อ
centipede	*tàkhàap*	ตะขาบ
cockroach	*malaeng sàap*	แมลงสาบ
cow	*wua*	วัว
civet	*chámót*	ชะมด
clouded leopard	*sẽua laai mêhk*	เสือลายเมฆ

crocodile	jaw-rákhêh	จระเข้
deer	kwaang	กวาง
dog	mǎa	หมา
dolphin	plaa lohmaa	ปลาโลมา
duck	pèt	เป็ด
elephant	cháang	ช้าง
fish	plaa	ปลา
fishing cat	sěua plaa	เสือปลา
fly	malaeng wan	แมลงวัน
frog	kòp	กบ
gaur	kràthing	กระทิง
gecko	túk-kae	ตุ๊กแก
gibbon	chánii	ชะนี
horse	máa	ม้า
monitor lizard	hào cháang	เห่าช้าง
leaf monkey	khàang	ค่าง
leopard	sěua dao	เสือดาว
Malayan sun bear	mǐi mǎa	หมีหมา
monkey	ling	ลิง
pangolin	lîn (nîm)	ลิ่น (นิ่ม)
rabbit	kràtài	กระต่าย
rhinoceros	râet	แรด
scorpion	malaeng pàwng	แมลงป่อง
shellfish (clams, oysters, etc)	hǎwy	หอย
shrimp, lobster	kûng	กุ้ง
snake	nguu	งู

snake (venomous)	*nguu phít*	งูพิษ
tapir	*sõm sèt*	สมเสร็จ
tiger	*sẽua*	เสือ
turtle	*tào*	เต่า
water buffalo	*khwaai*	ควาย
water fowl	*nók náam*	นกน้ำ
wild animals	*sàt pàa*	สัตว์ป่า
wild buffalo	*khwaai pàa*	ควาย
young animal, offspring	*lûuk*	ลูก

Trekking

(I/we) would like to hire a guide.

   yàak jâang khon pen kâi   อยากจ้างคนเป็นไก๊ด์

How far is it from ... to ...?

   jàak ... thẽung ... klai thâo   จาก...ถึง...ไกลเท่าไร?
   rai?

How many hours per day will we walk?

   jà doen wan-lá kìi   จะเดินวันละกี่ชั่วโมง?
   chûa-mohng?

Where is the trail to ...?

   thaang doen pai ... yàu   ทางเดินไป...อยู่ตรงไหน?
   trong nãi?

Is it a difficult walk?

   doen yâak mãi?   เดินยากไหม?

Can (I/we) stay in this village?
   phák thîi màu bâan níi dâi   พักที่หมู่บ้านนี้ได้ไหม?
   mãi?

Can (I/we) sleep here?
   nawn thîi nîi dâi mãi?   นอนที่นี่ได้ไหม?

Does the price include ...?	*raakhaa ruam kàp khâa ... mãi?*	ราคารวมกับค่า ...ไหม?
food	*aahãan*	อาหาร
transport	*khõn-sng*	ขนส่ง

How many ...?	*kìi ...?*	กี่...
days	*wan*	วัน
hours	*chûa-mohng*	ชั่วโมง
kilometres	*ki-loh-mêht*	กิโลเมตร

Camping

Can (I/we) put a tent here?
   waang tên thîi nîi dâi mãi?   วางเต้นท์ที่นี่ได้ไหม?

Are there tents available for rent?
   mii tên hâi châo mãi?   มีเต้นท์ให้เช่าไหม?

Is it safe?
   plàwt phai mãi?   ปลอดภัยไหม?

Is drinking water available?
   mii náam dèum mãi?   มีน้ำดื่มไหม?

Where is the park office?

aw-fít khăwng won-àtayaan   ออฟฟิสของวนอุทยานอยู่ที่ไหน?
yàu thîi năi?

sleeping bag	*thŭng nawn*	ถุงนอน
tent	*tên*	เต็นท์

Useful Words

hill tribe	*chao khăo*	ชาวเขา
lodging	*thîi phák*	ที่พัก
medicine	*yaa*	ยา
mosquito(es)	*yung*	ยุง
mosquito coil	*yaa kan yung*	ยากันยุง (แบบจุด)
	(bàep jàt)	
opium	*fin*	ฝิ่น
raft	*phae*	แพ
village headman	*phûu yài bâan*	ผู้ใหญ่บ้าน

Food

Thai meals are usually ordered family-style: that is, diners serve themselves from dishes placed in the centre of the table. Soup most often is not served in individual bowls. You serve yourself from the common bowl. Most Thai dishes are eaten with a fork and tablespoon. The fork (*sáwm*) is held in the left hand and used to push food onto the spoon (*cháwn*) from which you eat. To the Thais, pushing a fork into one's mouth is as uncouth as putting a knife into the mouth is in Western countries.

When serving yourself from a common platter, put no more than one or two spoonfuls onto your own plate at a time. It's customary at the start of a shared meal to eat a spoonful of plain rice first – a gesture that recognises rice as the most important part of the meal. Always leave some food on the serving platters as well as on your plate. To clean your plate and leave nothing on the serving platters would be a grave insult to your hosts – the more food is left on the table, the more generous the host appears.

Although Thais have words for morning meal (*aahǎan cháo*), noon meal (*aahǎan thîang*) and evening meal (*aahǎan yen*), there is no difference between types of dishes eaten during the day.

Eating Out

Please bring (a/the) ...	*khǎw ...*	ขอ...
bill (check)	*bin*	บิล
bowl	*chaam*	ชาม
chopsticks	*tà-kìap*	ตะเกียบ
fork	*sâwm*	ส้อม
glass	*kâew*	แก้ว
knife	*mîit*	มีด
menu	*meh-nuu*	เมนู
spoon	*cháwn*	ช้อน

What do you have that's special?
mii a-rai phí-sèt? มีอะไรพิเศษฯ

I eat only vegetarian food.
phǒm (m)/*dìi-chān* (f) *kin jeh* ผม/ดิฉันกินเจ

I can't eat pork.
phǒm (m)/*dìi-chān* (f) *kin* ผม/ดิฉันกินหมูไม่ได้
mǔu mâi dâi

Please don't use MSG.

    karúnaa mâi sài phōng   กรุณาไม่ใส่ผงชูรส
    chuu-rót

I didn't order this.

    níi phōm/dìi-chān mâi dâi   นี่ผม/ดีฉันไม่ได้สั่ง
    sàng

Typical Thai Dishes

steamed white rice	*khâo sūay*	ข้าวสวย
(literally 'beautiful rice')		
fried rice	*khâo phàt*	ข้าวผัด

tôm khàa kài   ต้มข่าไก่
   soup with chicken, galanga root & coconut

tôm yam kûng   ต้มยำกุ้ง
   prawn & lemon grass soup with mushrooms

kaeng jèut lûuk chín   แกงจืดลูกชิ้นปลา
   fish ball soup

yam   ยำ
   Thai-style salad (made with lots of chillies and lime juice)

kaeng phèt   แกงเผ็ด
   red Thai curry (usually very hot)

kaeng khīaw-wāan   แกงเขียวหวาน
   'green-sweet' curry (medium hot)

plaa dàk phàt phèt   ปลาดุกผัดเผ็ด
   catfish fried in fresh chilli paste and basil

kài phàt khīng   ไก่ผัดขิง
   chicken with ginger

mūu prîaw wăan sweet & sour pork		หมูเปรี้ยวหวาน
néua phàt náam-man hăwy beef in oyster sauce		เนื้อผัดนงมัน
phàt phàk ruam-mít stir-fried vegetables		ผัดผักรวมมิตร
phàt phàk bûng fai daeng morning glory vine fried in garlic and bean sauce		ผัดผักบุ้งไฟแดง

At the Market
Meat

beef	*néua (néua wua)*	เนื้อ (เนื้อวัว)
chicken	*kài*	ไก่
pork	*mūu*	หมู

Seafood

catfish	*plaa dàk*	ปลาดุก
fish	*plaa*	ปลา
freshwater eel	*plaa lăi*	ปลาไหล
green mussel	*hăwy malaeng phàu*	หอยแมลงภู่
oyster	*hăwy naang rom*	หอยนางรม
prawns/shrimp	*kûng*	กุ้ง
saltwater eel	*plaa lòt*	ปลาไหลทะเล
scallop	*hăwy phát*	หอยพัด
seafood	*aahăan thaleh*	อาหารทะเล
spiny lobster	*kûng mangkon*	กุ้งมังกร
squid	*plaa mèuk*	ปลาหมึก
tilapia	*plaa nin*	ปลานิล

Vegetables

angle bean	*thùa phuu*	ถั่วภู
bitter melon	*már -jiin*	มะระขึ้น
brinjal (round eggplant)	*mákhēua pràw*	มะเขือเปราะ
cabbage	*phàk kà-làm*	ผักกะหลง
	(kà-làm plii)	(กะหลงปลี)
cauliflower	*dàwk kà-làm*	ดอกกะหลง
Chinese radish (daikon)	*phàk kàat hūa*	ผักกาดหัว
corn	*khâo phôht*	ข้าวโพต
cucumber	*taeng kwaa*	แตงกวา
eggplant	*mákhēua yao*	มะเขือม่วง
garlic	*kràtiam*	กระเทียม
lettuce	*phàk kàat*	ผักกาต
long bean	*thùa fák yao*	ถ-วฝักยาว
okra (ladyfingers)	*krà-jíap*	กระเจยบ
onion (bulb)	*hūa hāwm*	หัวหอม
potato	*man faràng*	มันฝรั่ง
pumpkin	*fak thawng*	ฟักทอง
taro	*pheùak*	เผือก
tomato	*mákhēua thêt*	มะเขือเทศ

Fruit

banana	*klûay*	กล้วย
coconut	*máphráo*	มะพร้าว
custard-apple	*náwy nàa*	น้อยหน่า

durian	*thúrian*	ทุเรียน
guava	*fa-ràng*	ฝรั่ง
jackfruit	*kha-nūn*	ขนุน
lime	*má-nao*	มะนาว
longan	*lam yài*	ลำไย
mandarin	*sôm*	ส้ม
mango	*má-mûang*	มะม่วง
mangosteen	*mang-khút*	มังคุด
papaya	*málákaw*	มะละกอ
pineapple	*sàp-pàrót*	สับปะรด
pomelo	*sôm oh*	ส้มโอ
rambeh	*máfai*	มะไฟ
rambutan	*ngáw*	เงาะ
rose-apple	*chom-phûu*	ชมพู่
sapodilla	*lámút*	ละมุด
tamarind	*mákhāam*	มะขาม
watermelon	*taeng moh*	แตงโม

Condiments & Spices

black pepper	*phrík thai*	พริกไทย
chilli	*phrík*	พริก
coriander (cilantro)	*phàk chii*	ผักชี
crushed, roasted red chillies	*phrík phāo*	พริกเผา
dipping sauces	*náam jîm*	น้ำจิ้ม
fish sauce	*náam plaa*	น้ำปลา
ginger	*khīng*	ขิง

holy basil	*bai kà-phrao*	ใบกะเพรา
lime juice	*náam mánao*	นงมะนาว
sesame	*ngaa*	งา
shrimp paste	*kà-pì*	กะปิ
soy sauce	*náam sii-yú*	นงซีอิ๊ว
salt	*kleua*	เกลือ
Sri Racha sauce	*náam phrík sii raachaa*	นงพริกศรีราชา
sweet basil	*bai hohr phaa*	ใบโหระพา
tamarind	*makhãam*	มะขาม
vinegar	*náam sôm*	นงส้ม

Drinks
Nonalcholic

boiled water	*náam tôm*	นงต้ม
bottled drinking water	*náam dèum khàat*	นงต้มขวด
coffee	*kaafae*	กาแฟร้อน
tea	*chaa*	ชาร้อน
iced lime juice with sugar (usually with salt too)	*náam manao*	นงมะนาว
plain milk	*nom jèut*	นมจืต
plain water	*náam plào*	นงเปล่า
soda water	*náam soh-daa*	นงโซตา

Alcoholic

beer	*bia*	เบียร์
distilled spirits	*lâo*	เหล้า
draught beer	*bia sòt*	เบียร์สด
herbal liquors	*lâo yàa dong*	เหล้ายาดอง
'jungle liquor' (moonshine)	*lâo theuan*	เหล้าเถื่อน
Maekhong whisky	*mâe khõng*	แม่โขง

Shopping
Making a Purchase

How much?
thâo rai? เท่าไร?

How much altogether?
tháng mòt thâo rai? ทงหมดเท่าไร?

How much (for) ...?	... *thâo rai?*	...เท่าไร?
this	*níi*	นี่
per fruit	*lûuk-lá*	ลูกละ
per piece	*chín-lá*	ชิ้นละ
three pieces	*sāam chín*	สามชิ้น
per metre	*mêt-lá*	เมตรละ
both	*tháng sāwng*	ทั้งสอง

I'm looking for ...
phõm (m)/*dìi-chān* (f) *hāa* ... ผม/ดิฉันหา...

Do you have any ...?
mii ... mãi? มี...ไหม?

Do you have any more?
mii ìik māi?   มีอีกไหม?

I'd like to see another style.
khāw duu ìik bàep nèung   ขอดูอีกแบบหนึ่ง

Bargaining

Do you have something cheaper?
mii thàuk-kwàa níi māi?   มีถูกกว่านี้ไหม?

The price is very high.
raakhaa phaeng mâak   ราคาแพงมาก

I think that's too much.
khít wâa phaeng pai   คิดว่าแพงไป

Can you bring the price down?
lót raakhaa dâi māi?   ลดราคาได้ไหม?

Can you lower it more?
lót ìik dâi māi?   ลดอีกได้ไหม?

How about ... baht?
... bàat dâi māi?   ...บาทได้ไหม?

What's your lowest price?
raakhaa tàm sùt thâo rai?   ราคาต่ำสุดเท่าไร?

Souvenirs

baskets	*tà-krâa*	ตะกร้า
classical dance-drama masks	*hūa khōn*	หัวโขน
handicrafts	*kaan fīi-meu*	การฝีมือ
	(hàttakam)	(หัตถกรรม)

pottery/ceramics	*khrêuang pân/* *khrêuang thûay* *chaam*	เครื่องปั้น/เครื่อง ถ้วยชาม
Sawankhalok (Sangkhalok) style ceramics	*khrêuang thûay* *chaam* *(Sāngkhàlôk)*	เครื่องถ้วยชาม สังคโลก
Thai umbrellas	*rom thai*	ร่มไทย

Toiletries

Band-aid (plaster)	*phalaastoe*	พลาสเตอร์
bandage	*phâa phan phlâe*	ผ้าพันแผล
brush	*praeng*	แปรง
deodorant	*yaa kamjàt klìn tua*	ยากำจัดกลิ่นตัว
condoms	*thŭng yaang* *anaamai*	ถุงยางอนามัย
mosquito repellant	*yaa kan yung*	ยากันยุง
razor	*mîit kohn*	มีดโกน
razor blades	*bai mîit kohn*	ใบมีดโกน
sanitary napkins	*phâa anaamai*	ผ้าอนามัย
soap	*sa-bùu*	สะบู่
toilet paper	*kràdàat cham-rá*	กระดาษชำระ
toothbrush	*praeng sīi fan*	แปรงสีฟัน
toothpaste	*yaa sīi fan*	ยาสีฟัน

Photography

camera	*klâwng thàai rûup*	กล้องถ่ายรูป
develop	*láang fim*	ล้างฟิล์ม

film	*fim*	ฟิล์ม
colour	*sǐi*	สี
B&W	*khǎo dam*	ขาวดำ
lens	*lehn*	เลนส์
photograph (n)	*rûup (phâap)*	รูป (ภาพ)
slide film	*fim sàlai*	ฟิล์มสไลด์

How many days?
  kìi wan?　　　　　ก่วัน

Smoking

May I smoke?
  sùub buhrii dâi mǎi　　สูบบุหรี่ได้ไหม?
Please don't smoke.
  pràwtyaà sùub buhrii　　โปรดอย่าสูบบุหรี่
Are these cigarettes mild?
  buhrii lào níi jeùtmǎi　　บุหรี่เหล่านี้จืดไหม

cigarettes	*burìi*	บุหรี่
matches	*mái khìit fai*	ไม้ขีดไฟ

Sizes & Comparisons

size	*khanàat*	ขนาด
too large	*yài pai*	ใหญ่ไป
too long	*yao pai*	ยาวไป
too short	*sân pai*	สั้นไป
too small	*lék pai*	เล็กไป
too tight	*kâep pai*	แคบไป
too wide	*kwâang pai*	กว้างไป

Health

I need a ...	*phŏm* (m)/*dìi-chān* (f) *tâwng-kaan ...*	ผม/ดิฉันต้องการ...
doctor	*măw*	หมอ
dentist	*châang tham fan*	ช่างทำฟัน

At the Doctor

I'm tired.	*phŏm* (m)/*dìi-chān* (f) *nèuay*	ผม/ดิฉันเหนื่อย
I'm not well.	*phŏm* (m)/*dìi-chān* (f) *mâi sabai*	ผม/ดิฉันไม่สบาย
(I've) a cold.	*pen wàt*	เป็นหวัด
(I've) a fever.	*pen khâi*	เป็นไข้
It hurts here.	*pàat thîi-nîi*	ปวดที่นี่
(I) can't sleep.	*nawn mâi làp*	นอนไม่หลับ
(My) head aches.	*pàat sĭi-sà*	ปวดศรีษะ
There's pain in my chest.	*jèp nâa òk*	เจ็บหน้าอก
(My) back hurts.	*pùat lăng*	ปวดหลัง
(I've) a sore throat.	*jèp khaw*	เจ็บคอ
(I've) vomited several times.	*aajian lăai khráng*	อาเจียนหลายครั้ง

Ailments

AIDS	*rôhk éht*	โรคเอดส์
asthma	*rôhk hèut*	โรคหืด
cholera	*ahìwaa*	อหิวาต์
cough	*ai*	ไอ

cramps	*tàkhriu*	ตะคริว
dengue fever	*khâi sâa*	ไข้ส่า
diabetes	*rôhk bao wǎan*	โรคเบาหวาน
diarrhoea	*tháwng rûang*	ท้องร่วง
dysentery	*rôhk bìt*	โรคบิด
influenza	*khâi wàt yài*	ไข้หวัดใหญ่
malaria	*khâi jàp sàn*	ไข้จับสั่น
	(maalaaria)	(มาลาเรีย)
pneumonia	*rôhk pàwt àk sèhp*	โรคปอดอักเสบ
rabies	*rôhk klua náam*	โรคกลัวน้ำ
stomachache	*pàat tháwng*	ปวดท้อง
toothache	*pàat fan*	ปวดฟัน
veneral disease	*kaam rôhk*	กามโรค

Women's Health

I want to see a female doctor.

   chǎn tôngkarn phóp   ฉันต้องการพบหมอผู้หญิง
   mǎwphǔuyǐng

I'm pregnant.

   miikhan   มีครรภ์

I'm on the (contraceptive) pill.

   chǎn kin yàakhumkamnēut   ฉันกินยาคุมกำเนิด

I haven't had my period for ... weeks.

   chǎn mâi mii rāduu ... aathí   ฉันไม่มีระดู ... อาทิตย์แล้ว
   láo

Useful Words & Phrases

Is it serious?
  pen mâak mãi?   เป็นมากไหม?
I have health insurance.
  chãn mii pràkan   ฉันมีประกันสุขภาพ
  sàkhàphâap

addict	*khon tìt yaa*	คนติดยา
allergic (to)	*phae*	แพ้
hospital	*rohng phayaabaan*	โรงพยาบาล
ill	*pàay*	ป่วย
pain	*khwaam jèp-pùat*	ความเจ็บปวด

Parts of the Body

arm	*khãen*	แขน
back	*lãng*	หลัง
ear(s)	*hũu*	หู
eye(s)	*taa*	ตา
finger(s)	*níu meu*	นิ้วมือ
foot/feet	*tháo*	เท้า
hand(s)	*meu*	มือ
head	*sĩi-sà (hũa)*	ศรีษะ (หัว)
heart	*hũa jai*	หัวใจ
leg	*khãa*	ขา
mouth	*pàak*	ปาก
nose	*jà-mùuk*	จมูก
stomach	*th wng (kràpháw)*	ท้อง/กระเพาะ
teeth	*fan*	ฟัน

At the Chemist

chemist/pharmacy	ráan khăai yaa	ร้านขายยา

How many times a day?
　wan-lá kìi khráng?　วันละกี่ครั้ง?
Four times a day.
　wan-lá sìi khráng　วันละสี่ครั้ง
How much per tablet/pill?
　mét-lá thâo rai?　เม็ดละเท่าไร?

aspirin	yaa aet-sa-phai-rin	ยาแอสไพริน
injection	chìit yaa	ฉีดยา
insulin	yaa kâe rôhk bao wăan	ยาแก้เบาหวาน
painkiller	yaa kâe pàat	ยาแก้ปวด
pill/tablet	mét	เม็ด
sleeping pills	yaa nawn làp	ยานอนหลับ
vitamin	wí-taamin	วิตามิน

Time & Dates
Telling the Time

What's the time?	kìi mohng láew?	กี่โมงแล้ว?
The time is ...	... mohng láew	... โมงแล้ว

There are three ways of expressing time in Thailand: 'official' (*râatchakaan*) time, based on the 24-hour clock; the common 12-hour system; and the traditional six-hour system.

Official (24-Hour) Time

This is used by government agencies, in official documents and at bus and railway stations.

9 am (0900)	*kâo naalikaa*
midday (1200)	*sìp-sǎwng naalikaa*
1 pm (1300)	*sìp-sǎam naalikaa*
midnight	*yîi-sìp-sìi naalikaa*

The 12-Hour Clock

The 12-hour system divides the day into four sections (*tawn*): morning (*cháo*), afternoon (*bàai*), evening (*yen*) and night (*khâm*).

6 am to midday	*tawn cháo*
midday to 4 pm	*tawn bàai*
4 to 6 pm	*tawn yen*
6 to 11 pm	*tawn khâm*

After 11 pm time is referred to as *klaang kheun*. The 12-hour system is commonly used during the daylight hours.

9 am	*kâo mohng cháo*
midday	*thîang*
1 pm	*bai mohng*
6 pm	*hòk mohng yen*
midnight	*thîang kheun*

The Six-Hour Clock

From dusk to dawn, most Thais use the traditional six-hour system. In this system, times are expressed in the same way as with the 12-hour clock until 6 pm; from 7 pm to midnight the speaker uses *thûm*, counting from one to six; after midnight, it's back to one again with the hours referred to as *tii* (beats).

7 pm (1 *thûm*)	*neùng thûm*	
8 pm (2 *thûm*)	*sǎwng thûm*	
midnight	*hòk thûm*	
1 am (1 *tii*)	*tii neùng*	
3 am (3 *tii*)	*tii sǎam*	
6 am (daylight system again)	*hòk mohng cháo*	

Days of the Week

Sunday	*wan aathít*	วันอาทิตย์
Monday	*wan jan*	วันจันทร์
Tuesday	*wan angkhaan*	วันอังคาร
Wednesday	*wan phút*	วันพุธ
Thursday	*wan phréuhàt*	วันพฤหัส
Friday	*wan sùk*	วันศุกร์
Saturday	*wan sǎo*	วันเสาร์

Months

January	*deuan mókaraa-khom*	เดือนมกราคม
February	*deuan kumphaa-phan*	เดือนกุมภาพันธ์
March	*deuan miinaa-khom*	เดือนมีนาคม
April	*deuan mehsǎa-yon*	เดือนเมษายน
May	*deuan phréutsàphaa-khom*	เดือนพฤษภาคม
June	*deuan míthúnaa-yon*	เดือนมิถุนายน
July	*deuan kàrakàdaa-khom*	เดือนกรกฎาคม
August	*deuan sǐnghǎa-khom*	เดือนสิงหาคม
September	*deuan kanyaa-yon*	เดือนกันยายน
October	*deuan tàlaa-khom*	เดือนตุลาคม
November	*deuan phréutsàjìkaa-yon*	เดือนพฤศจิกายน
December	*deuan than waa-khom*	เดือนธันวาคม

Seasons

hot season (Mar-May)	*réuduu ráwn*	ฤดูร้อน
rainy season (Jun-Oct)	*réuduu fõn*	ฤดูฝน
cool season (Nov-Feb)	*réuduu não*	ฤดูหนาว

Dates

What date (is it)?
  wan thîi thâo-rai?   วันที่เท่าไร?

The thirteenth of January.
  wan thîi sìp-sāam deuan   วันที่สิบสามเดือนมกราคม
  mókaraa-khom

Present

today	*wan níi*	วันนี้
tonight	*kheun níi*	คืนนี้
this morning	*cháo níi*	เช้านี้

Past

yesterday	*mêua waan níi*	เมื่อวานนี้
the day before yesterday	*mêua waan seun*	เมื่อวานซืน
last week	*aathít kàwn*	อาทิตย์ก่อน

Future

tomorrow	*phrûng níi*	พรุ่งนี้
the day after tomorrow	*má-ruen níi*	มะรืนนี้
next week	*aathít nâa*	อาทิตย์หน้า
next month	*deuan nâa*	เดือนหน้า

Numbers
Cardinal Numbers

0	*sǔun*	ศูนย์
1	*nèung*	หนึ่ง
2	*sǎwng*	สอง
3	*sǎam*	สาม
4	*sìi*	สี่
5	*hâa*	ห้า
6	*hòk*	หก
7	*jèt*	เจ็ด
8	*pàet*	แปด
9	*kâo*	เก้า
10	*sìp*	สิบ
11	*sìp-èt*	สิบเอ็ด
12	*sìp-sǎwng*	สิบสอง
13	*sìp-sǎam*	สิบสาม
14	*sìp-sìi*	สิบสี่
...-teen	*sìp...*	สิบ...
20	*yîi-sìp*	ยี่สิบ
21	*yîi-sìp-èt*	ยี่สิบเอ็ด
30	*sǎam-sìp*	สามสิบ
40	*sìi-sìp*	สี่สิบ
100	*ráwy*	ร้อย
200	*sǎwng ráwy*	สองร้อย
1000	*phan*	พัน
10,000	*mèun*	หมื่น
one million	*láan*	ล้าน

Ordinal Numbers
These are formed by adding *thîi* before the cardinal numbers.

first	*thîi nèung*	ที่หนึ่ง
second	*thîi sǎwng*	ที่สอง

Emergencies

Help!	*chûay dûay*	ช่วยด้วย
Stop!	*yàt*	หยุด
Go away!	*bai sí*	ไปซี
Watch out!	*ráwang*	ระวัง
Thief!	*khamōhy*	ขโมย
Fire!	*fai mâi*	ไฟไหม้

I've lost my ...	*... hǎai láew*	...หายแล้ว
bags	*kràpǎo*	กระเป๋า
money	*ngoen*	เงิน
travellers' cheques	*chék doen thaang*	เช็คเดินทาง
passport	*nǎng sěu doen thaang*	หนังสือเดินทาง

I'm lost.
   chǎn lǒng thaang   ฉันหลงทาง ·
Call a doctor!
   chûay taam mǎw hâi dûay   ช่วยตาม หมอให้ด้วย
Call an ambulance!
   chûay rîak rót phayaabaan dûay   ช่วยเรียกรถพยาบาลด้วย

Call the police!

    chûay rîak tam-ràat dûay   ช่วยเรียกตำรวจด้วย

I've been robbed.

    chãn thàuk kha-mõhy   ฉันถูกขโมย

I've been raped.

    chãn thàuk khòm khẽun   ฉันถูกข่มขึ้น

Could I please use the telephone?

    chái thohr sàp dâi mãi?   ใช้โทรศัพท์ได้ไหม?

I wish to contact my embassy/
consulate.

    yàak tìt tàw kàp sathãan-   อยากติดต่อกับสถานทูตของฉัน
    thûut khãwng chãn

I didn't realise I was doing
anything wrong.

    chãn mâi rúu dâi tham   ฉันไม่รู้ได้ทำอะไรผิด
    a-rai phìt

I didn't do it.

    chãn mâi dâi tham   ฉันไม่ได้ทำ

I'm sorry, I apologise.

    khãw thôht, sĩa jai   ขอโทษ–เสียใจ

My blood group is (A,B,O,AB)
positive/negative

    lêuat phõm (m)/*dìi-chãn* (f)   เลือดผม/ดีฉันเป็นกรุ๊ป
    pen krúp ... bàak/lóp   (...) บวก/ลบ

VIETNAMESE

Vietnamese

Introduction

After nearly half a century of war and isolation, Vietnam became one of the poorest countries in the world. Today, however, people live with dignity and hope in this unfortunate country.

To help visitors begin to understand the Vietnamese culture, it is essential to describe some basic cultural norms. Elderly people in Vietnam, especially in rural areas, are particularly respected. The reasons are simple: they have spent their whole life fighting for the survival of their country, and they are the link between the dead and the living. While touring around Vietnam you may meet many young people with big smiles, laughter and curiosity. Don't be surprised or unsettled – they'd simply like to express their hospitality and friendliness to you. Their smiles or laughter have many meanings, however, one sure thing is that they are not provocative. They are meant as tokens of generosity and tolerance. What you might have to worry about, if anything, is that people keep away from you.

Vietnam's population is about 70 million. Over 84% of its population is ethnic Vietnamese. After regaining independence from Chinese rule in 939, the Vietnamese rebuilt their country in all aspects of life. One of these was to develop a system of writing, which became known as *Chữ Nôm*.

The system of *Chữ Nôm* used either a single Chinese character or the combination of two Chinese words. It was mainly used in the area of literature, and lasted until the beginning of this century.

The current writing system, called *Quốc Ngữ* (national written language), is based on the Roman alphabet. This system was developed in the first part of the 17th century by a European Catholic mission for religious purposes. *Quốc Ngữ* became popular, and today it is the formal, and only, writing system in Vietnam.

In Vietnamese culture, the foreign visitor who can speak some Vietnamese is appreciated and welcomed by the Vietnamese. This phrasebook aims to help you understand the spirit of the Vietnamese people, as well as to comunicate with them. We wish you good luck.

Southern & Northern Dialects

There are two main dialects in Vietnamese – the northern and the southern. In this chapter the southern dialect is used. Where both dialects appear, the southern dialect is indicated by *(S)* and the northern by *(N)*.

Pronunciation
Vowels

a	as in 'b**ah**'
ă	as in 'h**u**t'
â	as in American 's**h**ut'
e	as in 'k**e**g'
ê	as in French *et*
i/y	as in 'mach**i**ne'
o	as in 's**aw**'
ô	as in '**o**bey'
ơ	as in 'b**i**rd'
u	as in 'thr**ou**gh'
ư	between the 'i' in 'sister' and the 'u' in 'sugar'

Consonants

Consonants are pronounced as in English with the exception of the following:

c	as in 'cat' (not before *e, ê* and *i*)
ch	as in 'chop'
d or *gi*	as the 'z' in 'zoo'
đ	as in 'dog'
g	hard; as in 'game'
gh	as in 'game' (before *e, ê* and *i*)
k	as in 'kilo', (occurs only before *e, ê* and *i/y*)
ng/ngh	as in 'singer'
nh	as the 'ny' in 'canyon'
ph	as in 'photo'
q	a 'k' sound (only before *u*)
s	as in 'sugar'
t	unaspirated; as in 'stop'
th	as in 'thick'
x	as the 's' in 'soldier'

Tones

There are six tones:

dấu ngang	(no marker)	*ma*	'ghost'
dấu sắc	(marker)	*má*	'mother'
dấu huyền	(marker)	*mà*	'which'
dấu hỏi	(marker)	*mả*	'tomb'
dấu ngã	(marker)	*mã*	'horse'
dấu nặng	(marker)	*mạ*	'rice seedling'

A visual representation of these tones looks like this:

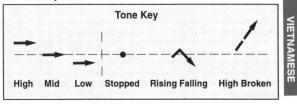

Tone Key

High   Mid   Low   Stopped   Rising Falling   High Broken

Greetings & Civilities
Greetings

'Hello' in Vietnamese is *chào*. To say *chào* only is not very polite. So you should add a personal pronoun ('you') after the word *chào*:

- To a man you first meet, and formally, you say:
  Chào ông.   'Hello Mr.'

- To a lady you first meet, and formally, you say:
  Chào bà.   'Hello Mrs.'

- To a man you know, and informally, you say:
  Chào anh.   'Hello older brother.'

- To a lady you know, and informally, you say:
  Chào chị.   'Hello older sister.'

- To an unmarried woman or a female teacher, you say:
  Chào cô.   'Hello Miss.'

- To a younger person, either male or female, you say:
  Chào em.   'Hello younger sibling.'

A common Vietnamese greeting is expressed in the following phrase:

What are you doing?   *Anh đang làm gì đó?*
                             (lit: you are doing what
                             there?)

The following is used when the person you meet is going somewhere:

Where are you going?   *Anh đang đi đâu đó?*
                             (lit: you are going where
                             there?)

Goodbyes
Chào is also used for 'Goodbye'. Again, you need to add a personal pronoun after it.

Civilities
Within family circles and among friends, the Vietnamese normally don't say 'Thank you' as much as Westerners. So if you do a favour for someone, don't be upset if you don't get a 'Thank you'. The expression for 'thanks' is *Cám ơn (bà/anh/chị/cô/em)*. A suitable response is *Không có chi/gì* (literally 'nothing'). Another way of expressing gratitude is in the phrase:

You are very kind to me.   *Ông quá tử-tế đối với tôi.*
                             (lit. you very kind to me)

VIETNAMESE

Requests & Apologies

When asking a question or making an apology, the Vietnamese normally use the expression *Xin lỗi* ('Excuse me') plus a personal pronoun at the beginning of the sentence.

Excuse me, where is the bank?	*Xin lỗi ông, ngân hàng ở đâu?* (lit: excuse me, bank is where?)
I'm sorry for being late. (to an unmarried woman)	*Xin lỗi cô, tôi đến trễ.* (lit: 'excuse me, I come late')

Forms of Address

The Vietnamese usually use the terms *ông,* 'Mr', and *bà,* 'Mrs', or *cô,* 'Miss', when they address people or on the first meeting. Once they have met someone many times, they change the form of address. They can call you *nội,* 'grand-father', if you are at the age of their grandparent, or *chú,* 'father's younger brother'. If you are younger than them, they will call you *em.*

The form of address varies according to the addressee's social position and age. If you hold a position of importance, the Vietnamese will normally address you by your title. Only very close friends will use both your title and name.

Ông Giáo sư	Mr Professor
Bà Bác sĩ	Mrs Doctor
Ông Giám đốc	Mr Director
Bà Bộ trưởng	Mrs Minister

Pronouns

Vietnamese pronouns vary depending on age, sex, social position and level of intimacy.

1st Person

Singular		Plural	
I	*tôi*	we/we all	*chúng tôi/chúng ta*

2nd Person

See page 333 for the different ways to say 'you'.

3rd Person

Singular ('he/she/it'): these are the same as the 2nd person singular pronouns (see page 333) but add *ay* after them.

it (young child or animal)	*nó*

Plural ('they'): these are the same as the 2nd person singular pronouns, except you add *các* before and *ay* after them.

they (young children or animals)	*chúng nó*
they (general)	*họ*

Body Language

A male and female shaking hands is uncommon in Vietnam. However, being arm in arm with friends of the same sex is acceptable. Couples kissing each other are seen very rarely.

The sign of crossing two fingers together in front of a woman is considered very rude. It is also considered very impolite to use finger signs to call a friend or an employee.

VIETNAMESE

Language Difficulties

I don't speak …	*Tôi không nói …*
Do you speak English?	*Ông có nói tiếng Anh không?*
Do you understand?	*Ông có hiểu không?*
I understand.	*Tôi hiểu.*
I don't understand.	*Tôi không hiểu.*
Could you repeat that?	*Xin ông nhắc lại điều ấy?*
Please show me (in this book).	*Xin chỉ cho tôi (trong quyển sách này).*
What does this mean?	*Cái này nghĩa là gì?*

Small Talk
Meeting People

What is your name?	*Tên ông là gì?*
My name is …	*Tên tôi là …*
Pleased to meet you.	*Hân hạnh gặp ông.*

Nationalities

Where are you from?	*Ông từ đâu đến?*
I am from …	*Tôi đến từ …*
Africa	*Phi châu*
Australia	*Úc-đại-lợi*
Cambodia	*Miên (S)/Cam-bốt (N)*
Canada	*Ca-na-đa*
China	*Trung hoa (S)/ Trung quốc (N)*
England	*Anh*
Europe	*Âu châu*
Ireland	*Ái-nhĩ-lan*

Japan	*Nhật*
Laos	*Lào*
the Middle East	*Trung Đông*
New Zealand	*Tân Tây-lan*
Scotland	*Tô-cách-lan*
Latin America	*Nam Mỹ*
Thailand	*Thái-lan*
the USA	*Hoa-kỳ*
Vietnam	*Việt-Nam*
Wales	*Xứ Wales*

Age

How old are you?	*Ông bao nhiêu tuổi?*
I am ... years old.	*Tôi ... tuổi.*
18	*mười tám*
25	*hai mươi lăm*

Occupations

What do you do (for a living)?	*Ông làm nghề gì?*
What is your salary?	*Lương ông bao nhiêu?*
Do you enjoy your work?	*Ông có thích việc làm của ông không?*
I am a/an ...	*Tôi là ...*
artist	*nghệ sĩ*
business person	*thương gia*
doctor	*bác sĩ*
engineer	*kỹ sư*
farmer	*nông dân*
journalist	*nhà báo*

lawyer	*luật sư*
manual worker	*nhân công*
nurse	*y tá*
office worker/clerk	*nhân viên văn phòng*
scientist	*khoa học gia (S)/*
	nhà khoa học (N)
student	*học sinh*
teacher	*giáo viên*
waiter	*người bồi bàn (S)/*
	hầu bàn (N)
writer	*văn sĩ*

Religion

What is your religion?	*Ông theo đạo nào?*
I am ...	*Tôi theo ...*
Buddhist	*đạo Phật*
Catholic	*đạo Thiên chúa*
Christian	*đạo Tin lành*
Hindu	*đạo Ấn-độ*
Jewish	*đạo Do thái*
Muslim	*đạo Hồi giáo*
Taoist	*đạo Lão*
not religious	*không có đạo*

Family

Are you married?	*Ông đã có gia đình chưa?*
I am single.	*Tôi độc thân.*
How many children do you have?	*Ông có bao nhiêu con?*

I don't have any children.	*Tôi không có đứa con nào cả.*
I have a daughter/son.	*Tôi có một đứa con gái/trai.*
How many brothers/sisters do you have?	*Ông có bao nhiêu anh/chị em?*
Is your husband/wife here?	*Chồng bà/vợ ông có ở đây không?*
Do you have a boyfriend/ girlfriend?	*Ông có bạn trai/bạn gái không?*

Vietnamese terms for kinship are very complicated, as there are separate titles for paternal and maternal sides, as well as for older and younger siblings. Listed here are words for immediate family member.

older/younger brother	*anh/em*
children	*con*
daughter	*con gái*
family	*gia đình*
father	*cha (S)/bố (N)*
grandfather (paternal)	*ông nội*
(maternal)	*ngoại*
grandmother (paternal)	*bà nội*
(maternal)	*ngoại*
husband	*chồng*
mother	*mẹ*
older/younger sister	*chị/em*
son	*con trai*
wife	*vợ*

Interests

What do you do in your spare time?	*Ông làm gì lúc rảnh?*
I like …	*Tôi thích …*
I don't like …	*Tôi không thích …*
Do you like …?	*Ông có thích … không?*
discos	*nhạc đít-cô*
films	*phim xi-nê*
going shopping	*đi chợ*
music	*âm nhạc*
playing games	*chơi các trò chơi*
playing sport	*chơi thể thao*
reading	*đọc sách*
travelling	*đi du lịch*
watching football	*xem bóng đá*
watching TV	*xem truyền hình*

Making Conversation

Wait here!	*Đợi đây!*
Please sit down.	*Mời ông ngồi.*
Would you like something to drink?	*O ng uố ng gì khô ng.*
When were you born?	*Ong sanh ngày nào?*

Getting Around
Finding Your Way

Where is …?	*… ở đâu?*
How do I get to …?	*Làm sao tôi đến …?*

I want to go to the …	*Tôi muốn đi đến …*
bus stop	*trạm xe buýt*
train station	*trạm xe lửa*

Is it far?	*Có xa không?*
Can I walk there?	*Tôi có thể đi bộ đến đó được không?*
Can you show me (on the map)?	*Ông có thể chỉ cho tôi (trên bản đồ) được không?*
Are there other means of getting there?	*Có cách nào khác đến đó không?*

Directions

Go straight ahead.	*Đi thẳng tới trước.*
It's two blocks down.	*Hai dãy nhà phía dưới.*

Turn left …	*Quẹo trái …*
Turn right …	*Quẹo phải …*
at the next corner	*ở ngã tư sắp tới*
at the traffic lights	*ở nơi đèn lưu thông*

behind	*phía sau*
far	*xa*
in front of	*đằng trước*
near	*gần*
opposite	*đối diện*

north	*bắc*
south	*nam*
east	*đông*
west	*tây*

Buying Tickets

I want to go to …	*Tôi muốn đi tới …*
How much is it?	*Giá bao nhiêu?*
I'd like to book a seat to …	*Tôi muốn giữ một chỗ đi …*
I'd like a one-way ticket.	*Tôi muốn một cái vé đi một lượt.*
I'd like a return ticket.	*Tôi muốn một cái vé khứ hồi.*
Can I reserve a place?	*Tôi có thể giữ một chỗ được không?*
Is it completely full?	*Hết chỗ hẳn rồi phải không?*
Please refund my ticket.	*Xin trả lui tiền vé.*

Air

Is there a flight to …?	*Có chuyến máy bay đi … không?*
When is the next flight to …?	*Chuyến bay sắp tới đi … lúc nào?*
How long does the flight take?	*Chuyến bay phải mất bao lâu?*
airport tax	*thuế phi trường*
boarding pass	*thẻ lên máy bay*
customs	*quan thuế*
aeroplane	*máy bay*

Bus

bus	*xe buýt*
long-distance bus	*xe buýt đi đường xa*

Which bus goes to …?	*Chiếc xe buýt nào đi đến …?*
Could you let me know when we get to …?	*Xin cho tôi biết lúc nào thì chúng tôi đến …?*
I want to get off!	*Tôi muốn xuống xe!*

What time is the … bus?	*Mấy giờ thì có xe buýt …?*
next	*sắp tới*
first	*đầu tiên*
last	*sau cùng*

Train

Is it an express train?	*Có phải là xe lửa tốc hành không?*
I'd like a sleeper ticket.	*Tôi muốn một vé toa nằm.*
What is this station called?	*Trạm xe lửa này gọi là gì?*
What is the next station?	*Trạm xe lửa sắp tới là gì?*

dining car	*toa bán đồ ăn*
express (train)	*tốc hành (xe lửa)*
local (train)	*địa phương (xe lửa)*
railway station	*ga xe lửa*
sleeping car	*toa ngủ*
train	*xe lửa*

Taxi & Pedicab

Can you take me to …?	*Ông có thể đưa tôi đến … được không?*
How much does it cost to go to …?	*Giá bao nhiêu đi đến …?*
For two people?	*Cho hai người?*

VIETNAMESE

It's too much!	*Quá nhiều!*
Does that include the luggage?	*Có gồm cả hành lý không?*
I want a taxi to the airport.	*Tôi cần một chiếc tắc-xi đi phi trường.*

Instructions

Here is fine, thank you.	*Đây rồi, cám ơn.*
The next corner, please.	*Xin đến ngã tư kế.*
Continue!	*Tiếp tục!*
The next street to the left.	*Đường kế quẹo trái.*
Stop here!	*Ngừng ở đây!*
Please slow down.	*Xin chậm lại.*
Please hurry.	*Xin nhanh lên.*
Please wait here.	*Xin đợi ở đây.*

Useful Phrases

The (train) is delayed/ cancelled/on time.	*(Xe lửa) bị trễ/hủy/đúng giờ.*
How long will it be delayed?	*Xe lửa bị trễ bao lâu?*
Do I need to change?	*Tôi có cần đổi xe lửa không?*
You must change trains/buses/platform.	*Ông phải đổi xe lửa/xe buýt/sân ga.*
How long does the trip take?	*Hành trình mất bao lâu?*
Is it a direct route?	*Tuyến đường đi thẳng phải không?*
Is that seat taken?	*Cái chỗ kia đã có ai chiếm chưa?*

I want to get off at ...	*Tôi muốn xuống ở ...*
Excuse me.	*Xin lỗi.*
Where can I hire a bicycle?	*Tôi có thể thuê xe đạp ở đâu?*
Where is the restroom?	*Phòng vệ sinh ở đâu?*

Accommodation
Finding Accommodation

Where is a/the ...?	*... ở đâu?*
camping ground	*khu cắm trại*
guesthouse	*nhà khách*
hotel	*khách sạn*
youth hostel	*nhà trọ thanh niên*

I'm looking for a ...	*Tôi đang kiếm ...*
cheap hotel	*một khách sạn rẻ tiền*
clean hotel	*một khách sạn sạch sẽ*
good hotel	*một khách sạn tốt*
nearby hotel	*một khách sạn gần đây*

Could you write down the address please?	*Xin ông vui lòng viết ra địa chỉ?*

Checking In

Do you have any rooms available?	*Ông có phòng nào trống không?*

I would like ...	*Tôi muốn ...*
a single room	*một phòng chiếc/đơn*
a double room	*một phòng đôi*

a room with a private bathroom	*một phòng có buồng tắm riêng*
a room with a shared bathroom	*một phòng có phòng tắm chung*
to share a dorm	*chia một phòng ngư*
a bed	*một giường*

I want a room with a …	*Tôi muốn một phòng có …*
bathroom	*buồng tắm*
shower	*vòi tắm*
television	*đài truyền hình*
window	*cửa sổ*

How much is it per night/per person?	*Bao nhiêu mỗi đêm/mỗi người?*
Can I see the room?	*Tôi cò thể xem phòng được không?*
Are there any others?	*Cò phòng nào khác không?*
Are there any cheaper rooms?	*Có phòng nào rẻ hơn không?*
Does it include breakfast?	*Có bao ăn sáng không?*
Can I have my passport back?	*Tôi có thể nhận lại sổ hộ chiếu của tôi được không?*

I'm going to stay for …	*Tôi sẽ lại …*
one day	*một ngày*
two days	*hai ngày*
one week	*một tuần*

Where is the bathroom?	*Có phòng tắm không?*

Requests & Complaints

Is there hot water all day?	*Có nước nóng suốt ngày không?*
Do you have a safe where I can leave my valuables?	*Ông có tư sắt để cất các đồ quý không?*
Is there somewhere to wash clothes?	*Có chỗ nào để giặt áo quần không?*
Please wake me up at … tomorrow.	*Xin thức tôi dậy lúc … ngày mai.*
The room needs to be cleaned.	*Phòng cần quét dọn.*
Please change the sheets.	*Xin thay ra trãi giường.*
I've locked myself out of my room.	*Tôi vừa tự khóa không vào phòng được.*
The toilet won't flush.	*Cầu vệ sinh không thoát nước.*
The … doesn't work.	*… không hoạt động.*
Can you get it fixed?	*Ông có thể cho sửa được không?*
I don't like this room.	*Tôi không thích phòng này.*
It's too small.	*Phòng quá chật.*
It's too cold/hot.	*Phòng quá lạnh/nóng.*
It's noisy.	*Phòng ồn.*
It smells.	*Phòng có mùi hôi.*

Checking Out

I'd like to pay the bill.	*Tôi muốn trả tiền.*
Can I leave my luggage here?	*Tôi có thể gởi/gửi hành lý lại đây được không?*

I'd like to check out ...	Tôi muốn trả phòng ...
now	bây giờ
at noon	trưa
tomorrow	ngày mai

Useful Words

air-con	có điều hòa không khí
bill	hóa đơn
cold	lạnh
electricity	điện
excluded	không kể
fan	quạt
hot	nóng
included	bao gồm
key	chìa khóa
room	phòng
soap	xa phòng
toilet paper	giấy vệ sinh
towel	khăn tắm

Around Town

I'm looking for ...	Tôi đang tìm ...
a bank	ngân hàng
the city centre	trung tâm thành phố
the ... embassy	tòa đại sứ ...
my hotel	khách sạn của tôi
the police	cảnh sát
the post office	bưu điện
a public toilet	nhà vệ sinh công cộng
the telephone centre	trung tâm điện thoại

VIETNAMESE

Directions

What ... is this?	*... này là gì?*
street	*đường (S)/phố (N)*
street number	*số đường (S)/phố (N)*

At the Post Office

I'd like to send a ...	*Tôi muốn gởi ...*
letter	*một lá thư*
postcard	*một bưu thiếp*
parcel	*một bưu kiện*
telegram	*một điện tín*
How much is the postage?	*Tiền gởi (S) gửi (N) bao nhiêu?*
aerogram	*giấy bì thư (S)/phong bì (N)*
airmail	*gởi (S)/gửi (N) máy bay*
envelope	*bì thư (S)/phong bì (N)*
registered mail	*thư bảo đảm*
surface mail	*thư thường*

Telephone

I want to call ...	*Tôi muốn gọi ...*
The number is ...	*Số là ...*
I want to speak for three minutes.	*Tôi muốn nói trong ba phút.*
I want to make a reverse-charges phone call.	*Tôi muốn gọi điện thoại bên kia trả.*
Hello, is ... there?	*He-lo, có phải ... đó không?*
It's engaged.	*Điện thoại bận.*
Operator, I've been cut off.	*Tổng đài, điện thoại vừa bị cắt.*

VIETNAMESE

At the Bank

I want to exchange some money.	*Tôi muốn đổi một ít tiền.*
I want to change travellers' cheques.	*Tôi muốn đổi chi phiếu (S)/séc du lịch (N).*
What is the exchange rate?	*Giá đổi là bao nhiêu?*
Can I have money transferred here from my bank?	*Tôi có thể lấy tiền chuyển từ ngân hàng của tôi đến đây được không?*
How long will it take to arrive?	*Bao lâu thì tiền đến?*
Has my money arrived yet?	*Tiền của tôi đã đến chưa?*

Sightseeing

Where is the tourist office?	*Phòng du lịch ở đâu?*
What time does it open?	*Mấy giờ thì mở cửa?*
What time does it close?	*Mấy giờ thì đóng cửa?*
Do you have a local map?	*Ông (bà) có bản đồ địa phương không?*
Can I take photographs?	*Tôi có thể chụp hình (S)/ảnh (N) được không?*
Can I take your photograph?	*Tôi có thể chụp hình (S)/ảnh (N) Ông (bà) được không?*
I will send you the photograph.	*Tôi sẽ gởi hình (S)/ảnh (N) đến ông (bà).*
What's ...?	*... là gì?*
this/that building	*tòa nhà này/kia*
this/that monument	*công trình này/kia*

VIETNAMESE

art gallery	*phòng triển lãm*
beach	*bờ biển*
botanical garden	*vườn bách thảo*
building	*tòa nhà*
church	*nhà thờ*
market	*chợ*
monastery	*tu viện*
museum	*viện bảo tàng*
old city	*thành phố cũ*
pagoda	*chùa*
palace	*cung (N)/điện/dinh (S)*
park	*công viên*
statues	*tượng*
temple	*đền, miếu*
theatre	*rạp hát*
university	*đại học*
zoo	*sở thú*

Paperwork

address	*địa chỉ*
age	*tuổi*
birth certificate	*giấy khai sinh*
border	*biên giới*
customs	*thuế quan*
date of birth	*ngày sinh*
driving licence	*bằng lái xe*
identification	*chứng minh thư*
immigration	*di trú*
internal travel permit	*giấy phép đi lại trong nước*
marital status	*tình trạng gia đình*
name	*tên*

nationality	*quốc tịch*
passport	*hộ chiếu*
passport number	*số hộ chiếu*
place of birth	*nơi sinh*
port of arrival/departure	*cửa vào/ra*
profession	*nghề nghiệp*
reason for travel	*lý do đi du lịch*
registration	*đăng ký*
religion	*tôn giáo*
sex (gender)	*phái*
tour	*chuyến*
tourist card	*thẻ du lịch*
visa	*thị thực*
business	*doanh thương*
extension	*gia hạn*
family	*gia đình*
journalist	*nhà báo*
tourist	*du khách*

In the Country
Weather

What's the weather like?	*Thời tiết như thế nào?*
Will it be ... tomorrow?	*Thời tiết sẽ ... ngày mai?*
cold	*lạnh*
cloudy	*có mây*
hot	*nóng*
humid	*ẩm ướt*
raining	*mưa*
snowing	*đổ tuyết*
windy	*gió*

dry season	*mùa khô*
rainy season	*mùa mưa*
storm	*bão*
sun	*mặt trời*

Geographical Terms

cave	*động*
farm	*nông trại (S)/nông trườ ng (N)*
forest	*rừng*
harbour	*hải cảng*
hill	*đồi*
island	*đảo*
jungle	*rừng*
lake	*hồ*
mountain	*núi*
national park	*công viên quốc gia*
ocean	*đại dương*
ricefield	*ruộng lúa*
river	*sông*
valley	*thung lũng*
village	*làng*
waterfall	*thác nước*

Flora

cactus	*cây xương rồng*
carnation	*cây cẩm chướng*
chrysanthemum	*cây hoa cúc*
coffee bushes	*cây cà-phê*

firewood	củi
flower	hoa
leaf	lá
lily	cây huệ
orchid	cây phong lan
palm tree	cây cọ
stick	cây gậy
sugar cane	cây mía
tree	cây
vegetation	cây cối
wood	gỗ

Fauna

bird	chim
cat	mèo
chicken	gà
cockroach	gián
cow	bò
deer	nai
dog	chó
horse	ngựa
leech	đỉa
lizard	thằn lằn
monkey	khỉ
mosquito	muỗi
ox	bò đực
pig	heo (S)/lợn (N)
sheep	cừu
snake	rắn
spider	nhện

VIETNAMESE

Camping

Am I allowed to camp here?	*Tôi có được phép cắm trại ở đây không?*
Is there a campsite nearby?	*Có chỗ cắm trại ở gần đây không?*
I want to hire a tent.	*Tôi muốn thuê một cái lều vải.*
It is waterproof?	*Không thấm nước phải không?*

can opener	*cái mở hộp*
firewood	*củi*
penknife	*dao nhíp*
rope	*sợi thừng*
tent	*cái lều vải*
torch (flashlight)	*đèn pin*
sleeping bag	*túi ngủ*

Food

restaurant	*tiệm ăn (S)/nhà hàng (N)*
food stall	*dãy thực phẩm*
grocery store/delicatessen	*tiệm (S)/cửa (N)hàng tạp hóa*
breakfast	*bữa ăn sáng*
lunch	*bữa ăn trưa*
dinner	*bữa ăn tối*

Eating Out

Table for ... people, please.	*Xin cho một bàn ... người.*
Do you have a menu in English?	*(Ông/Cô) có bản thực đơn bằng tiếng Anh không?*

Is service included in the bill?	*Tiền phục vụ có bao gồm trong phiếu tính tiền không?*
What is this/that?	*Món này/món kia là gì?*
I want the same as his.	*Tôi muốn món ăn như anh ấy.*
Not too spicy please.	*Xin đừng cho quá nhiều gia vị.*
It's not hot.	*Không cay.*
No MSG please.	*Xin đừng cho bột ngọt.*
I am a vegetarian.	*Tôi ăn chay.*
I don't eat meat. (implies red meat)	*Tôi không ăn thịt.*

Typical Vietnamese Dishes

chả giò	spring rolls
phở	beef noodle soup
bún bò Huế	Huế-style beef noodle soup
cơm trắng	steamed rice
cơm chiên (S)/rang (N)	fried rice
lẩu thập cẩm	mixed meat and seafood pot
thịt heo (S)/lợn (N) xào đậu cô-ve	pork cooked with green bean
tôm hùm xào hành, gừng	lobster cooked with ginger and onion
cua rang muối	crab fried with salt
gà xào sả ớt	chicken fried with lemon grass and chilli
cánh gà chiên bơ	chicken wing fried with butter
bông cải (S)/hoa (N) lơ xào thịt heo	cauliflower cooked with pork

VIETNAMESE

đậu phụ tôm thịt	bean curd cooked with prawn and pork
nấm xào hành	mushroom cooked with onion
giá xào thịt bò	bean sprouts cooked with beef
măng xào thịt heo	bamboo shoots cooked with pork
cải xà lách dầu giấm	lettuce with oil and vinegar
cá hấp	steamed eggplant
chè đậu xanh	green pea sweet soup
chè đậu đen	black bean sweet soup
đậu (S)/tương (N)	soya cake

At the Market
Meat

beef	*thịt bò*
chicken	*thịt gà*
duck	*thịt vịt*
goat	*thịt dê*
ham	*chả thịt heo* (S)/*lợn* (N)
lamb	*thịt cừu non*
meat	*thịt*
mutton	*thịt cừu*
pork	*thịt heo* (S)/*thịt lợn* (N)
tripe	*dạ dày bò*

Seafood

crab	*cua*
eel	*lươn*
fish	*cá*
lobster	*tôm hùm*

VIETNAMESE

mussels	*con trai*
oyster	*con sò*
prawns/shrimps	*tôm*
sardines	*cá mòi*
shark	*cá mập*
squid	*mực*
trout	*cá hồi*

Vegetables

bamboo sprouts	*măng*
bean sprouts	*giá*
beancurd (tofu)	*hũ (S)/đậu phụ (N)*
beans	*đậu*
cabbage	*bắp cải*
cauliflower	*bông cải (S)/hoa lơ (N)*
celery	*cần tây*
corn	*bắp (S)/ngô (N)*
cucumber	*dưa leo (S)/dưa chuột (N)*
eggplant (aubergine)	*cà pháo*
green beans	*đậu xanh*
lentils	*đậu lăng-ti*
mushrooms	*nấm*
olives	*ô-liu*
peas	*đậu Hà-lan*
potato	*khoai tây*
pumpkin	*bí đỏ (S)/bí ngô (N)*
spinach	*rau muống*
sweet potato	*khoai lang*
tomato	*cà chua*
turnip	*củ cải*
vegetable	*rau cải*

VIETNAMESE

Fruit

apple	*trái/quả táo*
apricot	*trái/quả lê*
avocado	*trái/quả bơ*
banana	*trái/quả chuối*
blackberry	*trái/quả dâu đen*
carambola	*trái/quả khế*
cherries	*trái/quả dâu*
coconut	*trái/quả dừa*
custard apple	*trái/quả mãng cầu dai/ trái na*
dates	*trái/quả chà là*
fig	*trái/quả sung*
fruit	*trái/quả cây/hoa quả*
grape	*trái/quả nho*
grapefruit (red)	*trái/quả thanh trà*
grapefruit (white or red)	*trái/quả bưởi*
green dragon	*trái/quả thanh long*
guava	*trái/quả ổi*
lemon	*trái/quả chanh*
longan	*nhãn*
lychee	*trái/quả vải*
mandarin	*trái/quả quýt*
melon	*trái/quả dưa tây*
orange	*trái/quả cam*
papaya	*trái/quả đu đủ*
passion fruit	*trái/quả lạc tiên*
peach	*trái/quả đào*
pear	*trái/quả lê*
pineapple	*trái/quả thơm/dứa*
plum	*trái/quả mận/roi*

pomegranate	*trái/quả lựu*
rambutan	*trái/quả chôm chôm*
raisins	*trái/quả nho khô*
star-apple	*trái/quả vú sữa*
strawberry	*trái/quả dâu tây*
watermelon	*trái/quả dưa hấu*

Spices & Condiments

chilli	*ớt*
cinnamon	*quế*
cloves	*hành con*
coriander	*rau mùi (S)/ngò (N)*
garlic	*tỏi*
ginger	*gừng*
mint	*rau thơm*
paprika	*ớt Hung*
pepper	*tiêu*
saffron	*nghệ*
salt	*muối*
soy sauce	*nước tương*
vinegar	*dấm*

Drinks
Cold Drinks

beer	*bia*
coconut milk	*nước dừa*
juice	*nước trái cây*
mineral water	*nước suối*
red wine	*rượu chát đỏ*

spirit	*rượu mạnh*
water	*nước*
white wine	*rượu chát trắng (S)/*
	rượu vang trắng (N)
without ice	*không có đá*

Hot Drinks

coffee	*cà-phê*
espresso coffee	*cà-phê hơi*
camomile tea	*trà cúc la mã*
herb tea	*trà dược thảo*
hot chocolate	*sô-cô-la nóng*
tea	*trà (S)/chè (N)*
with lemon	*với chanh*

Useful Words

ashtray	*cái gạt tàn thuốc*
bill	*phiếu tính tiền (S)/*
	hóa đơn (N)
bowl	*cái tô (S)/bát (N)*
fork	*cái nĩa*
glass	*cái ly (S)/cái cốc (N)*
knife	*con dao*
napkin	*khăn ăn*
plate	*cái đĩa*
spoon	*cái muỗng (S)/cái thìa (N)*
stale	*cũ (S)/ôi (N) nhạt nhẽo*
toothpick	*cái tăm (S)/tăm xỉa răng (N)*

VIETNAMESE

Shopping

Where is the nearest ...?	... gần nhất ở đâu?
bookshop	nhà (S)/cửa (N) hàng sách
chemist/pharmacy	nhà (S)/cửa (N) hàng thuốc tây
clothing store	tiệm (S)/cửa (N) hàng áo quần
laundry	tiệm giặt
market	chợ
shop	tiệm (S)/cửa (N) hàng
souvenir shop	tiệm (S)/cửa (N) hàng bán đồ kỷ niệm

Making a Purchase

I'd like to buy ...	Tôi muốn mua ...
How much is it?	Giá bao nhiêu?
Do you have others?	(Ông/Cô) có các thứ khác không?
I don't like it.	Tôi không thích cái ấy.
Which one?	Cái nào?
This one?	Cái này?
I'm just looking.	Tôi chỉ xem.
Can you write down the price?	(Ông/Cô) có thể viết giá ra được không?
Do you accept credit cards?	(Ông/Cô) có nhận thẻ tín dụng không?
What is it made of?	Cái ấy làm bằng gì?

VIETNAMESE

Bargaining

That's very expensive!	*Cái ấy rất đắt!*
That's too expensive for me.	*Cái ấy quá đắt đối với tôi.*
It costs a lot.	*Tốn quá.*
I'll buy it if you lower the price.	*Nếu (Ông/Cô) hạ giá xuống thì tôi sẽ mua.*
I don't have much money.	*Tôi không có nhiều tiền như thế.*
I'll give you … dong.	*Tôi sẽ tính cho Ông … đồng.*
No more than … dong.	*Không quá … đồng.*

Souvenirs

ceramics	*đồ gốm*
earrings	*hoa tai*
embroidered goods	*đồ thêu*
handicraft	*đồ thủ công*
hat made of latanier leaves	*nón lá*
lacquerware	*đồ sơn mài*
leatherwork	*đồ da*
mother-of pearl	*xà cừ*
necklace	*giây chuyền*
pottery	*đồ gốm*
silk paintings	*tranh lụa*
traditional musical instruments	*nhạc cụ cổ truyền*
wood-block prints	*tranh khắc gỗ*

Toiletries

chlorine tablets	*thuốc clo*
condoms	*áo mưa (S)/ bao ngừa thai (N)*

deodorant	*chất khử mùi*
insect repellent	*thuốc trừ sâu*
iodine	*i-ốt*
laxative	*thuốc nhuận trường*
moisturising cream	*kem dưỡng da*
razor	*dao cạo râu*
sanitary napkins	*băng vệ sinh*
shaving cream	*kem cạo râu*
soap	*xà-phòng*
sunblock cream	*kem chống nắng*
tampons	*tóc giả*
toilet paper	*giấy vệ sinh*
toothbrush	*bàn chải đánh răng*
toothpaste	*kem đánh răng*
water purification tablets	*thuốc lọc nước*

Photography

How much is it to develop?	*Sang (S)/Tráng (N) phim bao nhiêu?*
When will it be ready?	*Lúc nào thì xong?*
Do you fix cameras?	*(Ông/Cô) có sửa máy chụp hình (S)/ảnh (N) không?*
camera	*máy chụp hình (S)/ảnh (N)*
film	*phim*
B&W film	*phim trắng đen*
colour film	*phim màu*
colour slide	*phim âm bản màu*
flash	*đèn chụp hình*
lens	*ống kính*
light metre	*máy đo ánh sáng*

VIETNAMESE

Smoking

cigarettes	*thuốc lá*
lighter	*máy bật lửa*
matches	*diêm*
pipe	*ống vố (S)/tẩu thuốc (N)*
tobacco	*thuốc lá hút ống vố (S)/ tẩu (N)*

A packet of cigarettes, please.	*Xin cho một gói thuốc.*
Do you have a light?	*Ông có lửa không?*
Do you mind if I smoke?	*(Ông/Cô) có ngại tôi hút thuốc không?*
Please don't smoke.	*Xin đừng hút thuốc.*
I'm trying to give up.	*Tôi đang cố gắng bỏ hút thuốc.*

Sizes & Comparisons

big	*lớn*
bigger	*lớn hơn*
enough	*đủ*
less	*ít hơn*
a little bit	*một ít*
long	*lâu*
much/many	*nhiều*
more	*thêm nữa*
small	*nhỏ*
smaller	*nhỏ hơn*
some	*một ít*
too much/many	*quá nhiều*

Health

Where is a/the ...?	... *ở đâu?*
doctor	*bác sĩ*
hospital	*bệnh viện*
chemist	*nhà (S)/cửa (N) hàng thuốc tây*
dentist	*nha sĩ*

I'm sick. — *Tôi ốm/bệnh/bịnh.*
My friend is sick. — *Bạn tôi ốm/bệnh/bịnh.*

I need a doctor. — *Tôi cần bác sĩ.*
Where can I find a good doctor? — *Ở đâu tôi có thể kiếm được bác sĩ giỏi?*

At the Doctor

I feel dizzy. — *Tôi cảm thấy choáng váng.*
I feel weak. — *Tôi cảm thấy yếu.*
I've been bitten by something. — *Tôi vừa bị cái gì chích (S)/đâm vào (N).*

I'm having trouble breathing. — *Tôi đang bị khó thở.*

I've been vomiting. — *Tôi vừa nôn (S)/ói (N).*
I can't sleep. — *Tôi không ngủ được.*
I can't move my ... — *Tôi không nhúc nhích ... tôi được.*

It hurts here. — *Bị đau ở đây.*

VIETNAMESE

Ailments

I have (a/an) …	*Tôi bị …*
anaemia	*bệnh thiếu máu*
asthma	*bệnh suyễn*
burn	*phỏng (S)/bỏng (N)*
cold	*bị cảm*
constipation	*táo bón*
cough	*bị ho*
diarrhoea	*bệnh ỉa chảy*
fever	*bệnh sốt*
headache	*đau đầu*
hepatitis	*viêm gan*
infection	*nhiễm trùng*
influenza	*bệnh cúm*
lice	*chí (S)/chấy (N) rận*
low/high blood pressure	*áp huyết thấp/cao*
malaria	*bệnh sốt rét*
nausea	*nôn mửa*
pain	*đau*
stomachache	*đau dạ dày*
venereal disease	*bệnh hoa liễu*

Women's Health

I'm on the (contraceptive) pill.	*Tôi đang dùng thuốc ngừa (S)/chống (N) thụ thai.*
I haven't had my period for … months.	*Tôi chưa có kinh từ … tháng nay.*
I'm pregnant.	*Tôi có thai.*
maternity hospital	*bệnh viện sản khoa.*
menstruation	*kinh nguyệt*

VIETNAMESE

Specific Needs

I'm diabetic.	*Tôi bị bệnh đái đường.*
I'm epileptic.	*Tôi bị kinh phong (S)/động kinh (N).*
I'm allergic to …	*Tôi bị dị ứng với …*
antibiotics	*thuốc kháng sinh*
penicillin	*thuốc pê-ni-xi-lin*
I've been vaccinated.	*Tôi vừa chích ngừa (S)/ tiêm phòng (N).*
I have my own syringe.	*Tôi có kim chích (S)/ tiêm riêng (N).*
I have a heart condition.	*Tôi bị tim.*
I have medical insurance.	*Tôi có bảo hiểm y tế.*
accident	*tai nạn*
acupuncture	*châm cứu*
addiction	*nghiện (S)/ghiền (N)*
injection	*chích*

Parts of the Body

arm	*cánh tay*
ear	*tai*
eye	*mắt*
foot	*chân*
hand	*tay*
head	*đầu*
kidney	*cật (S)/thận (N)*
leg	*đùi chân*
mouth	*miệng*

VIETNAMESE

muscle	*gân*
neck	*cổ*
shoulder	*vai*
spine	*xương sống*
stomach	*dạ dày*
teeth	*răng*
tongue	*lưỡi*

At the Chemist

I need something for ...	*Tôi cần thuốc cho ...*
Do I need a prescription for ...	*Tôi có cần toa cho ...*
How many times a day?	*Bao nhiêu lần mỗi ngày?*
antibiotics	*thuốc kháng sinh*
antidiarrhoeal drug	*thuốc chống ỉa chảy*
antiseptic	*thuốc sát trùng*
aspirin	*thuốc át-pi-rin*
laxative	*thuốc nhuận trường (S)/ tràng (N)*
vitamins	*sinh tố*

Time & Dates
Telling the Time

What time is it?	*Mấy giờ rồi?*
It's 1 am.	*Một giờ sáng.*
It's 4.15.	*Bốn giờ mười lăm.*
It's 4.30.	*Bốn giờ ba mươi or bốn giờ rưỡi.*
It's 4.40.	*Bốn giờ bốn mươi.*
It's 4.45.	*Bốn giờ bốn mươi lăm.*

o'clock	*giờ*
am	*sáng*
pm	*chiều (tối* after 7 pm)
in the morning	*buổi sáng*
in the afternoon	*buổi chiều*
in the evening	*buổi tối*

VIETNAMESE

Days of the Week

Monday	*Thứ hai*
Tuesday	*Thứ ba*
Wednesday	*Thứ tư*
Thursday	*Thứ năm*
Friday	*Thứ sáu*
Saturday	*Thứ bảy*
Sunday	*Chủ nhật*

Months

January	*Tháng giêng*
February	*Tháng hai*
March	*Tháng ba*
April	*Tháng tư*
May	*Tháng năm*
June	*Tháng sáu*
July	*Tháng bảy*
August	*Tháng tám*
September	*Tháng chín*
October	*Tháng mười*
November	*Tháng mười một*
December	*Tháng mười hai*

Seasons

spring	*mùa xuân*
summer	*mùa hè (S)/mùa hạ (N)*
autumn	*mùa thu*
winter	*mùa đông*

Dates

What date is it today?	*Hôm nay là ngày mấy?*
It's 28 June.	*Ngày 28 Tháng sáu.*
It's 3 June.	*Ngày 3 Tháng sáu.*
It's 1 April.	*Ngày 1 Tháng tư.*

Present

today	*hôm nay*
this morning	*sáng nay*
this afternoon	*chiều nay*
tonight	*đêm nay*
this week	*tuần này*
this month	*tháng này*
this year	*năm này*

Past

yesterday	*hôm qua*
day before yesterday	*ngày kia*
yesterday morning	*sáng qua*
yesterday afternoon/evening	*chiều qua/tối qua*
last night	*đêm qua*
last week	*tuần trước (vừa qua)*
last month	*tháng trước (vừa qua)*
last year	*năm trước (vừa qua)*

Future

tomorrow	*ngày mai*
day after tomorrow	*ngày mốt (S)/kia (N)*
tomorrow morning	*sáng mai*
tomorrow afternoon	*chiều mai*
tomorrow evening	*tối mai*
next week	*tuần tới*
next month	*tháng tới*
next year	*năm tới*

During the Day

sunrise	*mặt trời mọc*
dawn, very early morning	*bình minh, lúc rạng đông*
morning	*sáng*
noon	*trưa*
afternoon	*chiều*
evening	*tối*
sundown	*hoàng hôn*
midnight	*nửa đêm*

Numbers
Cardinal Numbers

0	*không*	9	*chín*
1	*một*	10	*mười*
2	*hai*	11	*mười một*
3	*ba*	12	*mười hai*
4	*bốn*	13	*mười ba*
5	*năm*	14	*mười bốn*
6	*sáu*	15	*mười lăm* (not *mười năm*)
7	*bảy*	16	*mười sáu*
8	*tám*	17	*mười bảy*

VIETNAMESE

VIETNAMESE

18	*mười tám*	60	*sáu mươi*
19	*mười chín*	70	*bảy mươi*
20	*hai mươi*	80	*tám mươi*
21	*hai mươi mốt/*	90	*chín mươi*
	hăm mốt		
22	*hai mươi hai/*	100	*một trăm*
	hăm hai		
30	*ba mươi*	1000	*một ngàn*
40	*bốn mươi*	100,000	*một trăm ngàn*
50	*năm mươi*	one million	*một triệu*

Ordinal Numbers

1st	*thứ nhất*	6th	*thứ sáu*
2nd	*thứ hai*	7th	*thứ bảy*
3rd	*thứ ba*	8th	*thứ tám*
4th	*thứ tư*	9th	*thứ chín*
5th	*thứ năm*	10th	*thứ mười*

Emergencies

Help!	*Cứu với!*
Stop!	*Ngừng lại!*
Watch out!	*Coi chừng!*
Thief!	*Kẻ ăn cắp!*
Fire!	*Cháy!*
Go away!	*Đi đi!*
Call a doctor!	*Xin gọi bác sĩ!*
Call an ambulance!	*Xin gọi xe cứu thương!*
Call the police!	*Xin gọi cảnh sát!*
I've been raped.	*Tôi vừa bị hãm.*
I've been robbed.	*Tôi vừa bị móc túi*

VIETNAMESE

I've lost my ...
   bags
   money
   travellers' cheques
   passport

Tôi vừa mất ...
   cái xách tay của tôi
   tiền của tôi
   chi phiếu du lịch
   sổ hộ chiếu của tôi

I'm ill.
I'm lost.
Where is the police station?
Where are the toilets?
Could I please use the
telephone?
I wish to contact my
embassy/consulate.

Tôi bị bệnh.
Tôi bị lạc đường.
Đồn cảnh sát ở đâu?
Nhà vệ sinh ở đâu?
Tôi có thể dùng điện thoại
được không?
Tôi muốn liên lạc với tòa
đại sứ/tòa lãnh sự.

I didn't realise I was doing
anything wrong.
I didn't do it.
I'm sorry.
Contact number
(next of kin)

Tôi không nghĩ là tôi đã
làm điều gì sai.
Tôi không làm việc ấy.
Xin lỗi.
Số liên lạc (người trực hệ)

My blood group is (A, B,
O, AB) positive/negative.

Máu của tôi thuộc nhóm
(A, B, O, AB) dương/âm.

Index

Indonesian & Malay 64

Khmer 118

Lao..174

Thai 274

Vietnamese *332*

Quick Reference Pages..............................*385-398*

Quick Reference BURMESE

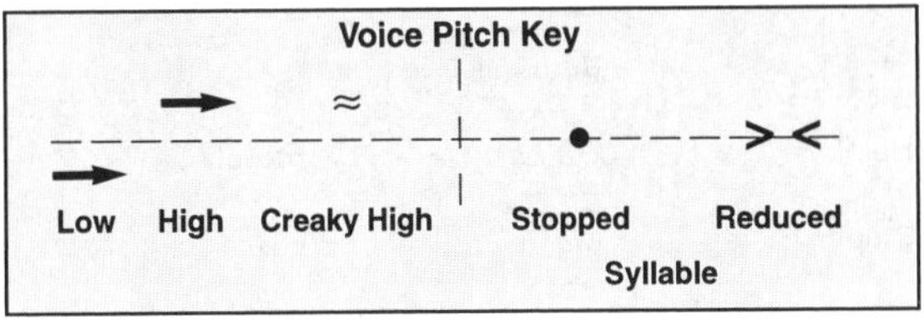
Voice Pitch Key
Low
High
Creaky High
Stopped
Reduced
Syllable

Hello.

k'ămyà (m)/shin (f) ne-kaùn-yéh-là?

ခင်ဗျား/ရှင် နေကောင်းရဲ့လား။

Goodbye. (when you are leaving)	*thwà-ba-oùn-meh*	သွားပါအုံးမယ်။
Goodbye. (when you are staying)	*kaùn-ba-bi*	ကောင်းပါပြီ။
Thanks.	*cè-zù-bèh*	ကျေးဇူးပဲ။
(I) don't understand.	*nà-măleh-ba-bù*	နားမလည်ပါဘူး။
Where is (a/the) ...?	*... beh-hma-lèh?*	... ဘယ်မှာလဲ။
Left/Right.	*beh-beq/nya-beq*	ဘယ်ဘက်/ညာဘက်
Straight (ahead).	*téh-déh*	တည့်တည့်

BURMESE *Quick Reference*

How much?	*beh-lauq-lèh?*	ဘယ်လောက်လဲ။
What time is it?	*beh-ăc'ein* *shí-bi-lèh?*	ဘယ်အချိန်ရှိပြီလဲ။
Help!	*keh-ba*	ကယ်ပါ။
Stop!	*yaq*	ရပ်။
I am ill.	*ne-măkàun-bù*	နေမကောင်းဘူး။
I am lost.	*làn pyauq-thwà-bi*	လမ်းပျောက်သွားပြီ။
today	*di-né*	ဒီနေ့
tomorrow	*măneq-p'yan*	မနက်ဖြန်

ENTRANCE	အဝင်
EXIT	အထွက်
NO ENTRY	မဝင်ရ
TELEPHONE	တယ်လီဖုန်း
TOILETS	အိမ်သာ
NO SMOKING	ဆေးလိပ် မသောက်ရ
NO PHOTOGRAPHS	ဓါတ်ပုံ မရိုက်ရ
DANGER	ရှိုသည်
STOP	ရပ်
WOMEN FORBIDDEN	အမျိုးသမီးများ မဝင်ရ

	INDONESIAN	MALAY
Good morning.	*Selamat pagi.*	*Selamat pagi.*
Hello/Good day.	*Selamat siang.*	*Selamat tengahari.*
Goodbye.		
(you are leaving)	*Selamat tinggal.*	*Selamat tinggal.*
(you are staying)	*Selamat jalan.*	*Selamat jalan.*
Please/Help.		
(request)	*Tolong.*	*Tolong.*
(offer)	*Silakan.*	*Silakan.*
Thank you.	*Terima kasih.*	*Terima kasih.*
You're welcome.	*Kembali/*	*Kembali/*
	Sama-sama. (slang)	*Sama-sama.* (slang)
Excuse me.	*Permisi/Ma'afkan*	*Permisi/Ma'afkan*
	saya.	*saya.*
I don't understand.	*Saya tidak mengerti.*	*Saya tidak faham.*
Where is the ...?	*Dimana ...?*	*Di mana ...?*
Go straight ahead!	*Jalan terus!*	*Jalan terus!*
Turn left.	*Belok kiri.*	*Belok kiri....*
Turn right.	*Belok kanan.*	*Belok kanan....*
How much is it?	*Berapa harganya*	*Berapa harganya*
	ini?	*ini?*

INDONESIAN & MALAY *Quick Reference*

	INDONESIAN	MALAY
What time is it?	*Jam berapa (sekarang)?*	*Pukul berapa (sekarang)?*
Help!	*Tolong!*	*Tolong!*
Stop!	*Stop!*	*Berhenti!*
I'm ill.	*Saya sakit.*	*Saya sakit.*
I'm lost.	*Saya kesasar.*	*Saya sesat.*
bus station	*terminal bis kota*	*terminal bas kota*
police station	*kantor polisi*	*stesen polis*
post office	*kantor pos*	*pejabat pos*
train station	*stasiun kereta api*	*stesen keretapi*
today	*hari ini*	*hari ini*
tonight	*malam ini*	*malam ini*
tomorrow	*besok*	*esok*

ENTRANCE	*MASUK*
EXIT	*KELUAR*
NO ENTRY	*DI LARANG MASUK*
EMERGENCY EXIT	*PINTU KECEMASAN*
INFORMATION	*INFORMASI*
NO SMOKING	*DI LARANG MEROKOK*
OPEN	*BUKA*
CLOSED	*TUTUP*
PROHIBITED	*DI LARANG*
TOILETS	*TANDAS/WC*

Hello.	*johm riab sua/* *sua s'dei*	ជំរាបសួរ / សួស្តី
Goodbye.	*lia suhn hao-y*	លាសិនហើយ
Please.	*sohm*	សូម
Thank you.	*aw kohn*	អរគុណ
Excuse me/I'm sorry.	*sohm toh*	សុំទោស
Yes. (men)	*baat*	បាទ
Yes. (women)	*jaa*	ចាស
No.	*te*	ទេ

I don't understand.
    kh'nyohm muhn yuhl te/   ខ្ញុំមិនយល់ទេ / ខ្ញុំស្តាប់មិនបានទេ
    kh'nyohm s'dap muhn baan te
What time is it?
    eileuv nih maong pohnmaan?   ពេលវេលានេះម៉ោងប៉ុន្មាន?

Where is (a/the) ...?	*... neuv ai naa?*	នៅឯណា?
Go straight ahead.	*teuv trawng*	ទៅត្រង់
Turn left ...	*bawt ch'weng*	បត់ឆ្វេង
Turn right ...	*bawt s'dam*	បត់ស្ដាំ

How much is it?   *nih th'lay pohnmaan?*   នេះថ្លៃប៉ុន្មាន?

Help!   *juay kh'nyohm phawng!*   ជួយខ្ញុំផង!

KHMER *Quick Reference*

Stop!	*chohp!*	ឈប់!
I'm ill.	*kh'nyohm cheu*	ខ្ញុំឈឺ
We are lost.		
yæng wohngweng phleuv		យើងវង្វេងផ្លូវ

bank	*th'niakia*	ធនាគារ
bus station	*kuhnlaing laan ch'nual*	កន្លែងឡានឈ្នួល
hotel	*sahnthaakia/ohtail*	សណ្ឋាគារ/អូតែល
police station	*poh polih/s'thaanii nohkohbaal*	ប៉ុស្តប៉ូលីស / ស្ថានីយនគរបាល
post office	*praisuhnii*	ប្រៃសណីយ
train station	*s'thaanii roht plæng*	ស្ថានីយរថភ្លើង
today	*th'ngay nih*	ថ្ងៃនេះ
tonight	*yohp nih*	យប់នេះ
tomorrow	*th'ngay s'aik*	ថ្ងៃស្អែក

Pitch Key					
Low	Mid	High	Rising	High Falling	Low

Hello.	*sábaai-dii*	ສະບາຍດີ
Thank you.	*khàwp jai*	ຂອບໃຈ
Excuse me.	*khāw thôht*	ຂໍໂທດ
I don't understand.	*baw khào jai*	ບໍ່ເຂົ້າໃຈ
Where is ...?	*... yùu sāi?*	... ຢູ່ໃສ ?
Go straight ahead.	*pai seu-seu*	ໄປຊື່
Turn left/right.	*lîaw sâai/khwāa*	ລ້ຽວ ຊ້າຍ/ຂວາ
How much?	*thao dai?*	ເທົ່າໃດ ?
Where are the toilets?	*hàwng sùam yuu sāi?*	ຫ້ອງສ້ວມຢູ່ໃສ ?

LAO *Quick reference*

Help!	*suay dae*	ຊ່ວຍແດ່
Stop!	*yút*	ຢຸດ !
I am ill.	*khàwy puay*	ຂ້ອຍປ່ວຍ
I am lost.	*khàwy lõng tháang*	ຂ້ອຍຫລົງທາງ
today	*mêu nîi*	ມື້ນີ້
tonight	*khéun nîi*	ຄືນນີ້
tomorrow	*mêu eun*	ມື້ອື່ນ

ENTRANCE	ທາງເຂົ້າ
EXIT	ທາງອອກ
OPEN	ທ້ວນເຂົ້າ
CLOSED	ທ້ວນກ່ວຍຮູບ
NO ENTRY	ເປີດ
NO PHOTOGRAPHS	ປິດ
PROHIBITED	ທ້ວນ
TOILETS	ທ້ອງນ້ຳ
INFORMATION	ຂ້ນູນ

Quick Reference **TAGALOG**

Hello/Hi.	*Hoy/Uy.* (fam)
Goodbye.	*Paálam/Síge.* (fam)
Thank you.	*Salámat.*
Excuse me/Sorry. (pol)	*Ipagpaumanhin ninyo ako.*
Yes.	*Óo.*
No.	*Hindì.*
I (don't) understand.	*(Hindí) ko náiintindihan.*
Where is ...?	*Násaan ang ...?*
Straight ahead.	*Dirétso lámang.*
To the right.	*Papakánan.*
To the left.	*Papakaliwà.*
How much is this?	*Magkáno hó ito?*
What time is it?	*Anong óras na?*
Where are the toilets?	*Násaan hó ang CR?*
Help!	*Saklólo!*
Stop!	*Pára!*
I am ill.	*May sakit ako.*
I'm lost.	*Nawáwalá ako.*

bank	*bangko*
bus station	*terminal ng bus*
guesthouse	*báhay pára sa mga turist*
hotel	*hotel*
post office	*post office*
train station	*terminal ng tren*
today	*ngayon*
tonight	*ngayong gabi*
tomorrow	*búkas*

SIGNS

Most common signs in the Philippines are written in English but the following are sometimes in Tagalog:

HOT/COLD	*MAINIT/MAGINAW*
NO ENTRY	*BAWAL PUMASOK*
NO SMOKING	*BAWAL MANINGARILYO*
OPEN	*BUKAS*
CLOSED	*SARA*
PROHIBITED	*BAWAL*
TOILETS	*CR*

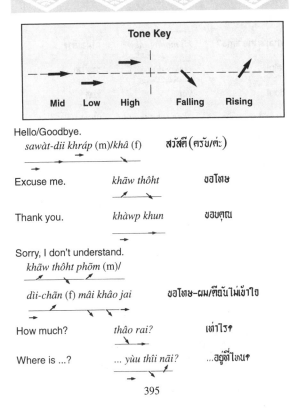

Tone Key

Mid Low High Falling Rising

Hello/Goodbye.
sawàt-dii khráp (m)/*khâ* (f)   สวัสดี (ครับ/ค่ะ)

Excuse me.   *khǎw thôht*   ขอโทษ

Thank you.   *khàwp khun*   ขอบคุณ

Sorry, I don't understand.
khǎw thôht phǒm (m)/
dì-chǎn (f) *mâi khâo jai*   ขอโทษ–ผม/ดีฉันไม่เข้าใจ

How much?   *thâo rai?*   เท่าไรฯ

Where is ...?   *... yùu thîi nǎi?*   ...อยู่ที่ไหนฯ

THAI   *Quick Reference*

Turn left/right.	*líaw sáai/khwāa*	เลี้ยว ซ้าย/ขวา
Straight ahead.	*trong pai*	ตรงไป
What's the time?	*kìi mohng láew?*	กี่โมงแล้ว?
Help!	*chûay dûay*	ช่วยด้วย
Stop!	*yàt*	หยุด
I'm lost.	*chãn lõng thaang*	ฉันหลงทาง
Call a doctor!		
chûay taam māw hâi dûay		ช่วยตาม หมอให้ด้วย
railway station	*sathãanii rót fai*	สถานีรถไฟ
today	*wan níi*	วันนี้
tonight	*kheun níi*	คืนนี้
tomorrow	*phrûng níi*	พรุ่งนี้

ENTRANCE	ทางเข้า
EXIT	ทางออก
OPEN	เปิด
CLOSED	ปิด
NO ENTRY	ห้ามเข้า
NO SMOKING	ห้ามสูบบุหรี่
NO PHOTOGRAPHS	ห้ามถ่ายรูป
ENQUIRIES	สอบถาม
TOILETS	ห้องสุขา

Quick Reference **VIETNAMESE**

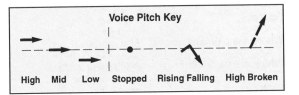

Voice Pitch Key

High | Mid | Low | Stopped | Rising | Falling | High Broken

Hello/Goodbye.
  (to a man) — *Chào anh*

  (to a woman) — *Chào chị*

Excuse me/I'm Sorry. — *Xin lỗi*

Thank you. — *Cám ơn*

I don't understand. — *Tôi không hiểu.*

How much is it? — *Giá bao nhiêu?*

Where is ...? — *... ở đâu?*

Go straight ahead. — *Đi thẳng tới trước.*

Turn left/right ... — *Quẹo trái/ phải ...*

What time is it? — *Mấy giờ rồi?*

Help!	*Cứu với!*
Stop!	*Ngừng lại!*
I'm lost.	*Tôi bị lạc đường.*
Where is the police station?	*Đồn cảnh sát ở đâu?*
Where are the toilets?	*Nhà vệ sinh ở đâu?*
bank	*ngân hàng*
post office	*bưu điện*
bus stop	*trạm xe buýt*
train station	*trạm xe lửa*
today	*hôm nay*
tonight	*đêm nay*
tomorrow	*ngày mai*

DANGER	*NGUY HIỂM*
ENTRANCE	*LỐI VÀO*
EXIT	*LỐI RA*
NO PHOTOGRAPHS!	*CẤM CHỤP HÌNH!*
NO SMOKING!	*CẤM HÚT THUỐC!*
STOP!	*NGỪNG!*

Phrasebooks

L onely Planet phrasebooks are packed with essential words and phrases to help travellers communicate with the locals. With colour tabs for quick reference, an extensive vocabulary and use of script, these handy pocket-sized language guides cover day-to-day travel situations.

- handy pocket-sized books
- easy to understand Pronunciation chapter
- clear & comprehensive Grammar chapter
- romanisation alongside script to allow ease of pronunciation
- script throughout so users can point to phrases for every situation
- full of cultural information and tips for the traveller

'...vital for a real DIY spirit and attitude in language learning'
– *Backpacker*

'the phrasebooks have good cultural backgrounders and offer solid advice for challenging situations in remote locations'
– *San Francisco Examiner*

Arabic (Egyptian) • Arabic (Moroccan) • Australian *(Australian English, Aboriginal and Torres Strait languages)* • Baltic States *(Estonian, Latvian, Lithuanian)* • Bengali • Brazilian • Burmese • British *(English, dialects, Scottish Gaelic, Welsh)* • Cantonese • Central Asia *(Kazakh, Kyrgyz, Pashto, Tajik, Tashkorghani, Turkmen, Uyghur, Uzbek & others)* • Central Europe *(Czech, German, Hungarian, Polish, Slovak, Slovene)* • Costa Rica Spanish • Eastern Europe *(Albanian, Bulgarian, Croatian, Czech, Hungarian, Macedonian, Polish, Romanian, Serbian, Slovak, Slovene)* • East Timor *(Tetun, Portuguese)* • Egyptian Arabic • Ethiopian *(Amharic)* • Europe *(Basque, Catalan, Dutch, French, German, Greek, Irish, Italian, Maltese, Portuguese, Scottish Gaelic, Spanish, Turkish, Welsh)* • Farsi *(Persian)* • Fijian • French • German • Greek • Hebrew • Hill Tribes *(Lahu, Akha, Lisu, Mong, Mien & others)* • Hindi/Urdu • Indonesian • Italian • Japanese • Korean • Lao • Latin American Spanish • Malay • Mandarin • Mongolian • Moroccan Arabic • Nepali • Papua New Guinea • Pidgin • Pilipino (Tagalog) • Polish • Portuguese • Quechua • Russian • Scandinavian *(Danish, Faroese, Finnish, Icelandic, Norwegian, Swedish)* • South-East Asia *(Burmese, Indonesian, Khmer, Lao, Malay, Tagalog Pilipino, Thai, Vietnamese)* • South Pacific *(Fijian, Hawaiian, Kanak languages, Maori, Niuean, Rapanui, Rarotongan Maori, Samoan, Tahitian, Tongan & others)* • Spanish *(Castilian, also includes Catalan, Galician & Basque)* • Sri Lanka • Swahili • Thai • Tibetan • Turkish • Ukrainian • USA *(US English, vernacular, Native American, Hawaiian)* • Vietnamese